STUDIES IN POLITICAL ECONOMY
Volume II: International Trade and
Domestic Economic Policy

STUDIES IN POLITICAL ECONOMY

VOLUME II: INTERNATIONAL TRADE AND
DOMESTIC ECONOMIC POLICY

Donald MacDougall

First published 1975 by
THE MACMILLAN PRESS LTD
London and Basingstoke
Associated companies in New York
Dublin Melbourne Johannesburg and Madras

SBN 333 15712 5

Typeset in Great Britain by
PREFACE LIMITED
Salisbury, Wiltshire
and printed and bound in Great Britain by
REDWOOD BURN LIMITED
Trowbridge & Esher

Contents

Introduction

This is the second of two volumes containing a selection of studies in political economy made over the past thirty-five years or so. I call them studies in 'political economy' because the majority of them attempt to use economic analysis (and usually a quantitative approach) to illuminate real problems of policy that have arisen both in the United Kingdom and elsewhere during this period. I have omitted some purely theoretical studies such as my very first article on 'The definition of prime and supplementary costs'.[1]

A good many of the studies were inspired by current controversy but I hope they will be of more than historical interest. First, many of the problems discussed are still very live issues today. Those that are not may well arise again; for history tends to repeat itself. Secondly, in the course of exploring particular problems I have, I believe, developed some techniques and methods of analysis which have proved to be of general and lasting interest.

After a good deal of thought I decided to divide the studies between the two volumes largely on a chronological basis. Thus, most of the studies in the first volume were written in the 1930s and 1940s, and those in the second volume in the 1950s and 1960s.

In the introduction to the first volume I explained how, towards the end of the war, I became interested in foreign trade questions, and the last five studies in that volume were in fact concerned with the particular foreign trade problem of the United Kingdom as it appeared in the early postwar years, and with the debate about the best form of international trade and monetary rules for the postwar world.

The first part of this second volume reflects my continuing interest during the 1950s and early 1960s in international economics, and is in many ways a natural development of the last five studies in Vol. 1. The second part is more concerned with domestic economic and social problems. The volume concludes, I hope fittingly, with an epilogue 'in praise of economics'.

[1] *Economic Journal*, September 1936.

COMPARATIVE COSTS AND ELASTICITIES IN INTERNATIONAL TRADE

This volume opens with what is perhaps my best known study: 'British and American Exports: A Study suggested by the Theory of Comparative Costs'. But, while the first part on the empirical testing of the comparative costs theory has found its way into the textbooks, the second part, dealing with price elasticities in international trade and with the importance of factors other than price in determining relative exports, is, I think, rather less well known.

I came to the subject by a number of routes. First, when arguing after the war with those who said that Britain could never compete with the U.S.,[1] I used to point out that, according to Rostas's famous calculations,[2] American output per head varied from little more than the British, in some industries, to four or five times the British in others. With American money wages so much higher than British, surely there must be quite a wide range of products where Britain could compete successfully.

Then again I found of doubtful value such statements as that in *The Times* for 23 September 1949: 'before devaluation British goods had been 25% higher in price than American'. It seemed to me likely that some British prices would normally be higher than American prices, some lower. The important question was how many were higher, how many lower, and by how much. Even if British and American prices were, according to some form of average, equal, this would not necessarily result in international equilibrium.

Finally, when teaching undergraduates economic theory I always liked to give practical examples where possible and, when we came to the theory of comparative costs, I used to give a few examples from Rostas's productivity figures and the U.S. and U.K. trade returns. For example, before the war American productivity in the manufacture of radio sets was 3½ times the British, and the U.S. exported far more than the U.K.; whereas American productivity in woollen and worsted was only a little above the British, and the U.K. did extremely well in export markets while the U.S. exported virtually nothing.

It was only after I had been giving these odd examples to undergraduates for several years that I thought of looking at all Rostas's sample of products and found to my astonishment how well his productivity figures, when combined with export figures and

---

[1] See, for example, *Economic Journal*, March 1948, p. 92-3 (Study 6 of Vol. 1).
[2] His first results were published in the *Economic Journal*, April 1943.

figures of relative wages, accorded with the labour theory of comparative costs. (This is, I think, quite an interesting example of how teaching can lead to fruitful ideas for research.)

Out of twenty-five products there were only five which did not obey the rule that, where U.S. productivity was more than twice the British (U.S. wages were twice the British before the war), the U.S. exported more than the U.K. and vice versa. I was interested to hear recently from Professor C. Major Wright his conclusion that four of these exceptions could be explained by restrictive business practices in international trade, and the fifth by differences in quality. The exceptions thus seem to prove the rule.

Another interesting finding was the 'scientific' nature of the U.S. tariff. So far as U.K. imports into the U.S. were concerned, U.S. import duties seemed to be carefully designed to offset America's apparent disadvantage in the various products. This was before the war (1937) and it was gratifying to find that, when the figures were redone for 1950 (see Study 2), this feature had disappeared, for three reasons: (a) U.S. wage costs per unit of output had in general risen in relation to the British, after allowing for the devaluation of sterling; (b) the incidence of U.S. tariffs generally had been reduced by cuts in rates of duty and by the effects of inflation on specific duties; (c) most interesting, the reduction in the incidence of the U.S. tariff was particularly marked in products where she had a comparative disadvantage. As a result of this third change, whereas in 1937 the U.S. tariff was in general much higher on such products than it was on others, in 1950 there was no such tendency.

The original findings naturally raised a lot of questions. What about variations between industries in relative wage rates, indirect labour, other costs, relative export prices, the Ohlin theory, imperfect markets? These are all discussed in the Study. Relative export prices (U.S.:U.K.) were found to be as expected given relative labour productivities. Moreover, when relative prices were plotted against relative exports, on a double-logarithmic scale, the points tended to lie about a straight line. This got me excited, for it suggested a possible new way of throwing light on price elasticities in international trade, using a cross-section 'commodity comparison' approach rather than traditional time-series analysis. Moreover, the slope of the curve seemed to suggest rather a high elasticity, and I had always been sceptical of some of the very low elasticities found by analyses of time series, some of which were in any case known to involve serious biases.

So, with the help of a number of loyal assistants (this was before the days when all self-respecting economists expected access to computers), a much larger sample of products was taken (leaving productivity behind and concentrating on relative prices), covering a long run of years, and also other pairs of industrial countries besides the U.S. and the U.K. After allowing for bias due to errors of observation, the conclusion was reached that, so far as U.S. and U.K. exports in the later thirties were concerned, a difference of 1 per cent in relative prices may well have been associated with a difference of 4—4½ per cent in relative quantities. After discussing other possible causes of bias, and adjusting downwards for the difference between what I call 'product' and 'total' elasticities of substitution (using a concept which I christened the 'index of similarity'), I hazarded the guess that the elasticity of substitution between total U.S. and U.K. exports of manufactures might be of an order approaching —3. This was about ten times as high as the figure of —0.3 obtained by Mr. Chang — often quoted by 'elasticity pessimists' — and much more in line with the results of, for example, Professor A. J. Brown.

I was careful not to place too much weight on this precise result — it was only suggestive of an order of magnitude (nearer —3 than —0.3 or —30) but concluded:

> While it is dangerous to apply the results obtained to future changes, I believe that the evidence gives some grounds for thinking that, at least in conditions resembling those of the later 30's (an important proviso), changes in the relative prices of British and American exports of manufactures should lead to comparatively large changes in the relative quantities demanded in third markets, at least after a period of years.

The last phrase, and other passages in Study 1, hint at the likelihood that elasticities in international trade will be larger in the long than in the short run. This was brought out much more clearly in *The World Dollar Problem*,[3] which concluded that the responsiveness of trade to relative price changes was fairly small in the short run but moderately (though only moderately) large in the long run; also that it would take a good many years for the full effects of exchange-rate changes to become apparent. This, I believe, was one of the earliest hints of the existence of the now fairly widely accepted 'J-curve', and of the long lags which are now appearing in more and more of the econometricians' export and import equations.

Coming back to Study 1, the method of analysis used also enables

---

[3] See especially Chapters XIV and XV, including Appendix XVB, which attempts to quantify long-run price elasticities in trade between the U.S. and the rest of the world.

one to study the effects on export performance of factors other than price. One interesting result for the later 1930s is that, in the case of exports to Commonwealth countries, the U.K. sold far more of a product than the U.S. when their prices were equal, whereas in the case of exports to non-Commonwealth countries the U.S. sold more than the U.K. when prices were equal. Calculations suggested that it was unlikely that more than a small part of this striking difference could be attributed to Commonwealth Preference, leaving the major part to be explained by commercial and political ties and other non-price factors.

I think this finding is interesting in showing the importance of non-price factors. But false deductions must not be drawn from it. It is often claimed that the importance of such non-price factors means that relative price *changes* are unlikely to bring significant *changes* in relative export performance. But this does not necessarily follow at all. A purchaser may be prepared to buy from A rather than B, even though A's price is, say, 5 per cent higher; but if the margin rises to, say, 7 or 8 per cent he may well switch the bulk of his purchases to B. Thus I believe both that trade is quite responsive to relative price changes, at least in the longer run, and also that, at any moment in time, non-price factors can be of great importance in determining the pattern of trade. These two views are not inconsistent.

In 1961 and 1962, with the help of a number of assistants, I brought the analysis in Study 1 up to date using, among other more recent data, postwar estimates of relative productivities in the U.S. and U.K. prepared by Deborah Paige and Gottfried Bombach. As this work was nearing completion I discovered that, unknown to me, Mr. Stern in the U.S. had been similarly engaged. His results were published in the *Oxford Economic Papers* for October 1962. I published in the same issue an addendum which was limited to substantially different and additional results. This is reprinted as Study 2. By and large the original results were confirmed, apart from the changed nature of U.S. tariffs described above.

THE DOLLAR PROBLEM
In 1951, at about the time I was finishing the comparative cost study, Churchill again became Prime Minister and once again asked Lord Cherwell to be Paymaster-General. I in turn found myself spending another two years in Whitehall, where I was deeply involved in economic policy, particularly on the international side. When I left in 1953, I decided to write a book on British economic policy in general. I started with a chapter on the dollar problem which was obviously relevant to British policy but which I expected to be

relatively short. The matter proved more complex than I had
expected. At the time I suppose most people expected the dollar
shortage to go on for ever, but I soon found myself questioning
much of the conventional wisdom.

After perhaps six month's work, I gave a preliminary report in 'A
Lecture on the Dollar Problem' delivered at the London School of
Economics in March 1954, and reprinted as Study 3. In this I set out
the conventional arguments for chronic dollar shortage, added a few
more for good measure, but then proceeded to give a lot of
counter-arguments. For example, I cast doubt on the then current
view, which younger economists may find astonishing but which was
almost universally held at the time, that productivity grows faster in
the U.S. than in the rest of the world. (My doubts were fully
documented two years later in the *Review of Economics and
Statistics*.)[4] I also gave reasons why U.S. exports might be
potentially vulnerable, and U.S. imports what I called 'potentially
explosive'. I concluded in agnostic terms: 'it would require a very
courageous man to forecast either chronic dollar shortage or its
absence during the coming decades. I for one lack the necessary
courage'.

I wish now that I had left it at that! But instead I spent another
couple of years or so working away at the arguments, the facts and
the figures so that I could find the courage to come down on one
side of the fence or the other. Unfortunately, in *The World Dollar
Problem*, published in 1957, I came down on the wrong side and
concluded that the U.S. balance of payments was more likely to
improve than it was to worsen during the following couple of
decades: but in a reappraisal in 1960[5] — which is too long to reprint
here — I returned to my 1954 position of agnosticism.

It is a pity I reached the wrong general conclusion in *The World
Dollar Problem* because I believe it contains quite a lot of economic
analysis of general interest which is independent of the dollar
problem.

The only part of it which I have thought it worth while to reprint
here (as Study 4) is, however, a critique of Professor (now Sir John)
Hicks's model of the dollar problem itself which he published in 'An
Inaugural Lecture' in 1953. This Lecture led to a considerable
discussion, of a theoretical nature, to which Study 4 is a contribution. This study cast doubt both on the theoretical and on the
empirical bases of Hicks's analysis, which appeared to conclude that

---

[4] May 1956. 'Does productivity rise faster in the U.S.?'
[5] 'The Dollar Problem: A Reappraisal', Princeton Essays in International Finance, No. 35,
March 1960.

the rest of the world would suffer as a result of trade with the United States.

After completing *The World Dollar Problem* I decided to see a bit of the world and visited, among other places, Australia, India and Venezuela. These visits led to three of the studies in this volume.

INTERNATIONAL INVESTMENT

During a visit to Australia in 1959 the current controversy about the costs and benefits of private investment from abroad led me to make a largely theoretical study of the problem (Study 5). Though written in an Austrialian context — it allows, for example, for the possibility of more, or less, immigration — it has I believe general applicability; and parts of it are by no means irrelevant, *mutatis mutandis*, to the costs and benefits of investment abroad *by* a country. Though cautious in my conclusions, I can say now that I formed the view that private investment from abroad was a good bet for Australia, despite some of the criticisms of it at the time.

This is another of my better-known studies and has led to considerable further discussion of the question. It benefited greatly from the stimulating atmosphere of the Australian National University in Canberra. It is an example of a theoretical analysis which starts with a large number of simplifying assumptions (ten in this case) and relaxes them one by one. It has been criticised by some as too 'static' — and its mainly static nature is admitted in the article itself — but I still rather doubt whether a more 'dynamic' approach can add a great deal, at least to the general theory.

INDIA'S BALANCE OF PAYMENTS PROBLEM

During a visit to India in 1961 I made a study of her balance of payments problem (Study 6). This revealed that shortage of foreign exchange was severely holding up production. One of my main conclusions was that a massive increase in exports was required — considerably larger than many people were contemplating — especially of the 'newer' manufactures (i.e. other than the traditional ones of cotton and jute) — if the current targets for growth of the national output were to be achieved. I have reprinted the study here, although it may seem rather dated, because it continues to arouse interest in India, and because it may be of more general interest to other developing countries in a similar situation. I formed the impression at that time that one developing country after another would probably have to turn more and more to exports of manufactures to balance their international accounts; and how important it therefore was for the advanced countries to import such manufactures as freely as possible.

During this visit to India I found myself working in the Planning Commission in New Delhi and, to my delight, treated as if I were an Indian civil servant. I shall always be grateful for the friendship, help and stimulus from those with whom I worked.

BRITAIN AND EUROPE

The last two studies in the international economic section of this volume concern Europe. Study 7 is an account of Western European economic co-operation during the early years of O.E.E.C.[6] (where I was the first Economics Director – in Paris – in 1948–9). Study 8 was written a decade later when the Six had already built up a flourishing Community; it discusses the pros and cons of Britain joining.

Study 7 could well have gone in Vol. 1 alongside the articles discussing the problems of bilateral bargaining, discrimination and so on, for it illustrates the serious practical problems, and hideous complexities (not incomparable with those of the C.A.P.!), of breaking out of a straight-jacket of bilateral trade and exchange restrictions in a period of severe dollar shortage. But I have decided to put it with the article on the Common Market, because it shows the first stirrings of European economic co-operation. It also shows how we faced then, in a different form, some of the issues now connected with a move towards economic and monetary union. For example, will progress in economic co-operation automatically bring political co-operation in its train? Or should we place more emphasis on the fact that a 'strong desire for political co-operation is indispensable for economic co-operation, which can make little real progress without a readiness to sacrifice national interests'?[7] Again, should we try to run before we can walk? In 1947–9, proposals for customs unions, while enthusiastically received, had little relevance to immediate action. So the O.E.E.C., having learned also the practical difficulties of co-ordinating investment plans (which the study describes), set about the less ambitious but more practicable task of reducing quantitative trade restrictions and liberalising payments. In these fields it achieved very considerable success, and this was a necessary preliminary to much more ambitious forms of economic integration in Europe.

In 1961 controversy raged on the question of whether or not

---

[6] Organisation of European Economic Cooperation.
[7] Study 7, p. 170.

Britain should join the Common Market. I found this a fascinating and crucial question. I was therefore grateful for an invitation from a Dutch Bank Review to write an article on the subject, since this gave me an opportunity to clarify my own thoughts and to sort out the various facts and figures bearing on the question.

The article was published in December 1961. Shortly afterwards I joined the new National Economic Development Office as its first Economic Director and expected to hear no more of the article; for the *Rotterdamsche Bank Review* had, I imagined, a very limited circulation in Britain. I had tried hard to make the analysis as objective, impartial and balanced as possible, and to report faithfully the various views in Britain at the time; and I made no attempt to recommend whether or not, on balance, it was advantageous for Britain to join. I believe, too, that our negotiators in Brussels at the time regarded it as a fair assessment.

I was therefore a little surprised and mildly embarrassed when, in Scotland on a short Easter break in 1962, I was chased by reporters from the *Daily Express*, and when on the Tuesday after Easter that newspaper published an article with the headline 'Sir Donald rocks the Market boat' which began 'The Government faces a new embarrassment over the Common Market from one of its top "backroom" economic advisers.' It went on to pick out from my article many of the arguments against joining and largely ignored those in favour. The article thereupon became rather famous – or notorious – and was quite widely quoted during that year, those referring to it including Hugh Gaitskell in his speech to the Labour Party Conference, opposing British entry.

In the article I took the view that the most important arguments for and against Britain joining the Community were political rather than economic. None of the economic arguments for joining were, in my opinion, compelling. There were indeed economic risks in joining, especially perhaps in the short run, but these were not sufficiently important to stand in the way of our entering if the political arguments for such a course were strong.

Re-reading the article I think it has stood the test of time reasonably well, although I should naturally place different emphasis now on various parts of the argument. Among the advantages I should now include an argument that I hardly used at the time, namely that entry would be an insurance (for which we might well have to pay a premium) against both Europe and the U.S. becoming highly protectionist, thus leaving Britain with only a relatively small market and so endangering her prosperity. This I would now regard as one of the most important economic arguments for entry.

INFLATION

The second part of this volume, concerned with domestic economic policy, starts with a study on inflation in the United Kingdom (Study 9). It is a lecture that I gave in various parts of Australia and New Zealand in the latter part of 1959, and is a distillation of a series of lectures given in Oxford earlier that year.

As was so often the case with the studies in these volumes, it was inspired by a current controversy, this time about the efficacy of demand-reducing measures in controlling inflation. I was in particular very uneasy about the restrictive measures to this end taken in 1957, which had helped to raise unemployment to about 2½ per cent by the end of 1958, though there had admittedly also been a marked reduction in the pace of inflation; indeed retail prices did not rise at all between the spring of 1958 and the spring of 1959.

This tended to give support to those who, like Professors Paish and Phillips (and their conclusions were to some extent supported by the latest work of Dow and Dicks—Mireaux), had recently published articles arguing that inflation could, and would, be largely stopped if only we settled for a moderately higher level of unemployment than we had had since the war — a level which could still, at a stretch, be termed 'full employment'; and that, moreover, any incomes policy, or attempt to change the attitude of the trade unions, was not only unnecessary but also pointless because the rate of increase of wages was largely determined by the level of unemployment as though by an iron law that the unions could not do much about.

My lecture was in essence a refutation of these views based on analysis of the evidence. I was not convinced that the pace of inflation was so sensitive to demand as recent empirical studies had suggested; and I was unconvinced that we could combine reasonably full employment and reasonable price stability, at least without some kind of incomes policy. I recognised that such a policy bristled with difficulties, but I did not accept that, if one could be devised and agreed, it would have no effect on the pace of inflation.

Re-reading the lecture, I am rather astonished at its relevance to the current situation, although of course the numbers today are much higher — of price and wage increases and of unemployment. I must admit, too, that I was overoptimistic (p. 206) about the extent to which future research work, and the unwinding of events, would teach us more about the economic relationships involved. I rather doubt whether we know very much more about these than we did fifteen years ago.

But we have advanced in at least one respect. In *The World Dollar*

Problem, published in 1957, I felt bound to point out[8] that phrases such as 'full employment without inflation' were quite often used in economic analysis as if maximum output and price stability necessarily went together, and that this contained an element of wishful thinking and could lead to misleading conclusions. Few, if any, suffer from such an illusion today.

DISTRIBUTION OF INCOMES

Study 10 is about a domestic problem in Venezuela. In 1958 I was a member of a team advising on the fiscal system in that country shortly after the downfall of the dictator Pérez Jiménez. The team produced a book entitled *The Fiscal System of Venezuela*. Most of this was a detailed analysis by American colleagues who were tax experts. I wrote two introductory chapters. One, not reproduced here, analysed the economic situation and problems of Venezuela, which I found particularly interesting as a study of an economy receiving a lot of manna from heaven every year in the shape of royalties and taxation from foreign oil companies. My other chapter was on the distribution of incomes, and I have selected this for reprinting here. It was, I believe, one of the first quantitative analyses of this kind in a Latin American country, and I hope that both the methodology and the results will be of interest.

I was surprised to find how much information there was to piece together, partly because of the willingness of Government agencies to give us information on such things as income-tax returns and pay rolls, in a degree of detail that would have been quite impossible under the rules of confidentiality in a country like the United Kingdom; partly because a number of relevant surveys, both official and unofficial, had recently been carried out.

The degree of inequality revealed by the study was striking, not only between individual members of the population, but also between town and countryside, between regions of the country and between sectors of the economy. For example, I estimated that the average income in the capital (Caracas) was about ten times that in rural areas; and that oil workers earned nearly twenty times as much as agricultural labourers, and professional people about seventy times as much. The *campesino*, according to one survey, 'tills the soil with his hands, aided sometimes with the traditional pico, planting stick and machete; 66% of them have no other tools'.

[8] p. 382 of that book.

The premium on skill was high in a country where many did not go to school and where a high school education was confined to a tiny fraction of the population. Capital and land were very unequally distributed. A few families controlled many of the large businesses (although there was also a substantial middle class of smaller businessmen); 2½ per cent of the agricultural units accounted for 82 per cent of the total agricultural area, while some 80 per cent of the 'farmers' had only 4 per cent of the land. On top of this, the tax structure was only very mildly progressive, and it seemed quite possible that taxation and the pattern of Government expenditure taken together had no redistributive effects.

ECONOMIC PLANNING AND DEMAND MANAGEMENT

Early in 1962, as mentioned earlier, I left Oxford to join the National Economic Development Office (an institution which, together with N.E.D.C., has displayed a survival value greater than most such bodies). On the change of Government in October 1964 I moved over to the newly created Department of Economic Affairs as Director-General, and at the beginning of 1969 went to the Treasury as Chief Economic Adviser and Head of the Government Economic Service, a position I held until the autumn of 1973. Thus, for nearly twelve years, most of my writing, though voluminous, was strictly not for publication (at least until thirty years later) or where published was anonymous. One exception was the report in 1964 of the Richardson Committee on value-added tax, of which I was one of the three members and co-authors. I also, naturally, gave a good many public talks on various matters, including inevitably several on national economic planning and on short-term demand management. I have selected two of these for reproduction here.

The first (Study 11), on national economic planning, was prepared during my last days in the D.E.A., and delivered early in 1969. By that time we had had both the Neddy Plan of 1963 and the National Plan of 1965. In neither case was the growth objective achieved. In the light of this sobering experience (and of a third, much less ambitious, planning exercise then being started) I tried to say a little about the possible purposes and methods of national economic planning, and its value for both government and industry. So far as government is concerned, I am pretty sure that medium-term projections will continue to be made, at least for internal use, since these have obvious — even if limited — value in the formulation of public expenditure programmes, in making decisions on the investment programmes of the nationalised industries, and as a guide to general economic policy. So far as private business is concerned, I suspect that its interest in national economic planning in various forms will move in cycles, as will views on how far the economic performance of the country can be improved by bringing the private sector into a planning process.

Study 12 of this volume – a lecture given in 1970 – is on the short-term regulation of the national economy, a matter with which I have been concerned for a good many years. In this lecture I emphasised that such regulation was by no means the be-all and end-all of economic policy. It could make only a limited *positive* contribution to faster economic growth, the avoidance of inflation and the achievement of a healthy balance of payments. But sound demand management was a *necessary* – if not a sufficient – condition of all these things.

Apart from describing the process, and suggesting ways in which short-term regulation of the national economy was different from, and probably more difficult than, similar regulation of a private business, I tried to answer those who claimed that it was pointless, and possibly even dangerous and counter productive.

I still believe it to be unproven that demand management since the war has been destabilising rather than stabilising; and certainly, for one reason or another, our economic performance over the past quarter of a century has in many ways been a good deal better than it was before the war, at least as regards the level of employment and the rate of growth. Nor am I clear what would take the place of short-term regulation of the economy. It seems to me that the various simple rules for achieving our objectives that have been proposed, relating for example to fiscal balances and monetary aggregates, overestimate the present state of economic knowledge and underestimate the complexity of the real economic and political world in which we live.

I am the first to admit that margins of error in short-term forecasting are necessarily considerable, so that, for example, the error in a forecast of gross domestic product may be of the same order of magnitude as the effect on demand of a typical Budget. But this does not mean that forecasting is therefore useless. What it does mean, in my view, is that we must first make the best possible *central* forecast; then recognise, and attempt to *quantify*, the uncertainties; and finally take policy decisions in the light of the risks and uncertainties, and of the trade-offs between various national objectives. The lecture discusses some of the complexities in this procedure. I think a lot more work could usefully be done by economists in developing techniques in this field to enable policy makers to take more rational decisions.

EPILOGUE

The volume concludes with an Epilogue: 'In Praise of Economics'. This is my Presidential address to the Royal Economic Society in 1974. It had been common in recent Presidential addresses to such bodies for economists to criticise rather severely the present state of the subject and I thought it proper to do something, in a somewhat lighthearted manner, to redress the balance. After some forty years as an economist I have come to the conclusion that we are not such a hopeless lot as is sometimes supposed.

Part One: International Trade and Investment

Comparative Costs and Elasticities In International Trade

1 British and American exports: a study suggested by the theory of comparative costs[1]

A. EXPORTS AND LABOUR COSTS

THE LABOUR THEORY OF COMPARATIVE COSTS

The work of Mr. Rostas[2] and others on the productivity of British and American industries makes it possible to test some aspects of the theory of comparative costs. According to that theory, when based on a labour theory of value and assuming two countries, each will export those goods for which the ratio of its ouput per worker to that of the other exceeds the ratio of its money wage-rate to that of the other. Before the war, American weekly wages in manufacturing were roughly double the British,[3] and we find that, where American output per worker was more than twice the British, the United States

[1] *Economic Journal*, December 1951 (Sections A and B), and September 1952 (Sections C, D and E). Some provisional results were submitted to a meeting of the International Economic Association at Monaco in September 1950 and published, in a greatly abbreviated form, in the Spring 1951 issue of the *International Social Science Bulletin.*

I am indebted to Messrs. Corner, Dehn, Donnison, Lisle and Thackeray, Mrs. Little, Miss Brotman and Miss Orton for statistical assistance, and particularly indebted to Miss Verry, who performed a large part of the calculations. I am grateful for technical and other services provided by the Oxford University Institute of Statistics and for financial assistance from the Oxford University Social Studies Research Fund. Professors D. G. Champernowne and J. E. Meade, Messrs. A. I. Bloomfield, H. Klemmer, D. J. Morgan, R. V. Rosa, L. Rostas, R. L. Sammons, J. R. N. Stone, C. Winsten and others have kindly given valuable advice, but are, of course, in no way responsible for any shortcomings in this paper.

[2] L. Rostas, *Comparative Productivity in British and American Industry.*
[3] The Ministry of Labour's figure (*Ministry of Labour Gazette*, March 1951, p. 92) for average weekly earnings in manufacturing industries only in the United Kingdom in October 1938 is 50s. 4d. = $12 (at £1 = $4.769). The Department of Labour's figure for United States manufacturing for October 1938 is $23.98, and the N.I.C.B. figure $26.14. These are respectively 2.0 and 2.2 times the British figure. A comparison of the United States and United Kingdom Censuses of Production for 1935 suggests a figure nearer 1¾. The British and American figures are not, of course, strictly comparable, and the weights given to the various industries are not the same.

had in general the bulk of the export market, while for products
where it was less than twice as high the bulk of the market was held
by Britain. This is shown clearly in Table I, and more detailed figures
are given in Table II. Out of twenty-five products taken, twenty
(covering 97% of the sample by value) obey the general rule, and two

TABLE I

*U.S. and U.K. pre-war Output per Worker and Quantity of Exports in
in 1937*

U.S. output per worker more than twice the British:

Wireless sets and valves	U.S. exports 8 times U.K. exports
Pig iron	5
Motor cars	4
Glass containers	3½
Tin cans	3
Machinery	1½
Paper	1

U.S. output per worker 1.4–2.0 times the British:

Cigarettes	U.K. exports 2 times U.S. exports
Linoleum, oilcloth, etc.	3
Hosiery	3
Leather footwear	3
Coke	5
Rayon weaving	5
Cotton goods	9
Rayon making	11
Beer	18

U.S. output per worker less than 1.4 times the British:

Cement	11
Men's and boys' outer clothing of wool	23
Margarine	32
Woolen and worsted	250

Exceptions (U.S. output per worker more than twice the British, but U.K. exports exceeded
U.S. exports): Electric lamps, rubber tyres, soap, biscuits, matches.

See Table II for further details.

The following industries for which Mr. Rostas made estimates were omitted from the
analysis: pipe tobacco, cigars, and fish-curing, where Mr. Rostas's estimates are particularly
liable to error; steelworks, foundries, bricks and seed crushing, where it is hard to find
comparable export figures; manufactured ice (no recorded exports from either country);
grain-milling and beet sugar.

The sample used covered nearly half United Kingdom exports in 1937 of 'articles wholly
or mainly manufactured' plus 'tobacco, manufactured' and nearly half United States exports
of 'finished manufactures.' It also included a small value of manufactured foodstuffs
(biscuits, margarine and beer), and a small part of the exports classified in the United States
returns as 'semi-manufactures.'

of the remaining five would cease to be exceptions if a different measure of output per worker were chosen.[4]

But while in the normal text-book examples the exports of each country go to each other, the great bulk of the exports of the United States and the United Kingdom in 1937 went to third countries — more than 95% of British exports of all our sample products but three, more than 95% of American exports of all the products but six (see columns (4) and (5) of Table II). It is true that each country was nearly always a net exporter to the other of products in which it had a comparative advantage (see column (9) of Table II), but this is of limited interest, since trade between them was in general a negligible proportion of their total consumption, despite the large differences in the ratio of productivity, which enabled some British industries to sweep the board in third markets, while in other industries America swept the board. The lower part of column (8) of Table II shows that, even where Britain had a comparative advantage, and could undersell American producers in third markets, her exports to America were usually a small fraction of 1% of total American consumption. The upper part of column (8) shows that, where America had the comparative advantage, her exports to Britain were, in general, more substantial, but never more than a few per cent of total British consumption.

TARIFFS

Why was this so? Apart from costs of transport and the many difficulties of selling in a foreign country where there are rival domestic producers, there seems little doubt that tariffs were a decisive obstacle. The approximate *ad valorem* incidence of the American tariffs (adjusted where necessary for internal revenue taxes[5]) is shown in column (6) of Table II,[6] and Fig. 1 shows how

---

[4] See footnote 34 to Table II.

[5] Such adjustments were necessary only for beer (where the internal revenue tax was levied only on home production) and for margarine (where the internal revenue tax was higher for imports than it was for home production). Where internal revenue taxes were levied on other items, they applied equally to home production and to imports, and were additional to Customs duty.

[6] The tariff rate (before adjusting for internal revenue tax) was obtained by expressing the calculated duty on the relevant categories of imports from the United Kingdom as a percentage of the value, excluding duty, of imports from the United Kingdom. This states correctly the protective effect of the tariff where (as with motor cars) one rate of duty applies to all sub-categories and the rate is *ad valorem*. But where the rate is wholly or partly specific, or where there is more than one rate, the protective effect tends to be understated, since imports of types and qualities on which the *ad valorem* incidence of the tariff is highest will tend to be the most restricted and may even be eliminated; it is shown in the text that potential imports from the United Kingdom were in large part kept out by the United States tariff.

TABLE II

	(1) Output per worker U.S.:U.K., pre-war	(2) Quantity of exports U.S.:U.K., 1937	(3) Price of exports U.S.:U.K., 1937	(4) U.S. exports to U.K. as % of exports to all countries, 1937	(5) U.K. exports to U.S. as % of exports to all countries, 1937	(6) U.S. tariff %, 1937	(7) U.K. tariff %, 1937	(8) U.K. imports from U.S. as % of U.K. consumption, 1935	(9) A = U.S. export surplus to U.K. B = U.K. export surplus to U.S., 1937
I. U.S. Output per worker more than twice U.K.:[1]									
Tin cans	5.25	3.0	0.68	—	—	[31]	20	0.005	A
Pig iron	3.6	5.1[3]	0.84	30	—	5	Nil[4]	2.4[5]	A
Wireless receiving sets and valves	3.5[6]	7.6[7]	0.64	10	—	35	25[8]	4.7 sets / 8.2 valves	A
Motor cars	3.1	4.3[9]	0.91[31]	3	2[11]	10	33⅓[5]	2.7[5]	A
Machinery	2.7[10]	1.5[11]	[31]	13[11]	—	20	20[12]	3.2	A
Glass containers	2.4	3.5	0.69	2	—	75	25	0.2	A
Paper	2.2	1.0[13]	0.72	8	1	25	20	0.06	A

								U.S. imports from U.K. as % of U.S. consumption, 1939	
II. U.S.Output per worker not more than twice U.K.[1]									
Beer	2.0[16]	0.056	1.30	—	2	20[40]	30[17]	0.01	B
Linoleum, oilcloth, etc.	1.9[10]	0.34[18]	1.04	4	9	40	20	2.0	B
Coke	1.9	0.19	1.08	—	1	Nil	Nil	0.03	B
Hosiery	1.8	0.30[19]	1.24	6	10	65	20[20]	0.04	B
Cigarettes	1.7	0.47	1.08	2	—	115	70[21]	0.004	A
Rayon weaving	1.5	0.20	1.19	2	1	80	40[22]	0.0023	B
Cotton spinning and weaving	1.5[23]	0.11[24]	1.03	—	1	35	20[25]	{ 0.04 yarn / 0.14 cloth	B
Leather footwear	1.4	0.32[15]	1.31	11	4	20	20	0.03	[38]
Rayon making	1.4	0.091	1.53	—	—	55	55[26]	0.0014	A
Woollen and worsted	1.35	0.004[27]	1.42	2	4	85	20[28]	{ 0.08 yarn / 1.8 cloth	B
Men's and boys' outer clothing of wool	1.25[29]	0.044[30]	[31]	—[30]	16[30]	60[14]	20	[31]	B
Margarine	1.2	0.031	1.34	2	—	210[39]	10	—	B
Cement	1.1[32]	0.091	2.12	2	—	5	10	0.007	B
III. Exceptions:[2]									
Electric lamps	5.4[6]	0.94[33]	0.51	1	2	20	10		A
Biscuits	3.1	0.23	1.01	4	—	30	10		B
Matches	3.1[34]	0.99[35]	0.86	—[35]	—	30	45[36]		A
Rubber tyres	2.7[34]	0.74[37]	1.12[37]	1	—	10	33⅓		A
Soap	2.7	0.35	1.24	3	1	25	20		B

Sources and General Notes on each Column

Column (1). Rostas, *Comparative Productivity in British and American Industry*, except where otherwise stated. 1935, 1937 or 1939 in each country except where otherwise stated. Rounded figures.

Column (2) *Foreign Commerce and Navigation of the United States; Annual Statement of the Trade of the United Kingdom.* An attempt was made to find categories comparable to those used by Mr. Rostas. Weighted averages of sub-items have been calculated in several cases.

Column (3). Same sources as for column (2). Obtained by dividing index of value (in dollars) by index of quantity as in column (2). Price differences may reflect partly differences of quality, etc.

Columns (4) and (5). Same sources as for column (2). Quantity ratios, in some cases weighted averages of sub-items. The sign − in these columns means less than one-half of 1%. Some of the figures in column (5) may be underestimated where no United Kingdom exports to the United States are specified in United Kingdom trade accounts although some took place.

Column (6). *Foreign Commerce and Navigation of the United States; Annual Reports of the Commissioner of Internal Revenue.* Calculated duty on relevant categories of imports from the United Kingdom as percentage of value of imports from the United Kingdom, excluding duty. Allowance made where necessary for internal revenue taxes. Rounded figures.

Column (7). *Annual Statement of the Trade of the United Kindom; Customs and Excise Tariff of the United Kingdom, 1937.* Average non-preferential rates in round figures. Since it was not always very clear into which tariff category a product fell, some errors may have arisen. Allowance was made so far as possible for excise taxes on British-produced goods.

Column (8). *United Kingdom Census of Production, 1935; Annual Statement of the Trade of the United Kingdom*; British Iron and Steel Federation, *Statistics of the Iron and Steel Industries*; Society of Motor Manufacturers and Traders Ltd., *The Motor Industry of Great Britain; Foreign Commerce and Navigation of the United States*; U.S. Tariff Commission, *Post-war Imports and Domestic Production of Major Commodities, 1945.* The categories covered do not always correspond exactly with those used in other parts of the table.

Column (9). Same sources as for column (2).

Footnotes to Table II

[1] American pre-war weekly wages were roughly twice as high as the British.

[2] American output per worker more than twice British, but British exports greater than American.

[3] This ratio is typical of the years 1937−39, but much higher than in earlier years.

[4] A duty of $33\frac{1}{3}$% was removed during 1937.

[5] 1937.

[6] United Kingdom, 1935; United States, 1939.

[7] Weighted average of sets and valves.

[8] Weighted average of sets (20%) and valves ($33\frac{1}{3}$%).

[9] Weighted average of private and commercial vehicles.

[10] United Kingdom, 1935; United States, 1937.

[11] Based on value; approximately same coverage in the United States and the United Kingdom; includes electrical machinery and locomotives.

[12] Typical rate of duty; the average incidence was probably lower, allowing for imports exempt from duty.

[13] Partly estimated.

[14] Based on figures for miscellaneous woollen wearing apparel, not knit or crocheted.

[15] Weighted average of main types.

[16] Beer is included in Group II, although Mr. Rostas's index is 2.01.

[17] Customs (approximately 130% of import value) less excise (approximately 100% on equivalent beer). Based on imports from all foreign countries. No imports from the United States are separately recorded.

[18] Weighted average of various types (linoleum, oilcloth, felt base floor covering, etc.).

[19] Weighted average of stockings, knitted underwear, knitted outerwear (approximate).

[20] Excluding silk and rayon duty.

[21] Customs duty was 14/7d. per lb. There was no excise duty on home-produced cigarettes as such, but that on home-grown tobacco was equivalent to an excise duty of 11/5d. per lb. The difference, 3/2d. per lb., is about 70% of the import value of U.S. cigarettes..

[22] Rough figure for printed rayon tissues only, from all foreign countries, allowing for excise duty on home-produced yarn.

[23] Adjusted to 1937 in each country.

[24] Weighted average of yarn and cloth.

[25] Rate on tissues.

[26] Customs (approximately 75% of import value) less excise (approximately 20%). Based on imports from all foreign countries. No imports from the United States are separately recorded.

[27] Weighted average of yarn, cloth, carpets, felt.

[28] Rate on tissues and carpets.

[29] 1946. *Heavy Clothing Industry Working Party Report,* p. 153.

[30] Based on value; quantity data inadequate.

[31] Not available.

[32] United Kingdom, 1938; United States, 1939.

[33] This ratio would be lower if allowance were made for the higher proportion of larger bulbs in United Kingdom exports.

[34] In terms of value of net output per worker, the ratios are 1.0 for matches and 1.7 for rubber tyres and the two items cease to be exceptions.

[35] 1935.

[36] Customs (approximately 370% of import value) less excise (approximately 325%). Based on imports from all foreign countries. No imports from the United States are separately recorded.

[37] Automobile outer covers only.

[38] Men's shoes — large United Kingdom export surplus to United States. Women's shoes — large United States export surplus to United Kingdom.

[39] Imports paid customs duty of 14 cents per lb. and internal revenue tax of 15 cents per lb., making a total of 29 cents per lb. Margarine produced in the United States paid internal revenue tax of 10 cents per lb. if coloured and of ¼ cent per lb. if uncoloured. Assuming that all imports from the United Kingdom were coloured, the extra tax paid by them was 19 cents per lb., equivalent to approximately 210% of the average value of imports from the United Kingdom. On uncoloured imports the extra tax would be still higher.

[40] Customs (approximately 29% of import value) less internal revenue tax (approximately 9%), which was levied on beer produced in the United States, but not on imported beer.

far they offset Britain's comparative advantages. This diagram (drawn on a double logarithmic scale for reasons to be explained later) shows the ratio of American to British output per worker in each industry — measured vertically — and the ratio of American to British exports — measured horizontally — for all products in our sample save the exceptions noted above. Where United States output per worker is not more than twice the British (items on or below the horizontal line marked 2) the indicidence of the American tariff is shown by an upward-pointing arrow. In cotton spinning and weaving, for example, United States output per worker is estimated at 1.5 times the British, and since the United States tariff was on average about 35%, the arrow extends upwards to just over 2.0. This means that, assuming a labour theory of value and American weekly wages

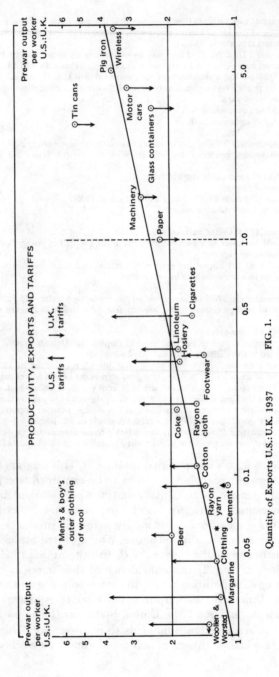

FIG. 1.

double the British, the price of United Kingdom goods would be three-quarters of the American in the world market, but as dear as the American in the American market after paying the tariff. Thus the tariff almost exactly offset Britain's comparative advantage in cotton goods, even ignoring the cost of transport.[7]

It will be seen that the American tariff fully offset Britain's comparative advantage in every product except cement and coke (where the cost of transport is high), and footwear, where the remaining margin was not large in relation to the transport and other special costs involved. (Figures given later show that the United States tariff also offset Britain's advantage as measured by *export prices* in every product save cement, coke, footwear and beer.[8]) It is perhaps significant that the American tariff was, in general, much higher on products where Britain had a comparative advantage than it was on the others. The unweighted average was 61% *ad valorem* where Britain had a comparative advantage, 28% where she had not.[9]

(It must be emphasised that all these conclusions refer to pre-war conditions. Since then, the *ad valorem* incidence of the U.S. tariff on many items has been substantially reduced, both through the reduction of rates and through the rise in prices, which has reduced the incidence of specific duties. There has, moreover, been a large rise in the ratio of American to British average dollar weekly earnings in manufacturing, from about 2 in October 1938 to nearly 3½ in April 1951. While in many industries output per worker may also have risen faster in the United States, there seems little doubt that, in most, American labour cost per unit of output must have risen in relation to the British. It seems likely, therefore, that the importance of the United States tariff in offsetting Britain's comparative advantages has in general been reduced.)

The British 1937 tariffs (Column (7) of Table II) were generally

---

[7] It will be seen later that the United States tariff on cotton goods offset, with a more substantial margin to spare, Britain's advantage as measured both by wage costs per unit of output and by export price.

[8] If, however, the *ad valorem* incidence of the (specific) beer duties is reckoned on the average value of the United Kingdom's total exports of beer, rather than on that of United States imports from the United Kingdom, the United States tariff (even after allowing for the internal revenue tax levied only on American-produced beer) fully offset Britain's price advantage.

[9] Groups II and I respectively in Table II.
Similar calculations covering 155 commodities showed that the average American tariff was 40% where the British *export price* was lower than the American and 26% where it was higher. They also showed that, in a (bare) majority of the cases where the British export price was lower than the American, the American tariff offset the British price advantage. (In these calculations, the *ad valorem* incidence of the American tariff was, for simplicity in computation, based on American imports from all sources, rather than on imports from the United Kingdom only.)

lower than the American; the unweighted average was 24% *ad valorem*[10] compared with an American average of 45%. The downward-pointing arrows in the diagram[11] show that the British tariffs fully offset America's comparative advantage in only paper and glass containers; British imports of these products from the United States were a negligible part of her total consumption. The British tariff failed to offset America's comparative advantage in machinery, motor cars, wireless sets and valves, pig iron and tin cans; in all but the last, where the cost of transport is high because of stowage difficulties, Britain's imports from the United States were a significant but still a small part of her consumption, ranging from 2½ to 8%. That they were not larger may perhaps be partly explained by transport and other special costs. The margins remaining after the tariff were small for machinery and motor cars, and for pig iron the cost of transport is heavy. Another possible reason will be given later for the low imports of these products into Britain.[12]

The more protective nature of the United States than of the United Kingdom tariff may help to explain the following facts: in 1937, only 4½% of Britain's exports of manufactures were sold in the United States, although that country accounted for about one-third of the world's consumption (not imports) of manufactures outside the United Kingdom; but as much as 11% of the United States' exports of manufactures were sold in the United Kingdom, roughly equal to the proportion which Britain represented of the world's consumption of manufactures outside the United States.[13]

VARYING RELATIVE WAGES

So far we have assumed that American weekly wages were roughly double the British in all the industries considered. In fact, there was some variation. It is, however, difficult to make allowance for this

[10] Omitting tin cans, for which no American figure was found.

[11] If the United Kingdom tariff was $100t\%$, and the ratio of United States to United Kingdom productivity R, the downward-pointing arrow brings the point down to $R(1 + t)$.

[12] See section on 'Indirect Labour.'

Figures given later show that America's advantage as measured by *export price* was fully offset by the United Kingdom tariff on motor cars, and the margins remaining after the tariff are reduced on tin cans, pig iron and wireless sets and valves. (For glass containers and paper, however, the American advantage is no longer offset).

[13] The figures in this paragraph are not all strictly comparable. The proportion of Britain's exports of manufactures sold in the United States is based on the United Kingdom's recorded exports of 'articles wholly or mainly manufactured.' The proportion of the United States' exports of manufactures sold in the United Kingdom is based on American recorded exports of 'finished manufactures' plus 'semi-manufactures.' The other two proportions quoted are calculated mainly from *Industrialisation and Foreign Trade*, League of Nations, 1945, and are based broadly on the classification 'manufactured articles' in the International (Brussels) Classification of 1913.

since the industrial classifications used by the two countries for the purpose of wage statistics differ considerably, and do not agree very closely with the classifications used in the productivity comparisons quoted. It was thought desirable, nevertheless, to make some very rough estimates of relative wage costs per unit of output, allowing for varying wage ratios, to test the validity of the general conclusions so far reached. The results for thirteen industries are shown in Table III. The 'exceptional' cases are excluded as before, together with other industries for which it seemed impossible to make even rough estimates of relative wages.

It was found that American weekly earnings ranged between about 1½ and 2½ times the British (see column (2)). Column (3) gives rough estimates of relative wage costs per unit of output, calculated from the relative output per worker and wage figures. It will be seen that, in all industries save cigarettes, American wage costs per unit of output were less than or greater than the British, according as

TABLE III

	(1) Output per worker U.S.:U.K. pre-war	(2) Weekly dollar earnings U.S.:U.K. Oct. 1938	(3) Wage costs per unit of output U.S.:U.K. (2) ÷ (1)	(4) Quantity of exports U.S.:U.K. 1937
Pig iron	3.6	1.5	0.4	5.1
Motor cars	3.1	2.0	0.6	4.3
Machinery	2.7	1.9	0.7	1.5
Glass containers	2.4	2.0	0.8	3.5
Paper	2.2	2.0	0.9	1.0
Cigarettes	1.7	1.5	0.9	0.47
Leather footwear	1.4	1.5	1.1	0.32
Hosiery	1.8	1.9	1.1	0.30
Cotton spinning and weaving	1.5	1.7	1.1	0.11
Beer	2.0	2.6	1.3	0.056
Cement	1.1	1.7	1.5	0.091
Woollen and worsted	1.35	2.0	1.5	0.004
Men's and boys' outer clothing of wool	1.25	2.3	1.8	0.044

Sources

Columns (1) and (4): from Table II.

Column (2): *Ministry of Labour Gazette.* November and December 1940, and *Monthly Labour Review*, February 1939 (U.S. Dept. of Labour; Bureau of Labour Statistics). The figures are rough orders of magnitude only and subject to a considerable margin of error. They often refer to industry groups that are neither exactly comparable in the two countries nor identical with those used in deriving the figures in columns (1) and (4).

American output per worker was or was not more than twice the British. There is also a clear inverse relation between relative wage costs per unit of output (column (3)) and relative exports (column (4)), rather clearer in fact than that between relative output per worker and relative exports. The earlier generalisations on tariffs also remain valid.[14]

Owing to the unsatisfactory nature of the statistics, no great significance should be attached to the detailed results shown, but the general impression derived from Table III is that the main conclusions reached earlier in the paper are unaffected by the fact that American wages were not exactly double the British in all industries.

THE OHLIN THEORY
The figures given so far tend to confirm the theory of comparative costs, even when based on a labour theory of value, so far as exports to third countries are concerned, and the small volume of trade in manufactures between Britain and America can be largely explained by tariffs that offset comparative advantages. The theory, as developed by Ohlin, that countries will export goods requiring a relatively high proportion of the factors with which they are well endowed, is not, however, confirmed by the statistics given by Mr. Rostas. If horse-power is taken as a rough index of capital employed, there is little tendency for Britain to export more than America of products requiring a low ratio of capital to labour, and vice versa. We find, for example, that Britain had the larger export market in linoleum, cement and coke, where the ratio of horse-power to labour is above the average for all factory trades in both countries, while the United States had the larger export market in tin cans, wireless, motor cars, machinery and glass containers, where the ratio of horse-power to labour is below the average.[15] Since, however, horse-power is probably an inadequate measure of capital employed, these negative results must not be taken as a refutation of the Ohlin theory.

IMPERFECT MARKETS
The usual labour theory of comparative costs assumes perfect markets and homogeneous products. If there were also no transport costs, Britain and America could both export the same commodity only where the productivity ratio equalled the wage ratio. Where either country had any comparative advantage, however small, she

---

[14] The only differences are that the American tariff now offsets the British advantage in leather footwear and fails to offset it in beer and in men's and boys' outer clothing of wool (but only by around 10% in each case).
[15] See Rostas, *op. cit,.*, pp. 68—70.

would get the whole export market. We find that, in fact, neither Britain nor America ever got the whole of the market (although this might be the case if we could take very narrow categories of goods). Each country tended rather to get the larger share of the market where it had a comparative advantage. But the figures show more than this. There is also a tendency for each country to get a larger and larger share of the market the greater its comparative advantage, especially when allowance is made for varying relative wages. This is what we should expect when there are imperfect markets, non-homogeneous products and transport costs, and the data thus tend to confirm the labour theory of comparative costs when these more realistic conditions are introduced.

A feature revealed by Fig. 1 that would not have been expected *a priori* is that the points lie fairly close to a straight line when plotted on a double logarithmic scale. The implications will be discussed later, but it may be well to consider for a moment the fact that the regression line passes through the horizontal line marked 2 (American output per worker twice the British) at a point well to the left of the vertical line marked 1.0 (American and British exports the same). This means that America tended to export considerably less than Britain (less than two-fifths as much) even in industries where her output per worker was double the British and so exceeded the British by as much as her wage level. America tended to export as much as Britain only when her output per worker was about 2½ times the British.[16] One possible reason is that Britain had on balance an advantage in the imperfect world market, including the advantage of Imperial Preference; this will be examined in more detail below. But there is another possible reason which must now be mentioned.

INDIRECT LABOUR

It seems likely that, where Mr. Rostas's figures show the Americans using half as much labour *within the factory* per unit of output, they were using more than half as much labour indirectly, to produce the goods and to transport them to the ports, in other sectors of the economy such as building, transport, distribution, commercial and other services. Even if in some non-manufacturing sectors, such as coal-mining, the Americans used less than half as much indirect labour per unit of output, it seems likely that on balance the figures of Mr. Rostas exaggerate the overall American superiority, except perhaps in products where they show American output per worker in

---

[16] If the 'exceptional' cases are included, the line is shifted still farther to the left.

the factory as considerably less than twice the British; in such cases the American superiority in output per worker may be less in the factory than in other sectors, and Mr. Rostas's figures may therefore understate the overall American superiority.[17]

If we could re-draw our diagram in terms of output per worker, including indirect workers, we should therefore expect the points on the right, referring to products where America had a comparative advantage, to be brought down nearer to the horizontal line marked 2; this would help to explain the small scale of Britain's imports even where her tariff did not appear to offset America's comparative advantage. On the left of the diagram, the higher points would tend to be lowered and some of the lower points might be raised. It seems that, in general, our conclusions on the protective nature of the American tariff would be unaffected. It is not unlikely that the regression line would be lowered and would cut the horizontal line marked 2 farther to the right, thus reducing the apparent dis-advantage of the United States in the imperfect world markets.

It is likely that the regression line, besides being shifted down-wards, would also become flatter, not only because the relative amounts of indirect labour per unit of output used in transport, distribution, etc., are largely independent of relative productivity in the factory,[18] but also in so far as individual factories used semi-finished products from a random selection of manufacturing industries in which the American relative superiority in output per worker tended to average 2:1. The importance of this latter

---

[17] Mr. Rostas (*op. cit.*, p. 89) suggests the following rough relative productivities per worker (United States:United Kingdom) in certain non-manufacturing sectors:

Transport of goods	1.0 (ignoring distance, which seems appropriate for this analysis)
Commercial and other services	1.0
Distribution	1.5
Building	1.15
Gas	1.7
Electricity	1.9
Communications	2.7
Mining	4.15

To find the indirect labour used in a manufactured product it is, of course, necessary to estimate also the amount of fuel, commercial services, etc., used per unit of output, but it is not thought that this would substantially alter the conclusions reached in the text. As regards labour used indirectly in replacing capital equipment, Mr. Rostas (*op. cit.*, pp. 56—8) finds no reason for supposing that this would greatly alter the average 2:1 superiority of United States industry in output per worker.

[18] It also seems that there is no observable relation between the relative amounts of capital (at least as measured by horse-power) used per unit of output and the relative productivities (see Rostas, *op. cit.*, p. 54). In so far as relatively high output per worker goes with relatively high capital per unit of output, the range of overall relative productivity would be still further reduced by the inclusion of labour used in capital replacement.

consideration must not, however, be exaggerated. Textile factories, for example, tend to use the semi-finished products of other textile factories, and Britain tended to have a comparative advantage over most of the textile field. Similarly, engineering works tend to use the products of other engineering works, and the United States had a comparative advantage over much of this field.

This may also help to explain the fairly good correlation between relative output per worker in the factory and relative exports. It is, after all, total cost and price rather than output per worker that is of importance in determining exports,[19] and, since the wage bill of the average British factory was only about one-fifth of the total value of the output, it might have been thought that the differences in other costs would swamp differences in wage costs.[20] But there is in fact, as we shall see, a distinct correlation between relative output per worker in the factory and relative export price, and this may well be because a large part of the semi-manufactures bought by the average firm comes from industries with an output per worker, in relation to America, similar to its own.

B. EXPORTS AND PRICES

We have already mentioned the rather surprising fact that, if relative output per worker is plotted against relative exports, the points tend to lie about a straight line if a double logarithmic scale is used. The correlation coefficient is 0.8, and the steeper of the two regression lines (that minimising the sum of the squares of the deviations in a horizontal direction) has a slope of about 4.[21] This is the regression line shown in Fig. 1. (If the 'exceptional' items are included the correlation coefficient is 0.7 and the slope is about 3.)[22] In other words, we find that, if the ratio of British to American output per worker in the factory was 1% higher for commodity A than for commodity B, the ratio of exports, according to the regression line shown, tended to be 3–4% higher. If *prices* in each country were proportional to direct *factory* labour used per unit of output the plotting of relative export prices against relative export quantities would show a downward slope of exactly the same magnitude, but if, as is less unlikely, prices were proportional to the *total* amount of

[19] Except in so far as high productivity includes the ability to keep up to date, etc.

[20] In round figures, the gross output of factory trades in the 1935 Census of Production was made up of 20% wages, 55% raw materials, etc., 25% other costs and profits.

[21] Throughout this study, for simplicity of exposition, dx/dy is used as a measure of slopes, not dy/dx, the more usual measure.

[22] The slope of the regression line, when the sum of the squares of the *vertical* deviations is minimised, is considerably flatter (5.7 excluding the exceptional cases and 6.0 including them).

labour used per unit of output, including indirect labour, we should expect the slope to be flatter for the reasons given above. The range of prices would, moreover, be still further reduced, and the curve still further flattened, if we took account of the use of raw materials entering into world trade and coming from neither the United States nor the United Kingdom, since their cost would tend to be the same for British and American manufacturers.

We do in fact find (in column (3) of Table II) that, disregarding our exceptional cases as before, the American export price was always lower than the British where America had a comparative advantage (output per worker in the factory more than twice the British) and exported more than Britain. Similarly, British export prices were always lower than the American where Britain had a comparative advantage and exported more than America.[23] The inverse relation between relative price and relative quantity is clearly illustrated in Table IV.[24] When relative exports are plotted against relative prices, rather than against relative output per worker in the factory, on a double logarithmic scale, the correlation coefficient is −0.8 and the steeper regression line has a slope of about −5. (If the five 'exceptional' cases are included, the correlation coefficient is −0.7 and the slope about −4.[25]) The slope of the line is flattened as we had expected.[26] A difference of 1% in relative price tends to be associated with a difference of 4–5% in relative quantity of exports. This result, and those that follow, are based on the steeper of the two regression lines. Reasons will be given later for supposing that such results tend to underestimate the true difference in relative quantity associated with a 1% difference in relative price. In the same way, the flatter of the two regression lines tends to give an overstimate.

The term 'price' is, of course, a misnomer in this context. It should, strictly, be replaced by 'average value' to take account of differing qualities and the like. This matter will be further discussed below. It is likely that, in other respects, some of the figures quoted

[23] No figures of price were available for machinery or for men's and boys' outer clothing of wool. Omitting these, the coefficient of correlation between the logarithms of relative output per worker and relative price was −0.83 excluding the exceptional cases and −0.70 including them.

[24] This table includes three of the five 'exceptional' cases: rubber tyres, soap and biscuits. It excludes the remaining two (electric lamps and matches), American exports of which were less than the British although American prices were lower.

[25] The slope of the other regression line is −7.6, both including and excluding the exceptional cases.

[26] The regression and correlation coefficients given here are broadly comparable with those in the previous paragraph, since the latter are hardly affected by the exclusion of machinery and clothing.

TABLE IV
Price and Quantity of American and British Exports, 1937

American price less than the British:

Wireless sets and valves	U.S. exports 8 times U.K. exports
Pig iron	5
Motor cars	4
Glass containers	3½
Tin cans	3
Paper	1

American price 1—1¼ times the British:

Rubber tyres	U.K. exports 1½ times U.S. exports
Cigarettes	2
Linoleum, oilcloth, etc.	3
Hosiery	3
Soap	3
Biscuits	4
Rayon weaving	5
Coke	5
Cotton goods	9

American price over 1¼ times the British:

Leather footwear	3
Rayon making	11
Cement	11
Beer	18
Margarine	32
Woollen and worsted	250

so far give a misleading picture of particular products. For this, apologies are due to experts in the various industries. It should be emphasised that the study is concerned only with an attempt to establish certain general conclusions, and it is hoped that these will not be upset by technical errors in the various fields. The detailed figures given should be interpreted in this light, and should not be taken as establishing anything about any particular industry or product; this would require more intensive study. In the rest of the paper no mention will be made of specific products.

A LARGER SAMPLE

The results given so far are based on a sample covering a substantial part of the British and American export trade in manufactures by value, but the number of observations is comparatively small. If, however, we leave productivity comparisons and the labour theory of value — the validity of which is in any case limited — we are no longer bound to the industrial groups for which Mr. Rostas and others have calculated figures. We can delve into the greater detail of the export trade returns.

This has been done, again for 1937, and 171 manufactures (including some semi-manufactures and manufactured foodstuffs) were found that seemed reasonably comparable and for which suitable quantity and value figures were given in the trade accounts of the two countries.[27] A correlation of the logarithms of relative dollar prices and relative quantities of exports gave a correlation coefficient of −0.62, and the regression line had a slope of −2.9, steeper than that derived from the smaller sample even when the 'exceptional' cases were included.

To test whether this result for 1937 was typical, similar calculations were made for each of the years 1922 to 1938. Owing to changes of classification in the trade accounts, it was impossible to get data for the same 171 products in each year. Reasonably comparable figures were, however, found for 109 items in each of the years 1928–38, for ninety-seven items in each of the years 1925–28 and for eighty-six items in each of the years 1922–25. (For the years before 1922, classification problems greatly reduced the number of comparable figures available.) The results are shown in Table V. Bearing in mind the changed coverage introduced in 1925 and 1928, for which years figures were calculated for both the smaller and the larger number of items, it is possible to analyse the trends over the whole period 1922–38.

When only 109 items are used, rather than 171, the correlation for 1937 is slightly better (−0.65) and the slope slightly flatter (−3.1). These figures turned out to be typical of the years 1934–38, each of which showed a correlation coefficient of between −0.64 and −0.68, and a slope of between −2.9 and −3.2. For the earlier years the slope was steeper and the correlation, at least before 1931, poorer. Neither the correlation nor the slope show any tendency to vary with the trade cycle. There is, however, a steady increase in the correlation coefficient and a fairly steady flattening of the slope from about 1924 until 1931. This may reflect the slow emergence of a new pattern of trade after the war and the gradual readjustment to a new price structure during a period of comparative exchange-rate stability following the post-war exchange-rate fluctuations, which no doubt upset price–quantity relationships. In February 1920 the pound had fallen, at its lowest point, to two-thirds of its pre-war dollar value; by 1922 it had recovered to about 90%, and subsequent fluctuations

[27] These covered approximately 40% of British exports of 'articles wholly or mainly manufactured' plus 'tobacco, manufactured,' 30% of American exports of 'finished manufactures' and 10% of American exports of 'semi-manufactures.' They also included a small number of manufactured foodstuffs. For statistical reasons, very few observations were possible in the important field of machinery.

TABLE V

Correlation between Logarithms of Relative Quantities (q) and Logarithms of Relative Dollar Prices (p) of United States and United Kingdom Exports of Individual Manufactured Products*

	(1) Number of manufactures	(2) Correlation co- efficient (r)	(3) Regression co- efficient (slope) (b_{qp})	(4) Rate of ex- change, pounds to dollars 1929 = 100
1913†	32	−0.54	−3.2	100
1922	86	−0.41	−2.0	91
1923	86	−0.40	−1.8	94
1924	86	−0.43	−1.9	91
1925	86	−0.47	−2.2	99
1925	97	−0.48	−2.1	99
1926	97	−0.50	−2.4	100
1927	97	−0.54	−2.4	100
1928	97	−0.55	−2.5	100
1928	109	−0.56	−2.5	100
1929	109	−0.57	−2.6	100
1930	109	−0.58	−2.6	100
1931	109	−0.66	−2.7	93
1932	109	−0.62	−2.6	72
1933	109	−0.65	−2.8	87
1934	109	−0.68	−3.2	104
1935	109	−0.64	−3.0	101
1936	109	−0.67	−2.9	102
1937	109 (171)	−0.65 (−0.62)	−3.1 (−2.9)	102
1938	109	−0.68	−3.1	101
1934—38‡	109	−0.73	−3.6	102
1937	118	−0.62	−3.0	102
1948	118	−0.34	−1.6	83

*Including some semi-manufactures and manufactured foodstuffs.
†Mid-1912 to mid-1913 for the United States.
‡See text.

were comparatively small until the return to the gold standard in 1925 ensured exchange-rate stability until September 1931.

In 1932 there was a reversal of the previous upward trend in both correlation coefficient and slope. Both fell, no doubt because of Britain's abandonment of the gold standard and the sharp fall in the dollar value of the pound, which might have been expected temporarily to upset price—quantity relationships.

Both correlation coefficient and slope increased again in 1933 and

1934, and from 1934 to 1938 remained generally at higher levels than previously, but showed no upward or downward trend. The flatter slope and higher correlation in these last five years is consistent with the trend observed in earlier years. It might have been thought that the Ottawa Agreements would have tended to weaken, rather than to strengthen, the relationship between relative prices (f.o.b. Britain and the United States) and relative quantities of exports to third countries, but, as will be seen later, the increased preference granted to British exports was probably not of great quantitative importance. The rather violent changes in exchange rates between September 1931 and the end of 1933 might have been expected to upset, at least temporarily, the price-quantity relationship, but, as the dollar-sterling rate had returned by 1934 to approximately the old parity, and as it varied little between 1934 and 1938, it may be that the fluctuations between September 1931 and the end of 1933 merely served to increase the price-consciousness of importers able to buy either British or American goods, and that this is one reason for the flatter slope in the later thirties. The fact that the exchange rate returned to approximately its old level may also help to explain the comparative stability of the slope and the correlation from 1934 onwards. After a substantial change in exchange rates that was *not* reversed, time might be required for a new pattern of trade to emerge, and during this period one might expect the correlation gradually to improve and the slope to flatten. It may be, of course, that such a tendency between 1934 and 1938 was offset by the growth of exchange and trade controls which weakened the relation between price and quantity. It is by no means easy to explain the observed changes in the correlation coefficient and in the slope. The suggestions made above are highly tentative.

Similar calculations were made for the years 1913 and 1948. For 1913 only thiry-two comparable products could be found. The correlation coefficient was −0.54 and the slope −3.2, but, in view of the much smaller number of observations, these results cannot be compared with those for the later years; nor should any great significance be attached to them. The calculation for 1948 covered 118 products.[28] The correlation coefficient was low (−0.34) and the slope only −1.6. Such a weak relation between relative price and

[28] It was impossible to obtain figures for the 109 products used in the calculations for 1928–38. The 118 products are, however, all included in the 171 used in the original calculation for 1937.

relative quantity was to be expected. Discriminatory regulation of trade was widespread, and the demand for many goods (particularly of British origin) at the ruling price was unsatisfied in varying degree owing to shortage of supply.

Similar calculations were also made, for 1929, for eight other pairs of the five major exporters of manufactures (the United Kingdom, the United States, Germany, Japan, France). The year 1929 was chosen rather than one in the late thirties, since by that time: (a) the German official rate of exchange was of doubtful value for conversion purposes, (b) German trade policy was such as to weaken greatly the relation between price and quantity, (c) the French franc was depreciating rapidly. The results are shown in Table VI, together with that for the United States and the United Kingdom for comparison. The number of observations obtainable was smaller than in the comparison of British and American exports. The data used were also, in general, less comparable. This may account for the lower slopes generally obtained. These ranged from −1.6 to −2.8, with a mean of −2.1, compared with −2.6 for the United States: United Kingdom comparison. The four comparisons of American exports with those of the other industrial countries gave very similar results, with slopes ranging between −2.4 and −2.8.

TABLE VI

Correlation between Logarithms of Relative Quantities and Relative Dollar Prices of Exports of Manufactures, 1929

	Number of observations.	Correlation coefficient.	Slope of regression line.
U.S.:U.K.	109	−0.57	−2.6
U.S.:Japan	41	−0.62	−2.8
U.S.:Germany	51	−0.60	−2.4
U.S.:France	56	−0.54	−2.4
U.K.:France	58	−0.48	−2.2
France:Japan	40	−0.52	−2.2
France:Germany	81	−0.47	−1.7
U.K.:Japan	44	−0.61	−1.6
U.K.:Germany	77	−0.43	−1.6

The calculations so far described were all made for single years. It was, however, observed that, in the United States: United Kingdom comparison, the price–quantity relationship for certain manufactures, although consistent over most years, went astray in particular

years. In an attempt to iron out these erratic movements, calculations were also made for the period 1934—38 as a whole.[29] This gave a
better correlation (—0.73) and a considerably flatter slope (—3.6).
The regression line is shown in Fig. 2. Almost identical results
(correlation —0.71; slope —3.6) were obtained by correlating relative
quantities in 1938 with relative prices in 1934—38, suggesting that
relative quantities in a given year are rather better explained by
relative prices over a period of years ending in that year than by
relative prices in that year alone, and that a 1% difference in relative
price over a period of years is associated with a larger difference in
relative quantity in the last year that is a 1% difference in relative
price in the last year only. This is what we might expect where
relative prices have changed in the last year, assuming that time is
required for relative quantities to be adjusted. As, however, relative
prices in 1938 were highly correlated with relative prices in earlier
years, the difference is not very great.[30]

BIAS DUE TO ERRORS OF OBSERVATION
The slopes of the regression lines derived from the data available are
consistent with flatter 'real' slopes, *i.e.*, with a larger difference in
relative quantity associated with a 1% difference in relative price, if
only truly comparable figures could be obtained.

One trouble is that the quality, design, etc., of products falling
into comparable categories in the two trade returns are not always
the same, and the proportion of different qualities exported by each
country may differ. If sufficient information were available the
figures could, in principle, be adjusted. In some cases this could be
done fairly precisely, *e.g.*, where there were well-established grades
(as with wheat), with fairly constant price differentials; but with

[29] The correlation was between:

$$\frac{\text{Total quantity of U.S. exports, 1934—38}}{\text{Total quantity of U.K. exports, 1934—38}}$$

and $$\frac{\text{Average value of U.S. exports, 1934—38}}{\text{Average value of U.K. exports, 1934—38}}$$

for each of the 109 manufactures. The average value of United States exports of
manufacture X was obtained by dividing the total value of United States exports of X, over
the period 1934 to 1938, by the total quantity exported.

[30] Several attempts were also made, using multiple correlation analysis, to explain relative
quantity in one year by relative price (*a*) in that year, (*b*) in one or more earlier years, but
this did not greatly improve the explanation; the correlation between relative prices in the
various years was high. However, the sum of the partial regression coefficients was generally
somewhat higher than the simple regression coefficient obtained by correlating relative price
and quantity in the last year only. This suggests that a 1% difference in relative price
maintained over a period of years is associated with a somewhat larger difference in relative
quantity than is a 1% difference in relative price in the year in question alone.

Relative prices and quantities of U.S. and U.K. exports of 109 manufactures 1934–8

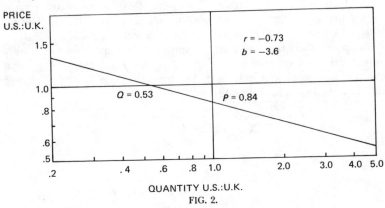

QUANTITY U.S.:U.K.

FIG. 2.

many manufactures the adjustment could only be rough and ready. The adjustments would affect both the relative price and the relative quantity figures, but in opposite senses. If, for example, it was known that the iron-ore exports[31] of country A had a 50% iron content and those of B a 25% iron content, and that importers were interested primarily in the iron content, the adjusted figures would show a relative price (A:B) half as great as the unadjusted relative price per ton of ore, and a relative quantity (A:B) twice as great as the unadjusted figure.[32]

A second difficulty is that a classification used by one country may include commodities not included at all in the most closely corresponding classification (or classifications) of the other. In this case, the required adjustment would change the figure of relative quantity, and might or might not change the figure of relative price either in the same or in the opposite sense.[33]

There is no reason why errors in the relative quantities (which are measured horizontally) should alter, in any particular sense, the slope of the regression line (which minimises the sum of the deviations in a

---

[31] Iron ore is not, of course, included in our sample of manufactures.

[32] This would mean that, on a double logarithmic scale, the adjustment would involve a shift in the point downwards and to the right, or upwards and to the left, along a line at an angle of 45° to the horizontal. In terms of logarithms the absolute price and quantity errors in the unadjusted figures would be equal. The implications are developed in Appendix A.

[33] Suppose the adjustment excluded a product from A's recorded exports within a certain category. This would increase, reduce or leave unaltered A's relative price, according as the product excluded had a price lower than, higher than or equal to that of the other products in the category.

horizontal direction). But errors in the relative prices (which are measured vertically) will tend to steepen the slope. This has been well illustrated by Mr. Orcutt,[34] and the matter is discussed in more detail in Appendix A to the present article. The following simple illustration of an extreme case may help to make the matter clear.

Suppose the figures were completely comparable and fully adjusted for differences in quality and the like, and suppose also that the market were perfect, with no transport costs. The observed points would then look like this:[35]

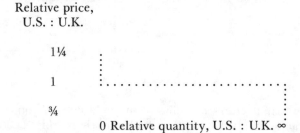

Relative price,
U.S. : U.K.

1¼

1

¾

0 Relative quantity, U.S. : U.K. ∞

Where America's price was above the British, she would export nothing; where it was less, Britain would export nothing; where it was the same, both could export. But if the observations were imperfect for the reasons given, the points might look like this:

Relative price,
U.S. : U.K.

1¼

1

¾

0   Relative quantity, U.S. : U.K.   ∞

The correlation would be very low and the regression line minimising the sum of the squares of the deviations in a horizontal direction nearly vertical. The imperfection of the data might thus lead us to suppose that there was little or no relationship between relative price

[34] G. H. Orcutt, 'Measurement of Price Elasticities in International Trade,' *Review of Economics and Statistics*, May 1950.
[35] Nought and infinity cannot in fact, of course, be shown on a logarthmic scale.

and relative quantity when in fact a small difference in relative price was associated with a very large difference in relative quantity.

It may, therefore, be that the 'real' slopes are flatter than those given by the calculations described above. The discussion in Appendix A gives reasons for believing that the slope of −3.6 for the years 1934−38 might easily have become −4 to −4½ if the observed data could have been corrected for errors of the type described, *i.e.*, that a 1% difference in relative price may well have been associated, in those years, with a difference of, say, 4−4½% in relative quantity.

The second half of this study will be concerned with the use of the data obtained to measure: (*a*) elasticities of substitution between British and American exports of manufactures and (*b*) the importance of factors other than price, and in particular of Imperial Preference, in determining the share of British and American exports in world markets.

C. ELASTICITY OF SUBSTITUTION

In Section B of this study we dealt with observed facts about the prices and quantities of British and American exports of a large number of manufactures in a given period of one or five years, and made some speculations about the possible effects of errors in the data used. We reached the conclusion that, in the years 1934−38 for example, where the relative price of product A was 1% lower than the relative price of product B, the relative quantity of product A tended to be at least 3½% greater than that of product B, and quite possibly 4−4½% greater when allowance is made for bias due to errors of observation. We made no examination of changes over time. It would, therefore, be a bold step to conclude from the facts observed that, in pre-war conditions, a 1% *fall* in a typical product's relative price would tend to lead to a 4−4½% (or even to a 3½%) *rise* in its relative quantity. In view, however, of the difficulties involved in most methods hitherto used for measuring elasticities in international trade,[36] it seems that this possible alternative approach, which might perhaps be called the 'commodity comparison' method, should be further explored. A similar type of cross-section analysis is, after all, used when conclusions are drawn about income elasticity of demand from family budgets observed in a given period; although admittedly one set of consumers may be more likely to behave like another set, given the conditions of the latter set, than one manufactured export is to behave like another.

[36] See Orcutt, *op. cit.*

THE 'COMMODITY COMPARISON' METHOD VERSUS THE 'TIME SERIES'
METHOD
Although the commodity comparison method of estimating elasticities in international trade is open to special objections, it avoids
certain other difficulties involved in the use of time series.

(1) The latter method often suffers from a paucity of observations. For example, Mr. Chang's estimate of the elasticity of
substitution between British and American exports of manufactures
in the inter-war years[37] was based on fifteen observations (for the
years 1924–38) compared with between 86 and 171 observations in
each of the calculations described above.[38]

(2) In the time series method the range of relevant price variation
(after allowance has been made for income changes) is often small in
relation to the errors of observation – in many cases only 5% or
10%.[39] For example, the standard deviation of the ratio of the U.S.
to the U.K. export price indices of manufactures over the period
1922–38 was only 7–8% of the mean, even before allowing for
trend or for world income, which, according to Professor A. J.
Brown,[40] was highly correlated with relative prices. In the calculations described above, the errors may be greater but the range of
price variation is much larger. For example, the standard deviation of
the 109 relative prices (U.S. : U.K.) used in the calculation for
1934–38 was 40% of the mean.[41]

(3) Mr. Orcutt has shown[42] that most time series analyses of
inter-war data can at best show the consequences of relatively small
changes in prices since the range of relative price variation was small.
He has also given reasons for supposing that elasticities are greater for
large than they are for small price changes, mainly because of the

[37] Tse Chun Chang, 'A Statistical Note on World Demand for Exports,' *Review of Economics and Statistics*, May 1948.
[38] Mr. Kubinski's method ('The Elasticity of Substitution between Sources of British Imports, 1921–38,' *Yorkshire Bulletin of Economic and Social Research*, January 1950) is based on an examination of 289 commodities imported into the U.K., but the number of observations in each correlation calculation is never more than eighteen (for each of the years 1921–38).
Messrs. D. J. Morgan and W. J. Corlett ('The Influence of Price in International Trade: A Study in Method,' *Journal of the Royal Statistical Society*, 1951) give the results of a few calculations with as many as forty-five observations (for the years 1870 to 1914), but the great majority of their calculations are based on less than twenty observations.
See also Orcutt, *op. cit.*, footnote 7, where it is argued that, in the time series method, the effective may be substantially less than the actual number of observations.
[39] See Orcutt, *op. cit.*, p. 121.
[40] *Oxford Studies in the Price Mechanism*, p. 95.
[41] The standard deviation of the 109 relative prices, U.K.:U.S., was 57% of the mean.
[42] *Op. cit.*, pp. 125–6.

cost and trouble to the buyer of shifting from one souce of supply to another. The commodity comparison method described above shows the extent to which relative quantities may vary when there are substantial differences in relative prices (at least as between different commodities at one time).

(4) According to Mr. Orcutt, the time series method may tend to give estimates of relatively short-run elasticities and underestimate the long-run elasticities. If this is so, the commodity comparison method may give a closer approximation to long-run elasticities, *i.e.*, to probable changes in relative quantities resulting from changes in relative prices if time were allowed for the consequences to work themselves out. This is, of course, an advantage only if it is desired to estimate long-run elasticities. Since the general pattern of relative export prices of British and American manufactures in our sample did not change greatly between 1934 and 1938, it may be that the regression coefficients for the later thirties give a fair idea of relatively long-run elasticities of substitution.

These apparent advantages of the commodity comparison method may justify its use, despite its limitations, at least as a complement to the time series method.[43] The last three of the four advantages just mentioned would lead one to expect higher elasticities than are obtained by the time series method. But, like the latter, the commodity comparison method may also tend to underestimate elasticities for a number of reasons. That connected with errors of observation was discussed in the last section, and there are two others that must now be explained.

FURTHER POSSIBLE BIAS IN THE COMMODITY COMPARISON METHOD

If we take the plunge and attempt to use the results of the commodity comparison method as some indication of what might happen to the relative demand for British and American exports of a particular product when relative prices change, we must assume that, for each product, there is a relationship between relative price and relative quantity demanded. Using our diagram measuring relative

[43] Mr. Orcutt has also shown (*op. cit.*, pp. 122—3) that, over time, supply and demand schedules are likely to move up and down together, and that this probably leads to an underestimate of elasticities of demand calculated from observed time series. We shall see later that, in the method described in the present article, there are schedules somewhat similar to demand and supply schedules and that these are not the same for each product, but there is no obvious reason why they should vary up and down together. This cannot, however, be counted as an advantage of the commodity comparison over the time series method, since Mr. Orcutt's criticism does not seem to apply to time series calculations using *relative* price and quantity indices. (See also footnote 45 of this study.)

prices vertically and relative quantities horizontally on a double logarithmic scale, we have 'demand substitution curves' for each product. Let us assume that these are straight lines and, for the moment, that they all have the same slope, which we wish to discover. There is, however, no reason why they should coincide. When, for example, British and American prices are equal (even after adjustment for 'quality' differences) the relative quantities demanded may vary; Britain may have an advantage in one imperfect market, America in another. We thus get a series of demand substitution curves lying between $D_1 D_1$ and $D_2 D_2$ in the following diagram:

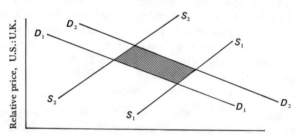

Relative quantity, U.S.:U.K.

We can also think of 'supply substitution curves' for each product, showing the relative quantities supplied at various relative prices.[44] These, likewise, are unlikely to coincide, because of differences in national factor endowments. When, for example, British and American prices are equal, Britain may supply much more of product A than the U.S., and much less of product B. We thus get a series of supply substitution curves lying between $S_1 S_1$ and $S_2 S_2$ which we assume for the time being to be upward sloping.

The observed points will lie at the intersection of the supply and demand substitution curves for each product, *i.e.*, within the shaded area. It is fairly clear (and this is demonstrated in Appendix B) that a regression line fitted to such points, so as to minimise the sum of the squares of the deviations in a horizontal direction, will tend to have a

[44]This is, of course, a simplification, since there may be an infinite number of pairs of prices that will give the same price ratio, and these different pairs of prices will normally lead to different ratios of quantity supplied unless the two national supply curves are related in a special way, *e.g.*, if they are parallel straight lines on a double logarithmic scale, *i.e.*, with equations of the type:

$$\log q = \log a_1 + b \log p$$

$$\log q = \log a_2 + b \log p$$

where p and q are relative price and relative quantity, and a_1, a_2 and b are constants. The two curves in this case have the same (constant) elasticity.

slope steeper than D_1D_1, and will thus underestimate the true slope of the demand substitution curves for each commodity.[45] The fact that negative rather than positive slopes are obtained for the regression lines means, presumably, that the position of the demand substitution curves varies less from product to product than the position of the supply substitution curves, *i.e.*, broadly, that differences in comparative national advantages in the imperfect markets for the various commodities have a less important effect than differences in national factor endowments on the position of the curves. This does not seem altogether unreasonable.

We must now remove the assumption that the demand substitution curves are parallel. It seems almost certain that some will be flatter than others, *e.g.*, where the market is more perfect or the product less heterogeneous. To isolate this point, let us suppose that, where British and American prices are equal, the ratio of the quantities demanded is the same for each product; *i.e.*, if either country has an advantage, it is the same in the market for each product. The various demand substitution curves will all pass through the point Z in the following diagram:

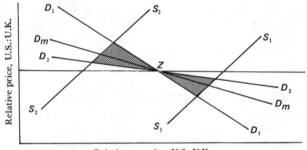

Relative quantity, U.S.:U.K.

[45] According to our conventions the nearer the curve to the horizontal the greater the slope (see footnote 21 of this study).

When a supply substitution curve is well to the right, *i.e.*, when national factor endowments are such that America supplies far more of the product than Britain at the same price, it is possible that the demand substitution curve will also tend to be well to the right, *i.e.*, that the demand for the American product will be far more than that for the British product at the same price. This might be so, because America's inevitably large share in the market has made her products better known to importers. Similarly, supply substitution curves towards the left may tend to be associated with demand substitution curves towards the left. In other words, high demand substitution curves may tend to be associated with low supply substitution curves and vice versa. If this is the case, the calculated regression line may tend to overestimate the true slope of the demand substitution curves for each commodity for reasons similar to those given by Mr. Orcutt (*op. cit.*, p. 123), where he shows that, in so far as demand and supply curves tend to move up and down together, the calculated regression line will tend to underestimate the true slope.

The steepest is $D_1 D_1$, the flattest $D_2 D_2$, the mean slope is that of $D_m D_m$.[46]

The observed points will lie within the shaded area. It is fairly clear (and this is also demonstrated in Appendix B) that the regression line fitted to such points will tend to have a slope steeper than $D_m D_m$, and will thus underestimate the true average slope of the demand substition curves for the various commodities.

The various demand substitution curves will, in fact, both have different slopes and cut the equal price axis at different points. The calculated slope will thus be steeper than the true average slope for both of these reasons.

This conclusion depends, however, on the assumption that the supply substitution curves slope upwards. If they are horizontal there is no bias, and if they are downward sloping the bias is in the other direction. This would necessitate downward sloping export-supply curves for individual British and American manufactures. It might be argued that, in the thirties at least, these curves did not slope appreciably upwards, since, *inter alia*, there was generally excess capacity and since exports were only a fraction of total output. For similar reasons it might be argued that the curves did not slope downwards and that, even in the long run, this would be unlikely where exports were not a large part of total output. The reader may make his private guess, but, for the purpose of this article, it seems safer to make no adjustment to our figures for the possible bias just discussed.

'PRODUCT' AND 'TOTAL' ELASTICITIES OF SUBSTITUTION

A 'product' elasticity of substitution of, say, —4 between British and American exports of individual manufactures would not necessarily mean, of course, that the elasticity of substitution between the two countries' total exports of manufactures was as high as —4, because of the different patterns of exports. Suppose, for example, that the total market for British and American exports together were fixed for each product, and that there were only two products, the U.K. exporting 99 yards of cloth and 1 radio, the U.S. 99 radios and 1 yard of cloth. A 1% fall in the British price for each product relative to the American would then increase the *ratio* of British to American exports of cloth by 4% (from 99 to about 103 times), but this would raise the *quantity* of Britain's cloth exports to only about 99.04 yards, while American exports fell to approximately 0.96 yards

---

[4] [6]The slope of $D_m D_m$ is the *arithmetic* mean of the individual slopes. For reasons for choosing this form of average see footnote 49 of this study.

[(99.04/0.96) = 103]. Britain's exports of cloth would then rise by only 0.04% and, since the weight given to her radio exports is very small, her total volume index of exports would also rise only slightly. Similarly, America's volume index would fall only slightly, and the ratio of the two volume indices would change by only a small fraction of 1%.

To get some idea of the importance of this factor, a calculation was made, covering the 109 products mentioned above for the years 1934–38, of the change that would result in the ratio of the two countries' export-volume indices for the 109 products if there were a small uniform percentage change in the price ratio for all products caused either by a uniform change in all the prices of one country or by this combined with a different uniform change in all the prices of the other. It was assumed that the total market for each good, for U.S. and U.K. exports taken together, remained the same or changed in the same proportion. It was found that, assuming a uniform 'product' elasticity of substitution for each commodity, the corresponding 'total' elasticity of substitution (relating to price and volume indices) would be 0.614 times as large. Thus, if the product elasticity of substitution is taken as (a) −3.6 (the calculated regression coefficient), or (b) −4 to −4½ (allowing for bias due to errors of observation), the total elasticity would be (a) −2.2 or (b) −2.5 to −2.8.

Similar calculations can be made for other years or groups of years, or for other pairs of countries. To find the total elasticity of substitution on the assumptions stated it is necessary to multiply the product elasticity of substitution by $(\Sigma V_a B/\Sigma V_a) + (\Sigma V_b A/\Sigma V_b)$, where V_a and V_b are the values of the two countries' exports of each product, and A and B the proportions of the market (in terms of quantity) held by each of them $(A + B = 1)$. The formula may perhaps be called an index of similarity of exports. Where the pattern of exports is exactly the same in the two countries the index is unity, where the exports are entirely different it is zero. Details are given in Appendix C.

Indices of similarity were calculated for the 109 British and American exports of manufactures for each of the years 1928 to 1938. These are shown in column (2) of Table VII, together with the results of multiplying the indices by the corresponding regression coefficients (called 'product elasticities of substitution' in the table). The resulting 'total elasticities of substitution' are in column (3). Apart from year-to-year fluctuations, they show a steady increase throughout the period, rising from under 1½ at the beginning to over 2 at the end.

TABLE VII

British and American Exports of 109 *Manufactures*

	Product elasticity of substitution*	Index of similarity	Total elasticity of substitution (1) x (2)
	(1)	(2)	(3)
1928	2.501	0.472	1.2
1929	2.601	0.572	1.5
1930	2.599	0.542	1.4
1931	2.713	0.656	1.8
1932	2.602	0.647	1.7
1933	2.826	0.683	1.9
1934	3.241	0.561	1.8
1935	2.958	0.679	2.0
1936	2.934	0.611	1.8
1937	3.128	0.701	2.2
1938	3.134	0.660	2.1
1934—38	3.624	0.614	2.2

*As in column (3) of Table V. Before allowing for bias due to errors of observation.

The assumption that the total market for each product remains constant, or changes in the same proportion, tends, however, to understate the total elasticity of substitution. Suppose, for example, that America had roughly the same share in the Anglo-American export market for both silk and rayon stockings (two products that are, in fact, included separately in the calculations described above). A relative fall in all American prices would induce foreign buyers to substitute American for British silk stockings, and American for British rayon stockings. It would also, probably, induce them to substitute American silk for British rayon stockings and American rayon for British silk stockings. But there is no obvious reason why the total market for either silk or rayon stockings should increase relatively to the other. If, however, America had a larger share in one market than in the other, the matter would be different. If, for example, America had the bulk of the market for silk stockings, and Britain the bulk of the market for rayon stockings, there would be much more scope for substitution of American silk for British rayon stockings than for the substitution of American rayon for British silk stockings, since exports of both these last two products would be small. It seems likely, therefore, that the total market for silk stockings (America's speciality) would increase in relation to the total market for rayon stockings (Britain's speciality). The increase in

America's total exports relative to Britain's would then be greater than it would have been had the total silk-stocking market not expanded in relation to the total market for rayon stockings. This means that the total elasticity of substitution will tend to be a greater fraction of the product elasticity than that given by the formula described above.

This formula showed that if, as had been suggested earlier, the product elasticity of substitution were −4 to −4½ the total elasticity would be −2.5 to −2.8. After what has just been said, we may perhaps hazard a guess that the total elasticity might be of an order approaching −3.[47] This is about ten times as high as the figure of −0.3 obtained by Mr. Chang for the prewar elasticity of substitution between British and American exports of manufactures.[48]

The assumptions are, of course, still unrealistic. Allowance should be made for elasticities of demand by third countries for the exports of America and Britain together that vary from product to product; this also would lead to varying changes in the size of the total markets. Allowance should also be made for product elasticities of substitution that vary from product to product,[49] for varying changes in price according to elasticity of supply and so on. Further adjustments of this kind might tend to increase or to decrease the value of the total elasticity, but the author has been unable to think of any obvious reasons for such bias.

CHANGES OVER TIME

The calculations described so far have all referred to one year or to an average of years. Some calculations have also been made for

[47] It is perhaps not necessary to remind the reader that we are talking of elasticity of substitution and that this may differ from the elasticity of demand for British or American exports. If we assume that the world import market for manufactures and the prices charged by our competitors remain constant, a given elasticity of substitution between British and *all other* exports of manufactures would mean an elasticity of demand for British exports four-fifths as great, since Britain supplied about one-fifth of the world's exports of manufactures before the war. The elasticity of demand would, however, be greater in so far as the world import market for manufactures was increased as a result of lower British prices, British manufactures being substituted both for manufactures produced in importing countries and for non-manufactures. Any changes in the definition of elasticy of demand so as to allow, for example, for price reactions by our competitors or for income changes would give correspondingly different results.

[48] Chang, *op. cit.*, p.112 . Based on the years 1924–38. Mr. Chang appears to compare total U.K. exports (which were mainly manufactures and semi-manufactures) with U.S. exports of semi-manufactures and manufactured goods only. Professor A. J. Brown (*op. cit.*, p. 95) has given reasons for the low figure obtained by Mr. Chang.

[49] Some reasons are given in Appendix C for thinking that the assumption that each product elasticity of substitution is equal to the arithmetic mean of the product elasticities does not introduce any bias into the derivation of the total elasticity. This provides some justification for taking the arithmetic rather than any other mean of the product elasticities as the magnitude we wish to find. (See footnote 46.)

changes over time using the figures obtained for the 109 products. These may be of some use in attempting to assess short-run elasticities of substitution in particular periods. Suppose, for example, we wish to examine the effects on relative quantities of British and American exports of the large changes in relative prices that took place after Britain left the gold standard in September 1931. The published price and volume indices of exports of manufactures by themselvex tell us relatively little. We find, for example, that, between 1930 and 1932, the American price index for exports of manufactures rose by 23% in relation to the British (in terms of dollars), while the American volume index fell relatively by 42%.[50] This suggests an elasticity of substitution of over − 2½.[51] Similarly, between 1932 and 1934, America's price index fell relatively by 27%, while her volume index rose relatively by 23%; this suggests an elasticity of substitution of only −$\frac{2}{3}$[52]. But it would be rash to rely on single observations of this type. We have reason to think, moreover, that American exports of manufactures are more sensitive than the British to cyclical fluctuations, since they contain a higher proportion of capital goods and of durable consumer goods for which the income elasticity of demand is high. This may account for part of the relative fall in American exports between 1930 and 1932, when activity was rapidly declining throughout the world. Then again, there might have been changes, between 1932 and 1934, in the imperfection of the world market that worked to the disadvantage of U.S. exports, for example, the Ottawa Agreements and the general spread of discriminatory practices. This might account in part for the comparatively small relative rise in American exports between 1932 and 1934.

More useful results may perhaps be obtained if we examine changes in individual products. A comparison was therefore made of changes, (*a*) between 1930 and 1932 and (*b*) between 1932 and 1934, in the relative quantities and relative prices of the 109 products mentioned above. In this way we can obtain 109 observations of short-period changes instead of only one (and there is also a substantial range of variation in relative prices). We can largely eliminate the complications that arise from the different patterns of

---

[50] Using the indices for U.S. exports of 'finished manufactures' and U.K. exports of 'articles wholly or mainly manufactured.' These are not wholly comparable, but this does not matter, since the figures are used here for illustration only.

[51] $\dfrac{\log 0.58}{\log 1.23} = \dfrac{-0.2366}{0.0899} = -2.63.$

[52] $\dfrac{\log 1.23}{\log 0.73} = \dfrac{0.0899}{-0.1367} = -0.66.$

British and American exports of manufactures, except in so far as there are differences within the commodity classifications used. We can isolate, in a general way, the effects of changes in the imperfections of the world market that work to the disadvantage of one country. Thus, in comparing 1932 and 1934, we plot the relative price index for each product in 1934 (1932 = 1) against the relative quantity index on a double logarithmic scale. The regression line cuts the horizontal axis, indicating no change in relative price, at a point where the relative quantity index is 0.72 (*A* in Fig. 3). This suggests that, where the relative price of a commodity remained unchanged betwwween 1932 and 1934, there was a fall of 28% in the American quantity relative to the British quantity. This may give some indication of the extent to which imperfections of the markets changed to the disadvantage of the U.S.;[53] although the later analysis (section D and Appendix D) shows the need for caution in drawing such a conclusion. The correlation coefficient is −0.62, and the slope of the regression line is −2.0. This suggests that, after allowing for the shift to America's disadvantage, a change of 1% in relative price of a product was accompanied by a change of 2% in relative quantity; in other words, that the product elasticity of substitution was −2.[54] A similar calculation for 1930−32 gave a correlation coefficient of −0.57 and an elasticity of −1.5.

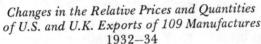

Changes in the Relative Prices and Quantities of U.S. and U.K. Exports of 109 Manufactures 1932−34

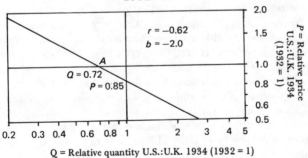

Q = Relative quantity U.S.:U.K. 1934 (1932 = 1)

FIG. 3

[53] In the case of nearly one-third of the 109 products, the American relative quantity fell despite a fall in the American relative price.

[54] The equation of the regression line is:

$$\log q = -2.0 \log p + \log 0.72$$

where *q* and *p* are indices of relative quantity and price (1934:1932)

These elasticities are considerably lower than those obtained by the other method, before allowing for downward bias. This may be partly because they can only show the comparatively short-run consequences of changes in relative prices, whereas the other method may give a better idea of long-run consequences. Even, however, when similar comparisons were made of changes over longer periods, relatively low figures were obtained. Thus, a comparison of 1929 and 1937, again for the 109 commodities, gave a correlation coefficient of only −0.45 and an elasticity of −1.8. A comparison of the four years 1928–31 against the five years 1934–38 gave a correlation coefficient of −0.48 and an elasticity of −1.7. These lower elasticities cannot be explained by the difference between long-run and short-run elasticities, unless it is thought that more than eight years are required for the full effects of price changes to be felt. It may be that they are biased towards zero more than the results of the earlier calculations, one important reason being that the range of variation in relative prices is much smaller. In general, one is hardly surprised to find rather a poor relation between relative price and relative quantity changes over a period of eight years, since so many things have happened, other than price changes, to affect the relative quantities demanded. The implications of the type of analysis just described probably deserve further examination, but this is not attempted here, as the present article is concerned primarily with the cross-section type of analysis.

CONCLUSIONS ON ELASTICITY OF SUBSTITUTION

This concludes the discussion of elasticity of substitution.[55] It cannot be too strongly emphasised that any numerical results that may be obtained by this or by other methods cannot be used to make precise forecasts. It is, however, useful to gather together all evidence that may provide some background for those who have to make forecasts and decisions, to consider as carefully as possible what the evidence means and what it does not mean, to examine possible biases and so on. Practical judgments about, for example, the effects of exchange-rate variations or the degree of difficulty involved in restoring international equilibrium do not depend upon a knowledge of whether elasticities of substitution are, say, −2.3 or −2.7, but they do require a knowledge of whether they are of the order of −0.03, or −0.3, or −3 or −30. Such judgments also, of

[55] Another type of analysis of the figures for the 109 products would be the correlation, for each product, of relative prices and relative quantities in the eleven years 1928–38, *i.e.*, 109 correlations with eleven observations each. This analysis, which would be similar to that made by Mr. Kubinski for imports into the U.K., has not been attempted.

course, require a knowledge of, or at least a view on, many other things (which will vary from time to time), such as the flexibility of supply, the reactions of producers and of their governments to changes in the prices charged by their competitors, the extent to which demand for the goods of competing nations is determined by supply of currency, speed of delivery, etc., rather than by price, and so on. Practical judgments of this type inevitably involve an act of faith; no one can work out the full implications on the world economy of an important change in the economic policy of a major country; no one can foretell the actions and reactions of millions of producers and consumers and of governments throughout the world. But this does not render futile the attempt to establish the likely order of magnitude of, for example, the elasticity of substitution between the exports of various countries, nor does it rob such a concept of all meaning.

This paper has suggested one method by which some relevant evidence can be collected and applied it to the particular case of American and British exports of manufactures, mainly in the years between the wars. There are doubtless difficulties involved in the method described other than those mentioned in this paper, and it is hoped that these will be explored by others. But is does seem fairly clear that there was some inverse relation between relative price and relative quantity and that variations in the former were associated with comparatively large variations in the latter. While it is dangerous to apply the results obtained to future changes, I believe that the evidence gives some grounds for thinking that, at least in conditions resembling those of the later thirties (an important proviso), changes in the relative prices of British and American exports of manufactures should lead to comparatively large changes in the relative quantities demanded in third markets, at least after a period of years.

D. EXPORTS AND FACTORS OTHER THAN PRICE

APPARENT AMERICAN DISADVANTAGE IN THE IMPERFECT WORLD MARKET

It will have been noticed that, according to the regression line in Fig. 2, which referred to the years 1934—38, the U.S. tended to export little more than half as much of a commodity as Britain when she charged the same price and that she exported as much only when her price was 16% below the British. As Table VIII shows, this was rather typical of the individual years 1933—38. When prices were equal, the U.S. tended to export between one-half and two-thirds as much as Britain and exported as much only when her price was 10—20%

lower. For the earlier years, 1928—32, the regression lines show the U.S. in a more favourable relative position; when prices were equal she tended to export roughly 80—90% as much as Britain, and she sold as much when her price was some 5—10% lower. For the years before 1928, allowing for lack of comparability, the figures tell roughly the same story, at least from 1924 onwards. (The results for 1948 show a striking improvement in the relative position of the U.S. compared with 1937 and, though the comparison is dangerous, there seems to have been a similar improvement between 1913 and the early 1920s.)

The figures for the years between the wars suggest that, in the period 1933—38 and, to a lesser extent, between 1924 and 1932, the U.S. had, on balance, a comparative disadvantage in the imperfect world market as the result of such factors as Imperial Preference, discrimination against dollar goods, differences in transport costs, stronger commercial ties between Britain and overseas markets, greater selling efforts by British exporters, etc. But before jumping to this conclusion we must consider other possible reasons for the low figures in Table VIII

(1) One possible explanation is that different methods of valuing exports in the two countries led to an artificial relative under-valuation of American exports. If this was so, regression lines based on the corrected figures would be above the lines we have obtained. They would show the U.S. exporting a higher fraction of the British quantity when prices were equal. There are two obvious corrections that should be made. First, U.S. exports are relatively under-valued because freight charges up to the Canadian border are not included in the recorded value of certain exports to Canada. This under-valuation probably represented about 1% of the value of U.S. exports to all countries before the war,[56] but may have been a smaller percentage of the value of manufactured exports, which tend to have a relatively high value per ton. Secondly, U.S. exports are in general valued f.a.s. (free along side), while U.K. exports are valued f.o.b. (free on board), the difference being the cost of loading. It is unlikely that this normally involved a difference of more than 1% of the value of manufactured exports. It is hard to discover any other important reason for American under-valuation, but the possibility should not be ruled out.

(2) A second possibility is that British exports were, on average, of a higher quality than the American, and that appropriate

---

[56] *Balance of International Payments of U.S.* (Department of Commerce). It is pointed out in *Foreign Commerce and Navigation of the United States* for 1946 that similar inaccuracies may occur in connection with ocean shipments.

TABLE VIII
Particular Values shown by Regression Lines

	No. of manufactures	Relative quantity (U.S.:U.K.) when price equal	Relative price (U.S.:U.K.) when quantity equal
	(1)	(2)	(3)
1913*	32	0.48	0.80
1922	86	1.01	1.01
1923	86	0.95	0.97
1924	86	0.82	0.90
1925	86	0.87	0.94
1925	97	0.81	0.91
1926	97	0.83	0.92
1927	97	0.78	0.90
1928	97	0.85	0.93
1928	109	0.90	0.96
1929	109	0.87	0.95
1930	109	0.79	0.91
1931	109	0.86	0.94
1932	109	0.84	0.93
1933	109	0.57	0.82
1934	109	0.51	0.81
1935	109	0.69	0.88
1936	109	0.59	0.83
1937	109	0.67	0.88
1938	109	0.61	0.85
1934—38	109	0.53	0.84
1937	118	0.50	0.79
1948	118	1.10	1.06
Commonwealth countries 1937	115	0.22	0.54
Non-Commonwealth countries 1937	115	1.36	1.16

*Mid-1912 to mid-1913 for U.S.

corrections would therefore raise the regression line.[54] This is a matter on which it is difficult to express an opinion.

(3) It has been shown above that the true average slopes of the lines are probably flatter than the calculated slopes because of errors of observation (other than a general tendency for the quality of one

---

[57] The correction would shift the observed points, on a double logarithmic scale, upwards and to the left at an angle of 45° to the horizontal. Since the regression lines obtained all have a slope flatter than −1, they would clearly be shifted upwards.

country's exports to be higher) and possibly for other reasons. The true regression lines would probably cut the equal-price and equal-quantity lines at different points, and this might reduce or eliminate the apparent American disadvantage. (This is discussed in Appendix D.)

For these reasons it seems unwise to conclude from the figures that, at least before 1933, the U.S. had a comparative disadvantage in the imperfect world market. For the later prewar years the presumption is stronger that this was the case, even allowing for possible errors. According to the regression line for the years 1934—38, the U.S. exported as much as the U.K. when her price was 84% of the British. It is hard to make allowance for the errors under (3) above, but it is suggested in Appendix D that this might well raise the figure to 86½%. A 2% allowance for under-valuation of U.S. exports (as in (1) above) would raise the figure farther to 88%. Thus we are left with a price margin of some 12%. If this cannot be explained by a higher average British quality ((2) above) and by immeasurable errors under (1) and (3) above, we may conclude that the U.S. had a comparative disadvantage in the later period.

That this was so is suggested in a more simple manner by the figures in columns (2) and (3) of Table IX. These are, in fact, unweighted quantity and price index numbers for the products in our sample. But, instead of comparing one year with another, they show for each year, or period of years, indices for the U.S., the U.K. being taken as unity. For the years 1934—38 taken as a whole, the recorded U.S. price was, on average, 93% of the British, but the U.S. instead of exporting more than Britain, as might have been expected, exported, on average, only 69% as much[58] If we assumed that a 2%

---

[58] These are geometric means. The arithmetic means are, of course, larger, and the harmonic means (*i.e.*, the reciprocals of the arithmetic means of relative price and quantity, U.K.:U.S. instead of U.S.:U.K.) are smaller. The various means are as follows:

	Arithmetic	Geometric	Harmonic
Relative quantity, U.S.:U.K.	4.75	0.69	0.03
Relative price, U.S.:U.K.	1.03	0.93	0.86

The arithmetic and harmonic means of relative *quantity* are greatly influenced by a few extreme cases which have a much smaller effect on the geometric mean. Nevertheless, the large difference between the arithmetic and harmonic means shows the need for caution in the use of the geometric mean. The differences between the various means of relative *price* are much less marked because the range of variation is much smaller in relative price than it is in relative quantity.

As a form of check on the geometric means, the medians were also calculated and these are shown in columns (4) and (5) of Table IX. The general picture is not very different, and the use of medians instead of geometric means does not greatly affect the arguments in the text.

TABLE IX
Geometric Means and Medians

	No. of manu-factures	Unweighted geometric means		Medians	
		Relative quantity (U.S.:U.K.)	Relative price (U.S.:U.K.)	Relative quantity (U.S.:U.K.)	Relative price (U.S.:U.K.)
	(1)	(2)	(3)	(4)	(5)
1913	32	0.69	0.90	0.55	0.89
1922	86	1.42	0.84	1.075	0.88
1923	86	1.14	0.90	1.04	0.94
1924	86	0.88	0.96	0.85	1.035
1925	86	1.03	0.93	0.89	0.98
1925	97	1.02	0.90	0.89	0.95
1926	97	1.00	0.92	0.99	0.98
1927	97	0.98	0.91	0.85	0.98
1928	97	1.05	0.92	1.01	0.99
1928	109	1.18	0.90	1.17	0.96
1929	109	1.13	0.90	1.10	0.96
1930	109	1.07	0.89	0.92	0.925
1931	109	0.94	0.97	0.98	0.99
1932	109	0.56	1.17	0.56	1.17
1933	109	0.57	1.00	0.45	1.03
1934	109	0.62	0.94	0.59	0.995
1935	109	0.59	1.05	0.50	1.02
1936	109	0.64	0.97	0.55	1.02
1937	109	0.76	0.96	0.58	0.99
1938	109	0.78	0.92	0.63	0.95
1934–38	109	0.69	0.93	0.58	1.00
1937	118	0.65	0.91	0.58	0.97
1948	118	1.37	0.87	1.33	0.91
Commonwealth countries 1937	115	0.235	0.97	0.24	0.96
Non-Commonwealth countries 1937	115	1.61	0.92	1.53	0.95

*Mid-1912 to mid-1913 for the U.S.

correction is adequate for under-valuation of U.S. exports ((1) above) this would raise the 93% to 95%; the general picture would not be materially altered. If we further assumed that British products were as much as, say, 10% better in quality than the American, this would further raise the average U.S. price to around 105% of the British, but it would also reduce the average U.S. quantity to around 63% of the British. Such a low American export could be explained by 5% higher prices only if there were an elasticity of substitution of more than -9,[59] and this seems improbable.

If median relative quantities and prices are used (columns (4) and (5) of Table IX), the result is less convincing, but, despite all the uncertainties, it seems not unlikely that, in the later thirties, the U.S. tended to export less of a commodity than Britain when the price was equal. It also seems likely that, in the earlier years, any American comparative disadvantage in the imperfect world market was smaller or non-existent. These tentative conclusions may not, however, apply to the whole range of manufactures; it should be remembered in particular that, for statistical reasons, the products in our sample include very few in the important field of machinery.

The figures in Table IX confirm the striking improvement in the relative position of the U.S. between 1937 and 1948, though it is not easy to assess the relative importance of various possible causes. While British exporters were out of the market during the war and early post-war years, American manufacturers doubtless built up goodwill and a preference for American models and qualities, and at the same time gained a lead in the development of new types of products. They were handicapped after the War by discrimination caused by dollar shortage, but this was limited by U.S. government loans and grants. On the other hand, the large change in the figures may reflect in part merely the inability of British exporters, in 1948, to meet demand at a given price.

Imperial Preference

It is tempting to try to discover how far the apparent disadvantage of the U.S. in the imperfect world market in the later thirties can be accounted for by Imperial Preference and how far the increase in preferences resulting from the Ottawa Agreements accounts for the apparent change to America's disadvantage after 1932. It is shown in Appendix E that, after Ottawa, the margin of preference on U.K. goods entering British Commonwealth markets was, on average, of the order of 10%, so that, as roughly one-half of British exports went

[59] $\dfrac{\log 0.63}{\log 1.05} = -9.5.$

to Commonwealth countries, the margin represented about 5% of the total value of British exports. The increase in the margin resulting from the Ottawa Agreements must have been considerably less than 5%. The reader may care to make his private deductions about the effects of Imperial Preference, but, in view of the difficulties described above, it does not seem that trustworthy conclusions can be drawn from the figures so far given.

A more fruitful approach is to consider separately British and American exports (*a*) to Commonwealth countries (excluding the U.K.) and (*b*) to non-Commonwealth countries (excluding the U.S.). This has been done, for 115 commodities, for the year 1937.[60] Owing to the labour involved, similar calculations were not made for other years. The two regression lines are shown in Fig. 4, and the main results are given in Tables VIII and IX.

It will be seen from Table IX that American prices were, on average, 92% of the British for exports to non-Commonwealth countries and 97% for exports to the Commonwealth.[61] This latter figure should perhaps be raised to about 100% to cover under-valuation of U.S. exports to Canada.[62] Other possible corrections for relative under-valuation or quality differences need not concern us here, since they would probably apply in more or less equal degree both to Commonwealth and to non-Commonwealth countries. We are concerned only with the fact that average relative prices were some 8% lower in trade with non-Commonwealth countries than they were in trade with the Commonwealth. There was, on the other hand, a very large difference in relative quantities. The U.S. exported, on average, 161% as much to non-Commonwealth countries as Britain and only 23½% as much as Britain to Commonwealth countries. In case these figures are biased by quality differences, it is safer to say that the relative quantities (U.S.:U.K.) were, on average, about 6.9 times as great for non-Commonwealth countries as they were for Commonwealth countries.[63] Such a large difference could be explained by the 8% difference in relative prices only if we

[60] For statistical reasons, it was impossible to obtain figures for the 171 or for the 109 commodities covered by the previous analyses.

[61] The geometric means are used in this paragraph and the next, but the argument is unaffected if the medians are used instead.

[62] Railway freight to the Canadian frontier not included in the recorded value of U.S. exports has been estimated at $34 million in 1937 (*The Balance of International Payments of the United States in 1937*, p. 28). This is 4% of U.S. exports to the British Commonwealth (excluding the U.K.), which totalled $827 million. Since the percentage for manufactures may have been smaller, and since there may have been offsetting factors, it seems reasonable to round up our observed figure of 97% to 100%.

[63] A comparison of the values of British and American exports of all manufactures to Commonwealth and non-Commonwealth countries shows a much smaller discrepancy.

Relative Prices and Quantities of U.S. and U.K. Exports
of 115 Manufactures in 1937:

(a) *to Commonwealth Countries*
(b) *to Non-Commonwealth Countries*

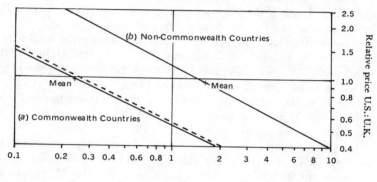

Relative quantity U.S.:U.K.

— — — — — = U.S. recorded prices raised by 3% to cover
freight to Canadian border.

FIG. 4

assumed an 'elasticity of substitution' as high as —23.[64] This is
unlikely, and it therefore seems almost certain that a large part of the
difference is to be explained by factors other than price.

Of these, Imperial Preference seems to provide only a partial
explanation. The margin of preference was about 10% of the value of
British exports to the Commonwealth, so that if, as the figures
suggest, the prices of British and American exports to the Commonwealth were, on average, the same excluding import duty, then
American prices, including duty, were some 110% of the British. In
non-Commonwealth countries they were 92% of the British, *i.e.*,
relative prices (U.S.:U.K.) were about 16% lower in non-
Commonwealth countries than they were in Commonwealth coun-

[64] $\dfrac{\log 6.9}{\log 0.92} = -23$.

This is a sort of 'spatial' elasticity of substitution. Questions of bias are not discussed, as the
figure is purely illustrative.

tries.[65] But, even allowing for this, the large difference in relative quantities could be explained solely by prices, including duty, only if we assumed an elasticity of substitution of at least -11.[66] It therefore seems likely that factors other than preferential duties were important.

An examination of the two regression lines may give some indication of the relative importance of Imperial Preference and other factors. It will be seen from Fig. 4 that the line for Commonwealth countries was far to the left of that for non-Commonwealth countries. Whatever corrections may be necessary, this seems to indicate a substantial difference in the relative advantages of America and Britain in these two markets at a given f.o.b. price ratio. According to the regression lines, U.S. exports to non-Commonwealth countries were 136% of the British when recorded prices were equal while her exports to the Commonwealth were only 22% of the British. It is suggested in Appendix D that, even allowing for corrections, it may still be fairly safe to say that, where British and American prices were equal in both markets,

---

[65] $0.92 \div 1.10 = 0.84$. It is assumed that the rate of duty on British and American goods in non-Commonwealth markets was the same. See also next footnote.

[66] $$\frac{\log 6.9}{\log 0.84} = -11.$$

This is an understatement for two reasons:

(a) Where duties are *ad valorem*, relative prices to Commonwealth countries, including duty (but excluding transport costs, the difference in which is small for most manufactures), would be:

$$\frac{1 + t_c + t_a}{1 + t_c} = 1 + \frac{t_a}{1 + t_c}$$

where t_c is the rate of common tariff and t_a the rate of additional duty on U.S. goods. Where t_a is 0.1 (10%), the relative price is thus less than 1.1, where t_c is not zero. Where duties are specific, relative prices, including duty, would be:

$$\frac{p + T_c + T_a}{p + T_c} = \frac{1 + \dfrac{T_c}{p} + \dfrac{T_a}{p}}{1 + \dfrac{T_c}{p}}$$

where T_c and T_a are the common and additional specific duties and p the American and British price. Where $T_a/p = 0.1$ this will again be less than 1.1.

(b) Relative prices of exports to non-Commonwealth countries, including duty, would be greater than 92% in so far as there are specific duties.

Relative prices to non-Commonwealth countries would thus be less than 16% lower than relative prices to Commonwealth countries, and the elasticity of substitution required to explain the difference in relative quantity would be higher than -11.

relative exports (U.S.:U.K.) were four times as great for non-Commonwealth as for Commonwealth countries.[67]

Now the margin of Imperial Preference was about 10% of the value of British exports to Commonwealth countries. Where British and American prices in Commonwealth markets were equal, including duty, the American price, excluding duty, was, therefore, on average, 9% less than the British price, excluding duty.[68] Assuming a product elasticity of substitution as high as −5, the relative quantity (U.S.:U.K.) was about 60% higher when prices were equal, including duty, than it was when prices were equal excluding duty.[69] If, therefore, the relative quantities were about four times as great in non-Commonwealth markets as they were in Commonwealth markets when prices, excluding duty, were equal, they were still about 4/1.6 = 2½ times as great when prices, including duty, were equal. There is thus still a margin of this order to be explained by factors other than Imperial Preference. The latter, in fact, explains directly only a comparatively small part of the relative advantage of the U.K. in Commonwealth as compared with non-Commonwealth markets. It would seem that factors such as commercial ties of Britain with the Commonwealth and of the U.S. with certain non-Commonwealth countries were considerably more important; although Britains's ties with the Commonwealth may, in part, have been indirectly fostered by the preferential duties. If the elasticity of substitution was less than −5, the importance of preferential duties was, of course, smaller.

It is interesting to speculate about the effect of preferential duties on the volume of Britain's export trade. Before the war, Commonwealth countries probably took around 37–38% of their imports of manufactures from Britain,[70] *i.e.*, the ratio of British to foreign

---

[67] According to the regression lines the U.S. exported the same amount as Britain to non-Commonwealth countries even when her price was 116% of the British, but the same amount to Commonwealth countries only when her price was 54% of the British. It is argued in Appendix D that the last figure may well be too low and the first too high.

[68] When duties are *ad valorem*, and prices are equal, including duty:

$$p_a(1 + t_c + t_a) = p_b(1 + t_c)$$

where p_a, p_b are the American and British prices, excluding duty, t_c the common rate of tariff and t_a the additional rate on U.S. goods (transport costs are ignored). *I.e.*,

$$\frac{p_a}{p_b} = \frac{1 + t_c}{1 + t_c + t_a} = \frac{1 + t_c}{1.1 + t_c}$$

which is greater than 1/1.1, *i.e.*, greater than 0.91. In so far as the true figure exceeds 0.91, the argument in the text is strengthened.

[69] Antilog $(−5 \log 0.91) = 1.6$.

[70] This is a rough calculation based on value; it is assumed that the figure for volume is the same.

exports of manufactures to Commonwealth countries was about 0.6.[71] If the preferences had been removed and prices, excluding duty, had remained the same, the ratio of British to foreign prices, including duty, would have risen by something like 10%. Assuming a *total* elasticity of substitution of −3 (the highest figure we dared to suggest for the *total* elasticity between British and U.S. exports of manufactures to all countries) the ratio of 0.6 would have fallen by about one-quarter,[72] *i.e.*, to 0.45, so that Britain's proportionate share would have fallen from about 37½% to about 31%.[73] If the total market had remained the same, the quantity of Britain's exports to Commonwealth countries would thus have fallen in the ratio 37½:31, *i.e.*, by about 17%, and, if her trade with other countries had been unaffected, her exports to all countries would have fallen by about 9%. Assuming a total elasticity of substitution of −2, the figure would be about 6%. In view, however, of the many indirect repercussions and of the danger, emphasised above, of using calculated elasticities, too much significance should not be attached to these results, which suggest that preferential duties safeguarded less than 10% of Britain's total exports.[74] It should be remembered, too, that they take no account of other preferential arrangements such as preferential import quotas.

E. GENERAL CONCLUSIONS

The studies described in this paper have ranged over a rather wide field; one thing led to another. It is hoped that they have illustrated, among other things, the usefulness of tackling problems of international trade through a study of individual commodities. The article is intended to be partly a study of method, but some of the results may be of more general interest.

It seems that the labour theory of value, crude as it is, does help to provide some explanation of British and American export trade in manufactures in an imperfect world market and to illustrate the importance of tariffs in limiting international commerce. It reminds us that a country can compete in certain lines, even with a rival

---

[71] $\dfrac{37\frac{1}{2}}{63\frac{1}{2}} = 0.6$

[72] $-3 \log 1.1 = -0.1242$, the antilog of which is 0.75.

[73] $\dfrac{31}{69} = 0.45$.

[74] This is not, of course, the same as the percentage of U.K. exports enjoying preference, which was considerably higher. Table XI shows that more than one-half of U.K. exports to Commonwealth countries enjoyed preference, *i.e.*, over one-quarter of all U.K. exports.

whose general level of productivity is much higher. (This does not, of course, mean that a high and rapidly rising level of productivity in, say, the U.S. may not aggravate the problem of international disequilibrium. For example, knowledge of the high American standard of living may increase any tendency of other countries to try to live beyond their means; high productivity, reflected partly in the ability to supply the latest products, creates a large demand for a country's exports; a more rapid growth of productivity than in other countries may mean continuous pressure on the international exchanges unless money wages also increase at an abnormally high rate; and so on.)

The fact that American weekly wages in manufacturing, which were about twice the British before the war, are now about 3½ times as high suggests that, despite changes in relative productivity, there may be important opportunities for British exporters in many new lines. Figures in Tables VIII and IX, however, are consistent with the common view that the war resulted in a substantial improvement in the relative position of the U.S. in the imperfect world market. Some allowance must be made for this fact in any estimate of British export prospects unless it is offset by special selling efforts by British exporters, by discrimination against American goods or in other ways.

Leaving labour costs and turning to prices, a similar picture emerged. There was a fairly clear inverse relation between relative prices of British and American exports and the relative quantities exported, variations in the former being associated with comparatively large variations in the latter. The range of relative prices showed, incidentally, the doubtful value of such statements as: 'before devaluation . . . British goods had been 25% higher in price than American.'[75] It seems likely that some British prices are usually higher than the American, some lower. The important question is how many are higher, how many lower, and by how much. Even if British and American prices were, according to some form of average, equal, this would not necessarily result in international equilibrium.

The results obtained suggested a possible method of estimating the elasticity of substitution between the exports of two countries by using data for a number of commodities in one period instead of data for one commodity (or group of commodities) in a number of periods. Although open to certain objections, this approach seems to avoid some of the difficulties connected with the more normal time series method.

[75] *The Times*, September 23, 1949.

A method was also suggested of using the 'product' elasticity of substitution so obtained to estimate the 'total' elasticity of substitution between groups of exports, which will normally be a lower figure. The calculations, allowing for possible bias, suggested a very much higher elasticity of substitution between British and American exports of manufactures than that obtained by Mr. Chang. An alternative method was also suggested of estimating short-period elasticities at particular times of rapid change.

Finally, the data for individual products were used in an attempt to estimate the importance of factors other than price in determining relative exports. The tentative conclusion was reached that, in the later thirties, the U.S. had on balance a comparative disadvantage in the imperfect world market, at least in the products studied. There was, however, a striking difference between Commonwealth and non-Commonwealth markets, the U.S. having a substantial disadvantage in the former and a substantial advantage in the latter. It seemed unlikely that more than a small part of this difference could be directly attributed to Imperial Preference, leaving the major part to be explained by commercial ties and other non-price factors. The importance of such factors in determining relative shares in export markets is not, however, inconsistent with a high price elasticity of substitution. A purchaser may be prepared to buy from A rather than B, even though A's price is, say, 5% higher; but if the margin rises to, say, 7% or 8% he may quickly switch the bulk of his custom to B.

It is hoped that the validity of the methods suggested in this article will be examined by others and that they may possibly be of some use in the study of other problems of international trade.

APPENDIX A

EFFECTS OF ERRORS OF OBSERVATION ON THE SLOPES OF THE REGRESSION LINES*

Suppose the true relationship between relative quantity and relative price of each product is given by the equation

$$X_1{}' = A + BX_2{}' \qquad (A.1)$$

where $X_1{}'$ and $X_2{}'$ are the logarithms of the true values (after all necessary adjustments) of relative quantity and relative price respectively, and A and B are constants.

*It will be evident that this Appendix owes much to Mr. Orcutt, *op. cit.*

Let X_1 and X_2 (without the primes) be the observed values, and let

$$X_1 = X_1' + E_1 \text{ and } X_2 = X_2' + E_2 \tag{A.2}$$

so that E_1 and E_2 are errors of observation.

From (A.1) and (A.2) we have

$$X_1 = A + BX_2 + E_1 - BE_2 \tag{A.3}$$

Let $\overline{X}_1, \overline{X}_2, \overline{E}_1$ and $\overline{E}_2$ be means and x_1, x_2, e_1 and e_2 the deviations from them, so that

$$X_1 = \overline{X}_1 + x_1, \text{ etc.} \tag{A.4}$$

(A.3) can then be re-written:

$$x_1 = Bx_2 + e_1 - Be_2 + (A - \overline{X}_1 + B\overline{X}_2 + \overline{E}_1 - B\overline{E}_2). \tag{A.5}$$

Multiplying through by x_2 and summing, we get

$$\Sigma x_1 x_2 = B\Sigma x_2^2 + \Sigma e_1 x_2 - B\Sigma e_2 x_2 \tag{A.6}$$

(Σx_2 multiplied by the constant expression in brackets in (A.5) is zero.)

Whence

$$B = \frac{\Sigma x_1 x_2 - \Sigma e_1 x_2}{\Sigma x_2^2 - \Sigma e_2 x_2} \tag{A.7}$$

i.e.,

$$B = \frac{\Sigma x_1 x_2 - \Sigma e_1 x_2' - \Sigma e_1 e_2}{\Sigma x_2^2 - \Sigma e_2 x_2' - \Sigma e_2^2} \tag{A.8}$$

This is the true slope we wish to find. The slope obtained by the method of least squares from the observed data (minimising the sum of the squares of the deviations of the logarithms of relative *quantity*) is, however,

$$b = \frac{\Sigma x_1 x_2}{\Sigma x_2^2} \tag{A.9}$$

We now compare the values of B and b. Four cases are considered.

I. Errors in Observed Values of Relative Quantities but not in Observed Values of Relative Prices

$e_2 = 0$, and hence, from (A.8),

$$B = \frac{\Sigma x_1 x_2 - \Sigma e_1 x_2'}{\Sigma x_2^2} \tag{A.10}$$

i.e.,
$$B = b - \frac{\Sigma e_1 x_2'}{\Sigma x_2^2} \tag{A.11}$$

If there is no reason to assume correlation between the true relative price (X_2') and the error in the relative quantity (E_1), there is no reason to expect the second term in (A.11) to be positive rather than negative, or vice versa. The value of b derived from the observed values is thus unbiased.

II. Errors in Relative Price but not in Relative Quantity

$e_1 = 0$ and, assuming no correlation between true relative price (X_2') and the error in relative price (E_2), equation (A.8) becomes

$$B = \frac{\Sigma x_1 x_2}{\Sigma x_2^2 - \Sigma e_2^2} \tag{A.12}$$

$$\therefore \frac{b}{B} = \frac{\Sigma x_2^2 - \Sigma e_2^2}{\Sigma x_2^2} \tag{A.13}$$

$$= 1 - \frac{\Sigma e_2^2}{\Sigma x_2^2} \tag{A.14}$$

$$\therefore \frac{b}{B} < 1 \tag{A.15}$$

Since b is negative, and we assume that B is negative, B is numerically greater than b, which is thus biased towards zero.

III. Errors both in Relative Quantity and in Relative Price, but no Correlation between these Errors

Then
$$B = \frac{\Sigma x_1 x_2}{\Sigma x_2^2 - \Sigma e_2^2} \tag{A.16}$$

as in equation (A.12), and b is biased towards zero, as in II.

IV. Errors in Logarithms of Relative Quantity and Relative Price of Equal Magnitude but Opposite Sign

This is the case described on pp. 26–27.

From (8), since $E_1 = -E_2$, and, therefore, $e_1 = -e_2$,

$$B = \frac{\Sigma x_1 x_2 + \Sigma e_2^2}{\Sigma x_2^2 - \Sigma e_2^2} \tag{A.17}$$

assuming no correlation between E_1 and X_2' or between E_2 and X_2'.

Starting with $b = \dfrac{\Sigma x_1 x_2}{\Sigma x_2^2}$, where $\Sigma x_1 x_2$ is negative, we are, in

(A.17), reducing the negative quantity in the numerator by the same amount as the positive quantity in the denominator. Since $|\Sigma x_1 x_2| > \Sigma_2^2$ in the results described in the text, B is therefore numerically greater than b, on the assumption that

$$\Sigma x_2^2 \geqslant \Sigma e_2^2 \,*$$

i.e., that $\Sigma(x_2' + e_2)^2 \geqslant \Sigma e_2^2$

i.e., that $\Sigma x_2'^2 + 2\Sigma x_2' e_2 \geqslant 0.$

This is so, assuming no correlation between X_2' and E_2. Hence b is biased towards zero.

It was shown in the text that errors of types III and IV exist in the data used. We may now consider what bias these may exercise on the regression coefficient obtained in the analysis of the five years, 1934–38. In this case there were 109 observations and

$$\Sigma x_1 x_2 = -12.25$$

$$\Sigma x_2^2 = 3.38$$

$$b = -3.624$$

Using equations (A.16) and (A.17), we may calculate B for various values of Σe_2^2.

Thus, for example, if $\Sigma e_2^2 = 0.6$, B is -4.4 or -4.2 according as the errors are wholly of type III or wholly of type IV. Columns (2) and (3) of Table X show the values of B on these assumptions for values of Σe_2^2 between 0.1 and 1.0.

Given Σe_2^2, the (arithmetic) *average* value of e_2 lies between $\sqrt{2\Sigma e_2^2}/109$ (the case where only two observed relative prices have errors different from the mean error† and $\sqrt{\Sigma e_2^2}/109$ (the case where all the errors differ from the mean by the same numerical amount‡). If Σe_2^2 were equal to 0.6, the average difference from the mean error of the logarithms of relative prices would lie between 0.01 and 0.0742, equivalent to between 2.3 and 18.7% of the

---

*If $\Sigma x_2^2 < \Sigma e_2^2 \leqslant |\Sigma x_1 x_2|$, B would be positive or zero, and if $\Sigma x_2^2 < \Sigma e_2^2 > |\Sigma x_1 x_2|$, B would be negative, but numerically less than unity, and therefore numerically less than b.

†It is impossible for only one observed price to have an error different from the mean error.

‡Strictly not possible with an odd number of observations.

TABLE X
109 *Products*, 1934–38 ($b = -3.624$)

$\Sigma e_2{}^2$	Value of B		Range of average values of $\lvert e_2 \rvert$		Equivalent average difference from the mean error in original relative price data, %[3]	
	Errors of type III only[1]	Errors of type IV only[2]	Minimum $\dfrac{\sqrt{2\Sigma e_2{}^2}}{109}$	Maximum $\sqrt{\dfrac{2\Sigma e_2{}^2}{109}}$	Minimum	Maximum
(1)	(2)	(3)	(4)	(5)	(6)	(7)
0.1	−3.7	−3.7	0.0041	0.0303	0.9	7.3
0.2	−3.9	−3.8	0.0058	0.0428	1.4	10.4
0.3	−4.0	−3.9	0.0071	0.0525	1.6	12.8
0.4	−4.1	−4.0	0.0082	0.0606	1.9	15.0
0.5	−4.3	−4.1	0.0092	0.0677	2.1	16.9
0.6	−4.4	−4.2	0.0100	0.0742	2.3	18.7
0.7	−4.6	−4.3	0.0109	0.0801	2.5	20.2
0.8	−4.7	−4.4	0.0116	0.0857	2.7	21.8
0.9	−4.9	−4.6	0.0123	0.0909	2.9	23.3
1.0	−5.1	−4.7	0.0130	0.0958	3.0	24.7

[1] $B = \dfrac{\Sigma x_1 x_2}{\Sigma x_2{}^2 - \Sigma e_2{}^2}.$ (Equation (A.16).)

[2] $B = \dfrac{\Sigma x_1 x_2 + \Sigma e_2{}^2}{\Sigma x_2{}^2 - \Sigma e_2{}^2}.$ (Equation (A.17).)

[3] As per cent of observed value or true value adjusted for the mean error if smaller.

$$\text{Col. (6) is } 100\left(\text{antilog } \frac{\sqrt{\Sigma e_2{}^2}}{109} - 1\right).$$

$$\text{Col. (7) is } 100\left(\text{antilog } \sqrt{\frac{\Sigma e_2{}^2}{109}} - 1\right).$$

observed value (or of the true value plus the mean error if smaller), and in practice well within these limits, say between 5 and 15%. Columns (4) to (7) of Table VII show the range of average difference from the mean error, measured in these two ways, for the various values of $\Sigma e_2{}^2$.

Now an average difference from the mean error of 5–15%, which means, assuming no biased errors in the observations, an average error of 5–15%, seems quite likely in the data used (the standard deviation of the 109 relative prices was 0.1761 in logarithms, equivalent to 50% in the original data). It thus seems quite possible that, if the observed data could have been corrected for errors of the type described, the slope of the regression line might have been of the order of −4 to −4½.

It may be mentioned in this connection that the slope of the other regression line, minimising the sum of the squares of the deviations in a vertical direction, was −6.9 and that the diagonal regression (the geometric mean of the slopes of the two regression lines) was −5.0. The diagonal regressions for the individual years 1922−38 ranged from −4.1 to −4.9.

APPENDIX B

OTHER POSSIBLE BIAS IN THE CALCULATED SLOPES OF THE REGRESSION LINES

Let the true demand substitution curve for product R be

$$X_1 = A_r + B_r X_2 \tag{B.1}$$

where X_1 and X_2 are the logarithms of relative quantity and relative price respectively. (It is assumed in this Appendix that there are no errors of observation.) A_r and B_r are not the same for each product. For product R, B_r is the slope of the demand substitution curve, A_r the value of X_1 when $X_2 = 0$, *i.e.*, the logarithm of the relative quantity when the British and American prices are equal.

Equation (B.1) may be re-written

$$(x_1 + \bar{X}_1) = (a_r + \bar{A}) + (b_r + \bar{B})(x_2 + \bar{X}_2) \tag{B.2}$$

where $\bar{X}_1$, $\bar{X}_2$, $\bar{A}$ and $\bar{B}$ are means and x_1, x_2, a_r, b_r deviations from them.

i.e., $$x_1 = \bar{B}x_2 + a_r + b_r x_2 + \bar{X}_2 b_r + (\bar{A} - \bar{X}_1 + \bar{B}\bar{X}_2) \tag{B.3}$$

Multiplying through by x_2, and summing, we get

$$\Sigma x_1 x_2 = \bar{B}\Sigma x_2{}^2 + \Sigma a_r x_2 + \Sigma b_r x_2{}^2 + \bar{X}_2 \Sigma b_r x_2 \tag{B.4}$$

(Σx_2 multiplied by the constant expression in brackets in (B.3) is zero)

Let b be the regression coefficient obtained by the method of least squares from the observed data (minimising the sum of the squares of the deviations of the logarithms of relative *quantity*). Then

$$b = \frac{\Sigma x_1 x_2}{\Sigma x_2{}^2} = \bar{B} + \frac{\Sigma a_r x_2}{\Sigma x_2{}^2} + \frac{\Sigma b_r x_2{}^2}{\Sigma x_2{}^2} + \bar{X}_2 \frac{\Sigma b_r x_2}{\Sigma x_2{}^2} \tag{B.5}$$

The second, third and fourth terms on the right-hand side of (B.5) will tend to be positive if the supply substitution curves slope upwards.

The second will tend to be positive because a positive value of a_r denotes a demand substitution curve towards the right, and this will tend to mean a relatively high relative price (since the supply substitution curves slope upwards), *i.e.*, a positive value of x_2. Similarly, negative values of a_r and x_2 will tend to go together.

The third term is a weighted average of the b_r's, the weights being the $x_2{}^2$'s. A positive b_r denotes a steeper than average slope, and it is with these commodities that the large $x_2{}^2$'s will tend to be found, since a large $x_2{}^2$ denotes a relative price which is well below, or well above, the mean. Similarly, a negative b_r will tend to be associated with a small $x_2{}^2$. Thus, while the unweighted average of the b_r's is zero, the weighted average will tend to be positive.

The fourth term will tend to be positive for the following reasons. When $\bar{X}_2 > 0$, *i.e.*, broadly, when the majority of the relative prices are greater than unity, a positive b_r (*i.e.*, a steeper than average slope) will tend to mean a positive x_2 (*i.e.*, a higher than average relative price) and $\Sigma b_r x_2$ will tend to be positive. The fourth term will thus tend to be positive. When $\bar{X}_2 < 0$, a positive b_r will tend to be associated with a negative x_2, and $\Sigma b_r x_2$ will tend to be negative. Again, the fourth term will tend to be positive.

Thus, from (B.5), b will tend to be greater than $\bar{B}$, *i.e.*, the calculated slope will tend to be steeper than the mean of the true slopes of the demand substitution curves if (i) the true curves are parallel but not coincident, or (ii) the true curves are not parallel but all cross the equal price line at the same point, or (iii) the true curves are not parallel and do not cross the equal price line at the same point.

If, however, the supply substitution curves are horizontal, it will readily be seen that these sources of bias disappear, and if they are downward sloping the bias is in the other direction.

APPENDIX C

RELATION BETWEEN THE 'PRODUCT' AND THE 'TOTAL' ELASTICITIES OF SUBSTITUTION (ON THE ASSUMPTIONS GIVEN ON P. 35)

If the quantitative *shares* of America and Britain in the exports of a commodity are A and B respectively ($A + B = 1$), the ratio of a small proportionate change in A to an accompanying small proportionate change in A/B will be

$$\frac{\frac{A}{B}}{A} \cdot \frac{dA}{d\left(\frac{A}{B}\right)} = \frac{1}{1-A} \cdot \frac{dA}{d\left(\frac{A}{1-A}\right)} = \frac{1}{1-A} \cdot (1-A)^{2*} = 1 - A = B$$

If, therefore, there is a small proportionate change K in the *ratio* of America's to Britain's exports of each commodity, there will be a proportionate change of KB_n in America's *share* in the total market for British and American exports of commodity n. If that total market changes in the ratio $1:(1+L)$ for each commodity, the *quantity* of America's exports of commodity n will change in the ration $1:(1 + KB_n)(1 + L)$. It can be shown, similarly, that the quantity of British exports will change in the ratio $1:(1 - KA_n)(1 + L)$.

The *volume indices* of American and British exports will then change in the ratios of, respectively†

$$1 : \frac{(1+L)\Sigma V_a(1+KB)}{\Sigma V_a} \quad \text{and} \quad 1 : \frac{(1+L)\Sigma V_b(1-KA)}{\Sigma V_b}$$

where V_a and V_b are the values of America's and Britain's exports of each commodity.

The proportionate change in the ratio of the American to the British volume index will be

$$\frac{\Sigma V_b \Sigma V_a(1+KB)}{\Sigma V_a \Sigma V_b(1-KA)} - 1 \qquad \qquad (C.1)$$

$$= K \frac{[\Sigma V_b \Sigma V_a B + \Sigma V_a \Sigma V_b A]}{\Sigma V_a \Sigma V_b - K \Sigma V_a \Sigma V_b A}$$

$$= K \frac{\left[\dfrac{\Sigma V_a B}{\Sigma V_a} + \dfrac{\Sigma V_b A}{\Sigma V_b}\right]}{1 - K \dfrac{\Sigma V_b A}{\Sigma V_b}} \text{(dividing numerator and denominator by } \Sigma V_a \Sigma V_b.)$$

* $\dfrac{d\left(\dfrac{A}{1-A}\right)}{dA} = \dfrac{A}{(1-A)^2} + \dfrac{1}{(1-A)} = \dfrac{1}{(1-A)^2}.$

† Using the formula $\dfrac{\Sigma p_0 q_1}{\Sigma p_0 q_0}.$

Since K is small, this equals

$$K\left[\frac{\Sigma V_a B}{\Sigma V_a} + \frac{\Sigma V_b A}{\Sigma V_b}\right] \tag{C.2}$$

If, now, the price of each American export changes in the ratio $1 : m_a$, and the price of each British export in the ratio $1 : m_b$, the price ratio for each product will change in the ratio $1 : m_a/m_b$. It is evident that the ratio of the price indices of the two countries will also change in the ratio $1 : m_a/m_b$. In other words, the proportionate change in the price ratio for each product and in the price-index ratio will be $m_a/m_b - 1$. Let us call this P.

The product elasticity of substitution will then be K/P, and the total elasticity of substitution will be

$$\frac{K}{P}\left[\frac{\Sigma V_a B}{\Sigma V_a} + \frac{\Sigma V_b A}{\Sigma V_b}\right]$$

The term in brackets has been called the index of similarity of exports. If the two countries have no exports in common it is zero. The first term is zero because, when America exports a product, Britain does not; hence when V_a is not zero, B is zero. The second term is zero for similar reasons.

When the (value) pattern of exports is exactly the same, the index is unity. V_a/V_b is constant, and the index may be re-written

$$\frac{\Sigma V_b(1-A)}{\Sigma V_b} + \frac{\Sigma V_b A}{\Sigma V_b} = 1$$

Where K is not the same for each product, the proportionate change in the ratio of the American to the British volume indices will be

$$\frac{\Sigma V_a K B}{\Sigma V_a} + \frac{\Sigma V_b K A}{\Sigma V_b}$$

$$= \overline{K}\left[\frac{\Sigma V_a B}{\Sigma V_a} + \frac{\Sigma V_b A}{\Sigma V_b}\right] + \left[\frac{\Sigma V_a B k}{\Sigma V_a} + \frac{\Sigma V_b A k}{\Sigma V_b}\right]$$

where $\overline{K}$ is the (arithmetic) mean of K, and k the deviation from it. The first set of terms is the same as (C.2) with $\overline{K}$ substituted for K. An examination of the second set of terms suggests no obvious reason why they should be biased away from zero, so that the assumption that K is the same, for each commodity, as the arithmetic mean of the individual K's does not seem to introduce any bias into the derivation of the total elasticity.

APPENDIX D

ERRORS IN THE INTERCEPTS OF THE REGRESSION LINES ON THE EQUAL QUANTITY AND EQUAL PRICE AXES

Using the notation of Appendices A and B, let the true demand substitution schedule from commodity R be

$$X_1' = A_r + B_r X_2'$$

i.e., $$(\overline{X}_1 + x_1 - \overline{E}_1 - e_1) = (\overline{A} + a_r) + (\overline{B} + b_r)(\overline{X}_2 + x_2 - \overline{E}_2 - e_2)$$

Summing and dividing by N (the number of observations), we get

$$\overline{X}_1 = \overline{A} + \overline{B}\overline{X}_2 + \frac{\Sigma b_r x_2}{N} + \frac{1}{N}(\Sigma a_r + \overline{B}\Sigma x_2 - \overline{B}\Sigma e_2 + \overline{X}_2\Sigma b_r$$

$$- \overline{E}_2 \Sigma b_r - \Sigma x_1 + \Sigma e_1) + (\overline{E}_1 - \overline{B}\overline{E}_2) - \frac{\Sigma b_r e_2}{N}$$

The terms in the first bracket are necessarily zero. Those in the second are zero, assuming that the errors of observation are unbiased (the case of biased errors is dealt with on pp. 42–3). The last term tends to zero, since there seems no reason to expect correlation between b_r and e_2. We are thus left with

$$\overline{A} = \overline{X}_1 - \overline{B}\overline{X}_2 - \frac{\Sigma b_r x_2}{N} \tag{D.1}$$

$\overline{A}$ is the average intercept on the equal price axis (*i.e.,* the value of X_1 when $X_2 = 0$) that we wish to discover. The equation of the regression line we find by the method of least squares is

$$(X_1 - \overline{X}_1) = b(X_2 - \overline{X}_2)$$

i.e., $$X_1 = (\overline{X}_1 - b\overline{X}_2) + bX_2$$

The intercept on equal-price axis that we find is thus

$$a = \overline{X}_1 - b\overline{X}_2 \tag{D.2}$$

Hence

$$\overline{A} - a = \overline{X}_2(b - \overline{B}) - \frac{\Sigma b_r x_2}{N} \tag{D.3}$$

Since we assume that the true average slope is flatter than the observed slope, and since both b and $\bar{B}$ are negative, $(b - \bar{B}) > 0$. When $\bar{X}_2 > 0$, the first term on the right-hand side of (D.3) is thus positive and, when $\bar{X}_2 < 0$, it is negative. But, assuming upward sloping supply substitution curves, when $\bar{X}_2 > 0$, steep slopes of the demand substitution curves (*i.e.* positive b_r's) will tend to be associated with high relative prices (*i.e.*, positive x_2's), and therefore the second term will tend to be negative. Similarly, when $\bar{X}_2 < 0$, the second term will tend to be positive. We therefore cannot say whether the calculated intercept on the equal-price axis is biased to left or to right. If, however, the supply substitution curves are horizontal or downward sloping, we can say that the calculated intercept will be biased to the left when $\bar{X}_2 > 0$, and to the right when $\bar{X}_2 < 0$. In any case it will be unbiased when $\bar{X}_2 = 0.$, *i.e.*, when average relative price is unity.

For exports to Commonwealth and non-Commonwealth countries, $\bar{X}_2$ equals -0.0128 and -0.0357 respectively. If the supply substitution curves are horizontal, the last term in (D.3) tends to zero, so that

$$\bar{A} = a + \bar{X}_2 (b - \bar{B}) \tag{D.4}$$

Assuming $\bar{B}$'s of -3, -4 or -5, the intercept for exports to Commonwealth countries falls from the calculated figure of 0.22 to 0.21, 0.20 or 0.19, while that for exports to non-Commonwealth countries falls from the calculated figure of 1.36 to 1.26, 1.16 or 1.07. The ratio of the intercepts falls from the calculated figure of 6.2 to not less than 5½.

If the supply substitution curves are downward sloping, both intercepts will tend to fall further, and the ratio may also fall further, but there seems to be no way of estimating the probable amount.

If the supply substitution curves are upward sloping, the last term in (D.3) tends to be positive, since $\bar{X}_2$ is negative in both cases. A lower limit for the true value of the intercept for exports to non-Commonwealth countries is thus given by (D.4), *i.e.*, 1.07 for a true $\bar{B}$ of -5. The corresponding figure of 0.19 for exports to Commonwealth countries will tend to be raised by the positive last term in (D.3), but, as $\bar{X}_2$ is not greatly below zero, we may perhaps guess that the true intercept is not greatly in excess of, say, 0.25, even after allowing for the correction necessitated by underestimation of U.S. exports to Canada. If this is correct, the ratio of the true intercepts is thus at least 4.

There may have been quality differences and differences in

methods of valuation that applied equally to exports to each group of countries, but, provided these were not too large, and provided the true slopes for the two groups of countries were not very different, it does not seem unreasonable to assume that, when price (corrected where necessary) was equal, relative quantity (U.S.:U.K.) was probably at least four times as great for non-Commonwealth as it was for Commonwealth countries.

We now turn to the intercept on the equal quantity axis, *i.e.*, the value of X_2 when $X_1 = 0$. The intercept we wish to find is

$$I = \frac{-\overline{A}}{\overline{B}} = \frac{-\overline{X}_1}{\overline{B}} + \overline{X}_2 + \frac{\Sigma b_r x_2}{N\overline{B}}$$

The calculated intercept is

$$i = -\frac{a}{b} = -\frac{\overline{X}_1}{b} + \overline{X}_2$$

Hence

$$I - i = \overline{X}_1\left(\frac{1}{b} - \frac{1}{\overline{B}}\right) + \frac{\Sigma b_r x_2}{N\overline{B}}$$

Now $1/b - 1/\overline{B} < 0$ and $\Sigma b_r x_2/N\overline{B}$ tends to have the opposite sign from $\overline{X}_2$ if the supply substitution curves slope upwards, the same sign if they slope downwards and to be zero if they are horizontal.

For exports to the Commonwealth, $X_1 < 0$ and $X_2 < 0$. Hence $I > i$ if the supply substitution curves are upward sloping or horizontal, while if they are downward sloping no conclusion can be drawn. For exports to non-Commonwealth countries, $\overline{X}_1 > 0$ and $\overline{X}_2 < 0$. Hence $I < i$ if the curves are downward sloping or horizontal, while if they are upward sloping no conclusion can be drawn. Hence the statement, in the foootnote 67 of this Study, that the figure obtained for relative price where the quantity of exports was equal may well be too low for exports to Commonwealth countries and too high for exports to non-Commonwealth countries.

For exports to all countries in 1934–38, $\overline{X}_1 < 0$ and $\overline{X}_2 < 0$. If the supply substitution curves are horizontal, and $\overline{B} = -5$, the antilogarithm of I works out at 0.864. If the supply substitution curves slope downwards, the true figure is lower, but if they slope upwards it is higher. Hence the figure of 86½% on p. 44.

APPENDIX E

IMPERIAL PREFERENCE*
It was stated in the text that the average margin of preference enjoyed by U.K. exports to British Commonwealth countries before the war, but after Ottawa, was of the order of 10%. This was based on a calculation for 1937 (or the financial year 1937–38) covering countries that took 97% of U.K. exports to the Commonwealth.† The main sources used were the trade returns and, where necessary, the tariff lists, of the various countries.

For each product imported into a Commonwealth country from the U.K., the percentage margin of preference is the difference between the duty that would have been paid had the product been American and the duty actually paid on the U.K. product, expressed as a percentage of the value of the imports from the U.K., excluding duty. The average percentage margin of preference on all imports from the U.K. is the average of the percentage margins of preference on the various products weighted according to the value of imports of each product from the U.K. This is the same as the difference between the duty that would have been paid on the total of imports from the U.K. had the goods been American and the duty actually paid, expressed as a percentage of the total value of imports from the U.K.

The average percentage margin of preference for each country is shown in column (5) of Table XI. It will be seen that the average of these figures, weighted according to U.K. exports to each country in 1937 (column (1)), was 9–10%. This represents the difference between the duty that would have been paid on all U.K. exports to Commonwealth countries had they been American and the duty actually paid, expressed as a percentage of the value of all U.K. exports to Commonwealth countries.

The method of calculation used tends to overstate the average margin of preference in so far as the existence of preference presumably tends to increase the proportion of U.K. exports enjoying higher preferences and to reduce the proportion enjoying lower preferences or none at all. Likewise, it might be expected to increase the proportion of U.K. exports sent to countries granting the higher average preferences. If the various margins of preference were weighted according to the pattern that exports would have

*This appendix is almost wholly the work of Miss Rosemary Orton. Much valuable help was obtained from London representatives of Dominion Governments.
†Defined for this purpose as countries classified as 'British' in the U.K. trade returns.

TABLE XI
Margins of Preference 1937

Country	(1) % of total U.K. exports to British countries	(2) % of trade covered	(3) % of imports from U.K. given preference. [4]	(4) % average margin of preference on goods given preference.	(5) % average margin of preference on all imports from U.K.
New Zealand	8.0	100.0	88–90	25–27	23–24
Canada	10.9	99.7	88	23	20
Southern Rhodesia	1.2	99.5	96	19–20	19
Australia	14.9	100.0	90[1]	19[1]	17[1]
British Guiana	0.5	99.8	93	18–19	17
Channel Islands	2.2	59.1	73–86	18–39	15–29
Jamaica	0.8	99.9	83	15	12–13
Trinidad and Tobago	1.0	99.4	64	19	12
Burma	1.3	98.6	62–93	10–21	9–13
Northern Rhodesia	0.4	99.8	93–97	9–11	9–10
Malta	0.5	100.0	71	12	8
Ceylon	1.6	97.2	70–86	8–21	7–8
Federated Malay States	1.2	97.9	44–58	11–19	6–8
India	14.2	96.0	50	12	6
Union of South Africa	16.5	99.3	39–43	5–8	2–4
Straits Settlements	3.4	100.0	24	13	3
Gibraltar	0.4	100.0	5–7	24–48	2
Hong Kong	1.3	100.0	5[2]	15	1
Eire	8.6	99.3	10	13–31[2]	1–2[3]
Territories granting no preference[6]	8.2	100.0	0	–	0
Total of above countries	97.1	98.6[5]	55–57[5]	15–18[5]	9–10[5]

[1] Taken directly from the official Year Book.
[2] Takes no account of additional duty of 10% on certain U.K. goods.
[3] Allows for additional 10% duty on certain U.K. goods.
[4] Refers to imports from the U.K. that were covered in this calculation.
[5] Weighted average.
[6] Nigeria (including British Cameroons), Gold Coast (including Togoland) most of British East Africa, Anglo-Egyptian Sudan, Palestine, Aden, New Guinea and Papua.

GENERAL NOTES ON TABLE XI

Column (1).
Calculated from *Annual Statement of Trade of the U.K.*

Columns (2)–(5)
Calendar year 1937 for New Zealand, Northern and Southern Rhodesia, Trinidad and Tobago, South Africa, Eire, British Guiana, Malta, Jamaica, Hong Kong; financial year 1937–38 for the rest.

In calculating the preference margins it was sometimes necessary to give upper and lower limits for a small percentage of items for which it was impossible to reconcile the classifications in the trade returns with those in the tariff lists. Several trade returns contained, for example, items such as 'other foods' and 'other textile manufactures'. It was impossible to find either the exact amounts given preference or the amount of preference, if any, conceded. This kind of difficulty accounts both for many of the percentages in Column 2 being less than 100 and for the outside limits in columns 3, 4 and 5 which take the place of precise figures. It also, together with rounding, accounts for the apparent slight inconsistencies between the last three columns.

WEIGHTING

A. *To obtain average figures for each country.*
The percentage margin of preference for each product was weighted by the value of imports from the U.K. as follows:

(*a*) Australia, Canada, Jamaica, Trinidad and Tobago, South Africa, India. Value of imports on which preference was granted.
(*b*) New Zealand, Northern and Southern Rhodesia, British Guiana, Malta, Eire, Hong Kong. Value of imports originating in the U.K. Since the qualification for preferential rates is that a certain percentage of an article's value should be the result of British labour (the percentage varying with the importing country), the figures given in columns (3) and (5) may be slightly above their true value.
(*c*) Channel Islands, Burma, Federated Malay States, Gibraltar, Ceylon, Straits Settlements. Value of U.K. exports as given in U.K. *Annual Statement of Trade,* Vol. IV. This will also give an upward bias to the figures in columns (3) and (5), since the U.K. figure includes all goods which in the U.K. have 'undergone operations' which do not 'leave them essentially unchanged.'

In the Canadian trade returns imports are attributed to the country from which they are consigned. The margins of preference on the separate items were weighted by the value of imports under the preferential tariff and then expressed as a percentage of the total value of imports *consigned from* U.K. (as opposed to the total value of imports *originating* in U.K. for other countries). The figures for Canada in columns (3) and (5) are therefore, relatively, underestimates.

B. *To obtain average figures for all British countries.*
For consistency the figures for each country were weighted by total exports of U.K. produce and manufactures to each country (column (1)).

taken without preference, or according to the value of U.S., rather than U.K., exports to Commonwealth countries, one would expect the final figure to be lower, though this tendency might, of course, be offset by other factors.

The notes to Table XI describe only some of the difficulties involved in the calculations. The main purpose of the table is to help to show how the final figure of 10% was reached. The results obtained for the various countries, although shown for convenience with some degree of precision, are subject to a considerable margin of error. The following broad picture is, however, probably correct and may be of some interest:

Of U.K. exports to Commonwealth countries, one-third went to

Canada, Australia and New Zealand, which gave an average preference of around 20%; one-third went to India and South Africa,
which gave an average preference of around 5%; one-sixth went to
Eire, which on balance gave little preference, or to territories giving
no preference at all; one-sixth went to miscellaneous countries,
which gave various rates of preference averaging about 10%.

It is hoped to publish more details at a later date.

No account has been taken of preference given through import
quotas or by any method other than import duties.

2 British and American productivity, prices, and exports: an addendum[1]

This note is an addendum to the preceding article by Mr. Stern and should be read in conjunction with articles published in 1951 and 1952.[2] We have been working for some time attempting to bring these articles more up to date, unaware that Mr. Stern was similarly engaged. Since most of his results are naturally similar to our own, we have limited this note to substantially different and additional results.[3]

I. A DIFFERENT SAMPLE AND METHOD OF CALCULATION

Our sample of products drawn from the work of Paige and Bombach, and our method of calculating the relative quantities of U.S. and U.K. exports, are both rather different from Stern's.[4] The results are shown in Table I and in the diagram. Our regression line of relative exports on relative productivity (taking logarithms in each case) has a flatter slope than his (1.89 against 1.27) and our correlation coefficient is also higher (0.61 against his 0.44).[5]

---

[1] *Oxford Economic Papers,* October 1962, with Monica Dowley, Pauline Fox and Senta Pugh.

[2] MacDougall, 'British and American Exports: A Study Suggested by the Theory of Comparative Costs', Parts I and II, *Economic Journal,* Dec. 1951 and Sept. 1952.

[3] Some of the calculations were made at the Oxford University Computing Laboratory. We are grateful to Dr. Mayers for the use of his General Multiple Regression programme and for his help.

[4] In particular, we have attempted to calculate export ratios for entire industry groups, whereas Stern has calculated them only for the products used as indicators by Paige and Bombach, although their estimates of relative output per worker referred to the industry groups as a whole.

[5] p. 290 of Stern. Our equation corresponding to that on p. 290 of Stern is $x = -2.19 + 1.89y$. As in the 1951 article (p. 711, n. 1), dx/dy is used as a measure of slopes, not dy/dx.

TABLE I

I.S.I.C. subgroup	Industry	Code no. on chart	Output per worker U.S.:U.K. 1950 (1)	Quantity of exports U.S.:U;K. 1950 (2)	U.K. tariff % 1950 (3)	U.S. tariff % 1950 (4)
3510	Metal cans	1	5.61	2.12	20	23
3530	Heating, cooking, and plumbing equipment	2	5.03	2.59*	19	24
38A	Automobiles, trucks, and tractors	3	4.70	1.58*	30	10
3191	Medicinal and pharmaceutical preparations	4	4.63	2.54*	10	14[1]
3651	Refrigeration machinery	5	4.46	3.85*	19[2]	15
2110	Distilling, rectifying, and blending of spirits	6	4.37	0.20	7	26
3610	Agricultural machinery	7	4.29	3.79*	15	free
2721	Paper, containers, boxes, and envelopes	8	4.28	3.20*	19	16
2722	Miscellaneous paper and board products	9	4.26	1.04*	19	15
3681	Laundry machinery	10	4.16	1.34*	16	18
3751	Storage batteries	11	4.11	1.48[3]*	15	20
3411	Blast furnaces	12	4.08	1.63[4]	24[5]	4[5]
3731	Radio and television	13	4.00	1.85	20	15
3197	Matches	14	3.76	1.05*	15	27
3660	Mechanical handling equipment	15	3.75	1.82*	15	free
3670	Office machinery	16	3.69	5.65*	13	15
3194	Paint and varnish	17	3.63	0.78[6]*	19	27
3740	Electric light bulbs	18	3.56	1.76*	10	20
3733	Electronic tubes	19	3.56	0.75[7]*	33⅓	15
2710	Pulp, paper, and board	20	3.38	1.20*	6	13
3652	Pumps and compressors	21	3.22	1.24	18	15
3621	Construction and mining machinery	22	3.20	3.38[8]*	16[9]	15
2130	Brewing and manufacture of malt	23	3.00	0.87	9	11
2640	Metal furniture	24	2.98	1.02*	18	free
3321	Glass containers	25	2.74	3.36*	25	20
2437	Hats, caps, and millinery	26	2.70	0.29	20	22
2391	Linoleum and leathercloth	27	2.56	0.28[10]	18[11]	16[11]
2610	Furniture and upholstery	28	2.54	1.36*	10	14
2200	Tobacco manufacture	29	2.51	0.98	39	5
2311/12	Cotton spinning and weaving	30	2.49	0.79[12]	17	25
3192	Soap, candles, and glycerine	31	2.49	0.64[13]	10	9[14]
3010	Tyres and tubes	32	2.41	0.84	30	10
2314	Rayon, nylon, and silk	33	2.26	0.52*	54[15,16]	20[16]
3630	Metal-working machinery	34	2.21	1.97*	21	15
3850	Motor-cycles and bicycles	35	2.16	0.04[17]*	22	12
3691	Ball- and roller-bearings	36	2.08	1.40*	20	25
3521	Cutlery	37	1.93	0.35*	19	20
2920	Leather products	38	1.92	0.42*	22	19
2317	Carpets	39	1.90	0.013[18]	10[19]	30[19]

TABLE I (*continued*)

I.S.I.C. subgroup	Industry	Code no. on chart	Output per worker U.S.:U.K. 1950 (1)	Quantity of exports U.S.:U.K. 1950 (2)	U.K. tariff % 1950 (3)	U.S. Tariff % 1950 (4)
2320	Knitting mills	40	1.87	0.90[20]	25	26
2313	Woollen and worsted	41	1.85	0.039[21]	5	18
2435	Gloves	42	1.83	0.12	30[22]	29[22]
3622	Textile machinery	43	1.83	0.47*	19	16
2410	Footwear except rubber	44	1.71	0.47[23]	16	10
2431 2432 2433 2439	Outerwear, underwear, and infants' wear	45	1.70	0.58	23[24]	24[24]
3020	Rubber footwear	46	1.55	0.28[25]	18	16
3822	Railroad and street cars	47	1.30	0.21*	11	18
3340	Cement	48	1.16	0.27	10	4
3810	Shipbuilding and repairing	49	1.11	0.35*	10[26]	15

Sources and methods of calculation

Column (1): Paige and Bombach, *A Comparison of National Output and Productivity of the United Kingdom and the United States*, O.E.E.C., Paris, 1959. Industry Tables, pp. 130–89.

Column (2): *U.S. Bureau of the Census, Report F.T. 410, 1950 Unites States Exports of Domestic and Foreign Merchandise.* Department of Commerce, Washington, D.C., 1951.

Annual Statement of the Trade of the United Kingdom with Commonwealth Countries and Foreign Countries, Vol. I, 1950, H.M.S.O., London 1952.

Indexes to the International Standard Industrial Classification of all Economic Activities. Statistical Papers Series M., No. 4. United Nations, New York.

Schedule B. Statistical Classification of Domestic and Foreign Commodities Exported from the United States. U.S. Department of Commerce. Bureau of Census. 1958 edition.

Since the relative productivity figures calculated by Paige and Bombach refer to I.S.I.C. subgroups as a whole, we have attempted to calculate relative export quantities for these subgroups as a whole (and not merely for the products used as indicators by Paige and Bombach). Relative export quantities were calculated using the mean of Paasche and Laspeyres index numbers, where data and conversion factors were available. Elsewhere (in cases marked by an asterisk*), relative export values were adjusted by the net cost ratios calculated by Paige and Bombach (admittedly a somewhat rough and ready method).

Column (3): *Annual Statement of the Trade of the U.K. with Commonwealth Countries and Foreign Countries — 1950*, Vol. II, and *Customs and Excise Tariff of the U.K. in Operation on 1 September 1950*, H.M.S.O., 1950.

As for 1937 (MacDougall, op. cit., Part I, p. 701), average non-preferential rates in round figures. Allowance was made for excise taxes levied on home production for spirits, beer, tobacco, and matches only.

Column (4): *Census Report No. F.T. 110 — U.S. Imports of Merchandise for Consumption, January 1950,* and *Schedule A — Statistical Classification of Commodities Imported into the U.S. — August 1950. Custom House Guide,* 1950 edition.

As for 1937, calculated duty on relevant categories of imports from the U.K. as percentage of value of imports from the U.K., excluding duty. (Tariff Concessions under G.A.T.T. include those negotiated at Annecy on 10 Oct. 1949 and were allowed for from their respective effective dates onwards; thus, on the items concerned, one rate was used for imports up to, say, May 1950, and another, lesser one, for imports during the rest of the year.)

Other notes to Table I

[1] Understated because for about one-fifth of the total value of imports, tariff is 'based on American selling price of a similar competitive American article'.

[2] Includes small refrigerators less than 12 cubic feet capacity.

[3] Automotive and radio batteries only.

[4] U.S. figure includes half of ferro-alloy exports as this is produced in blast furnaces in U.S. and exports of it are much higher than those of pig-iron.

[5] Includes ferro-manganese and spiegeleisen.

[6] Excludes manufactured pigments.

[7] This figure has slight positive adjustment for U.S., as U.K. data include values consigned in radio sets.

[8] Includes oilfield, well-drilling, and specialized mining machinery.

[9] Includes power tools employed in civil engineering.

[10] Includes coated fabric.

[11] Excludes felt.

[12] 'Unfinished' goods as far as possible.

[13] U.S. figure includes 'surface active agents'.

[14] Includes 'taxable oil imports excise duty' levied on soap and soap powder.

[15] Includes tyre cord fabric.

[16] Includes rayon waste, excludes silk waste.

[17] Excludes motor-scooters.

[18] Wool carpets only.

[19] Includes cotton carpets.

[20] Includes hosiery.

[21] 'Unfinished goods' as far as possible, includes 'semi-manufactures'.

[22] Excludes gloves in embroidery and lace.

[23] Excludes repair material

[24] Excludes articles of lace and embroidery, includes leather clothing.

[25] Includes repair material.

[26] Excludes 'ships for breaking up', which enter free.

II. TARIFFS

Stern has not calculated U.S. and U.K. rates of tariffs in 1950. These are shown in Table I and by the arrows in the diagram. It will be noticed that the upward-pointing arrows seldom reach the horizontal line representing U.S. output per worker 3.4 times the British (the average ratio of U.S. to U.K. wages). Thus in 1950 U.S. tariffs seldom offset America's comparative disadvantage (measured in this crude way[6]) whereas in 1937 they usually did so.[7] The change may be explained (*a*) by the fact that U.S. productivity generally rose less in relation to the British than U.S. wages did in relation to British wages, allowing for the devaluation of sterling, (*b*) by the reduction in the incidence of the U.S. tariff resulting from cuts in rates of duty and from the effect of inflation on such duties as are specific.[8]

The reduction in the incidence of the U.S. tariff was particularly marked in products where she had a comparative disadvantage. As a

[6] i.e. assuming a crude labour theory of value, all U.S. wages 3.4 times the British, and ignoring transport costs.

[7] MacDougall, op. cit., Part I, pp. 699 et seq.

[8] These changes were foreseen in the 1951 article (pp. 704—5).

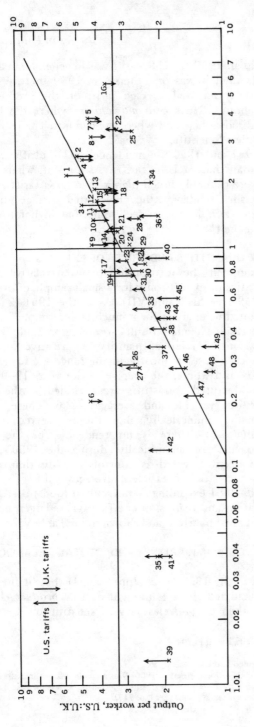

Fig. 1. Quantity of exports, U.S.:U.K. Productivity, exports, and tariffs, 1950.
(For key to numbers, see Table I.)

result, whereas in 1937 the U.S. tariff was in general much higher on such products than it was on others,[9] in 1950 there was no such tendency; the unweighted average tariff on the products in our sample was about 16 per cent *ad valorem* where the U.S. had a comparative disadvantage and where she had not. The U.S. tariff had become much less 'scientific'.

Between 1937 and 1950 the incidence of U.S. tariffs was reduced much more than that of U.K. tariffs. As a result, whereas in 1937 U.S. tariffs were generally much higher than U.K. tariffs,[10] in 1950 there was no such tendency; the unweighted average tariff on the products in our sample was in fact somewhat higher for the U.K. than it was for the U.S.

III. RELATIVE QUANTITIES AND PRICES OF EXPORTS

Stern has examined the relationship between relative prices and relative quantities of exports only for a small sample of products, for 1950 and 1959 (see his Table VII). As in the 1951–2 articles we have carried out this analysis for a much larger sample for each year from 1948 to 1959. The main results are shown in Table II.

The regression of relative quantity on relative price (taking logarithms in each case) is mostly in the range −2 to −3 as in the inter-war years as a whole, the average of the years 1949–59 being −2.3. If manufactured foodstuffs are excluded,[11] the regression coefficient is less variable and averages −2.6. These figures are somewhat smaller, numerically, than those observed in the later 1930's (around −3). There is no tendency for the regression coefficient to increase, numerically, during the 1950's, as might perhaps have been expected as controls and discrimination were relaxed. The correlation coefficient averages −0.54 for the years 1949–59, and −0.61 excluding manufactured foodstuffs.[12]

The correlation and regression coefficients are larger, numerically, than those obtained by Stern and shown in his Table VII.

IV. 'INDICES OF SIMILARITY' AND 'TOTAL ELASTICITIES OF SUBSTITUTION'

It was shown in the 1952 article (pp. 493–4) that, if the regression coefficient calculated above is thought of as a *'product* elasticity of substitution'; then a *'total* elasticity of substitution' between U.S.

---

[9] MacDougall, op. cit., Part I, p. 704.
[10] Ibid., Part I, p. 705.
[11] They were included in the pre-war figures.
[12] A correlation analysis for the period 1956–9 as a whole did not increase the numerical value of either the correlation or the regression coefficient, as was the case when the period 1934–8 as a whole was taken (ibid., Part I, p. 717).

TABLE II

Correlation between Logarithms of Relative Quantities (q) and Logarithms of Relative Dollar Prices (p) of U.S. and U.K. Exports of Individual Manufactured Products*

(Figures in brackets exclude manufactured foodstuffs)

	Number of manufactures (1)	*Correlation coefficient* (2)	*Regression coefficient (q on p)* (3)
1948†	90 (78)	−0.36 (−0.54)	−2.1 (−2.5)
1949‡	90 (78)	−0.53 (−0.59)	−3.0 (−2.7)
1949‡	95 (83)	−0.55 (−0.61)	−3.0 (−2.8)
1950	95 (83)	−0.62 (−0.59)	−2.7 (−2.7)
1951	95 (83)	−0.44 (−0.54)	−2.1 (−2.5)
1952	95 (83)	−0.49 (−0.60)	−2.3 (−2.8)
1953	95 (83)	−0.56 (−0.59)	−2.3 (−2.4)
1954	95 (83)	−0.55 (−0.61)	−2.1 (−2.3)
1955	95 (83)	−0.49 (−0.59)	−2.0 (−2.4)
1956	95 (83)	−0.58 (−0.63)	−2.6 (−2.9)
1957	95 (83)	−0.55 (−0.66)	−2.3 (−2.7)
1958	95 (83)	−0.56 (−0.65)	−2.2 (−2.5)
1959	95 (83)	−0.53 (−0.60)	−1.9 (−2.2)
1959†	113 (101)	−0.53 (−0.60)	−2.0 (−2.3)
1956−9	95 (83)	−0.49 (−0.58)	−1.9 (−2.2)

This table corresponds to Table V in the Dec. 1951 article (p. 715). The corresponding figures for 1948 in that table were: number of manufactures 118; correlation coefficient −0.34; regression coefficient −1.6. The same sample could not be taken for the present study since it was desirable to get comparable figures for subsequent years; and the U.S. trade classification in particular has been substantially changed in recent years.

*Including some semi-manufactures and manufactured foodstuffs.
†The largest practicable number of reasonably comparable manufactures was taken for 1959 only. For other years, the number was determined by the desire to get a comparable series for 1949−59. Five of the 95 products were not shown separately in 1948.
‡Average rate of exchange taken as \$3.68 = £1.

and U.K. exports can be obtained by multiplying the 'product elasticity' by an 'index of similarity'. This index has been calculated for 1949−59 and the results are shown in Table III, together with the resulting 'total elasticity of substitution'. The indices of similarity are of the same order as those calculated for the inter-war years, if anything a little higher. The resulting total elasticities of substitution are usually in the range −1½ to −2, again of the same order as before the war, but if anything a little lower. It should be remembered that, because of errors of observation and for other reasons, there may be a downward bias in these figures.[13]

[13]MacDougall, op. cit., Part I, pp. 718−20; Part II, pp. 494−5.

TABLE III

Elasticity of Substitution of British and American Exports of Manufactures

(Figures in brackets exclude manufactured foodstuffs)

	Number of manufactures (1)	Product elasticity of substitution* (2)	Index of similarity (3)	Total elasticity of substitution (2) × (3) (4)
1949	95 (83)	−3.041 (−2.779)	0.628 (0.692)	−1.9 (−1.9)
1950	95 (83)	−2.687 (−2.660)	0.677 (0.733)	−1.8 (−1.9)
1951	95 (83)	−2.079 (−2.477)	0.652 (0.707)	−1.4 (−1.8)
1952	95 (83)	−2.309 (−2.777)	0.682 (0.708)	−1.6 (−2.0)
1953	95 (83)	−2.328 (−2.434)	0.705 (0.752)	−1.6 (−1.8)
1954	95 (83)	−2.080 (−2.276)	0.699 (0.749)	−1.5 (−1.7)
1955	95 (83)	−2.006 (−2.392)	0.648 (0.695)	−1.3 (−1.7)
1956	95 (83)	−2.608 (−2.880)	0.645 (0.694)	−1.7 (−2.0)
1957	95 (83)	−2.284 (−2.741)	0.673 (0.703)	−1.5 (−1.9)
1958	95 (83)	−2.171 (−2.461)	0.740 (0.798)	−1.6 (−2.0)
1959	95 (83)	−1.927 (−2.199)	0.693 (0.778)	−1.3 (−1.7)

This table corresponds to Table VIII in the Sept. 1952 article (p. 494).
* As in Table II, column (3).

TABLE IV

Particular Values shown by Regression Lines

(Figures in brackets exclude manufactured foodstuffs)

	No. of manufactures	Relative quantity (U.S.:U.K.) when price equal	Relative price (U.S.:U.K.) when quantity equal
1948	90 (78)	1.27 (0.86)	1.12 (0.94)
1949	90 (78)	0.93 (0.72)	0.98 (0.89)
1949	95 (83)	0.94 (0.74)	0.98 (0.90)
1950	95 (83)	1.00 (0.85)	1.00 (0.94)
1951	95 (83)	1.09 (0.96)	1.04 (0.99)
1952	95 (83)	0.94 (0.78)	0.97 (0.91)
1953	95 (83)	0.91 (0.77)	0.96 (0.90)
1954	95 (83)	0.94 (0.80)	0.96 (0.91)
1955	95 (83)	0.93 (0.79)	0.97 (0.90)
1956	95 (83)	0.99 (0.88)	1.00 (0.96)
1957	95 (83)	0.97 (0.93)	0.99 (0.97)
1958	95 (83)	0.86 (0.76)	0.93 (0.90)
1959	95 (83)	0.78 (0.71)	0.88 (0.85)
1959	113 (101)	0.89 (0.83)	0.94 (0.92)
1956−59	95 (83)	0.91 (0.81)	0.95 (0.91)

This table corresponds to Table IX in the Sept. 1952 article (p. 501). The corresponding figures for 1948 in that table were: 118; 1.10; 1.06.

V. OTHER RESULTS

The 1952 article (pp. 500–4) showed that, according to the regression lines for the years 1933–8, the U.S. tended to export much less than the U.K. when the prices charged by the two countries were equal; even allowing for possible errors, there was a presumption that the U.S. had a 'comparative disadvantage in the imperfect world market'. Table IV shows that in the post-war years, according to our regression lines, the U.S. tended to export nearly as much as the U.K. when prices were equal. If manufactured foodstuffs are excluded, the U.S. tended to export significantly less but, in view of the limited nature of the sample, and of considerations mentioned in the 1952 article (pp. 510–2), it would be unwise to conclude that the U.S. had any longer any significant 'comparative disadvantage in the imperfect world market'.

In this study, interpretation of the results has been kept to a minimum and repetition of the discussion in the 1951–2 articles avoided. It is hoped that the figures given may be of some use to anyone working on those articles.

The Dollar Problem

3 A lecture on the dollar problem[1]

The title of this lecture is obviously too wide. It is impossible to deal with the whole dollar problem in fifty minutes. It is necessary to select a few aspects, and even some of these can be dealt with only superficially. I am not clear in my own mind about the answers to some of the questions I shall raise; so perhaps you will regard this as a preliminary report — a throwing out of ideas, some of which may, I hope, be at least provocative.

SOME DEFINITIONS

One of the things there is no time to discuss is the definition of the dollar problem, but I must say briefly what I shall mean by it. I shall be talking about the *world* dollar problem, and not the dollar problem of Britain, the Sterling Area, or Europe; and about the *United States* dollar problem, not the problem of balancing trade between the whole of North America and the rest of the world.

I shall define a solution of the dollar problem as a situation in which there is an easy balance of payments between the United States and the rest of the world on current account, but allowing for normal long-term loans and grants. This balance must be achieved, or expected to be achieved, over a longish period, without discriminatory restrictions against American goods, and while preserving a reasonably high and free level of trade in the rest of the world, a reasonably high level of employment and rate of expansion (an important point), and reasonable terms of trade between the United States and the rest of the world.

This is, of course, an imprecise and question-begging definition. But I think this is probably inevitable because the dollar problem is partly a political one. And, if I may be allowed to say so in this School of Economics and Political Science, politics is not a very

[1] *Economica*, August 1954. Delivered at the London School of Economics and Political Science on 2nd March, 1954. This version was written later from notes used during the lecture. Apart from minor changes, it is intended to be as faithful a record as possible of what was said. The statistical results are provisional.

precise subject. The dollar problem is political in the sense that, for example, though it might be soluble if the rest of the world made sufficient sacrifices, yet, if it is thought politically undesirable or impracticable for these sacrifices to be made, the dollar problem remains.

I might mention in passing that, according to this definition, there can be a dollar problem even if currencies are convertible. Others have taken a different view. For example, Professor Mikesell, the American economist, has claimed that 'during the 1930's there was no general dollar shortage since the key currencies were all convertible into dollars'. This is true in the sense that no special shortage of dollars was apparent to the monetary authorities of the various countries, since other currencies could be freely converted into dollars. But there may still be a real dollar problem in such circumstances, according to my definition, if convertibility is maintained only at the expense of, for example, heavy unemployment in the rest of the world, as in the 1930's, or severe import restrictions against American goods.

So much for definitions. The main question I wish to consider is whether the dollar problem is chronic, whether it will be with us for the rest of our lives. But, to clear the ground, I should like to give brief answers to two preliminary questions:

First, has the dollar problem ever existed?

Secondly, does it still exist?

HAS THE DOLLAR PROBLEM EVER EXISTED?

The first question may seem a strange one to a British audience that has lived through the past eight years. But it has been argued, mainly perhaps in America, but also over here, that there never can be a real dollar shortage, because it is always curable by sufficient devaluation of non-dollar currencies and sufficient deflation in the non-dollar world. I have unfortunately no time to discuss this question. I can only say, briefly and brutally, that, in my view and according to my definition, the dollar problem could not have been solved in this way, at least in the early post-war years.

IS THERE STILL A DOLLAR PROBLEM?

It is not so easy to answer my second preliminary question — is there still a dollar problem? — because there has been a great improvement since the early post-war years.

In the free world outside the United States, industrial production has nearly doubled since 1946, and is now about half as great again as it was before the war. Food production in the free world outside

North America has risen by perhaps one-quarter, although it has, unfortunately, not caught up with the rise in population since before the war, expecially in the Far East.

Mainly as a result of this great recovery of production in the rest of the world the United States balance of payments has become much less one-sided. In the first two post-war years — 1946–47 — the rest of the world paid for only one-half of its purchases from the United States by earnings in that country. In the next two years — I am taking pairs of years because of the two-year cycle that has been apparent in the American balance of payments during most of the post-war period — the fraction was two-thirds; in the following two years, six-sevenths; and in the last two years — 1952–53 — the rest of the world has paid for about 95 per cent of its purchases from the United States, leaving out of account throughout military goods and services supplied free by the American Government.

This improvement has, moreover, been accompanied by, I should say, a relaxation of discriminatory restrictions against American goods, and, on the whole, of restrictions on non-dollar trade. The terms of trade have become better for the rest of the world, not worse; and there has not been much serious unemployment. There has therefore, according to my definition, been a great easing of the dollar problem.

There is also the much publicised fact that, during the fifteen months from the summer of 1952 to the autumn of 1953, the United States was actually losing gold and dollars to the rest of the world at a rate of $2½ billion per annum.

In the light of all these encouraging facts, it is tempting to think that the dollar problem has been virtually solved. I think this would be a false deduction. A gain of $2½ billion per annum is by no means excessive for rebuilding the still exiguous reserves of the non-dollar world, especially as the United States was very prosperous during the period in question. It is right and proper that a surplus of at least this size should be earned in such periods to offset deficits when the United States is less prosperous.

A margin of $2½ billion is only about 5 per cent of the rest of the world's annual transactions with the United States, and we know from experience how quickly the position can be reversed. For example, in the year following the outbreak of war in Korea, the rest of the world was gaining gold and dollars from America at a considerably greater rate; and within a few months we were in the middle of another dollar crisis.

I therefore suggest that the margin during these fifteen months should, in prudence, be wholly discounted; and we are left with, at best, a balance. But this was not an easy balance. It was a precarious one, since it depended on, first, $2 billion a year of U.S. government loans and grants, other than military supplies. This is broadly 'economic aid', which the Randall Commission has recommended should be brought to an end as soon as possible, at least on a grant basis.

The balance depended, secondly, on nearly $2½ billion a year of American military expenditure abroad. A considerable part of this expenditure is temporary, or at best precarious (though I am not suggesting that there is any danger of a large reduction in the near future), since it consists of off-shore purchases and of expenditure on military works abroad which will, presumably, sooner or later be completed.

The balance depended in the third place on $4 billionworth of military supplies given free by the American Government. If this form of aid ceased or was reduced, it might have to be replaced, in part at least, by the recipient countries.

Lastly, the balance depended on the suppression of demand for American goods through discriminatory restrictions imposed by other countries. I do not propose to put a figure to this nor to the total of the four points I have mentioned, but I am prepared to say that, in my view, there is still a real underlying gap of, shall we say, "a good many billions of dollars'.

The gap is certainly much smaller than it was seven or eight years ago. But it is still uncomfortably large and it would be a grave mistake to think that it could be at all easily closed by devaluation or deflation or in any other way, without risking other serious difficulties.

IS THE DOLLAR PROBLEM CHRONIC?

I have answered two questions and that is enough. The dollar problem has existed and still exists. I am afraid I do not propose to answer my third and main question — Is the dollar problem chronic? — for the good reason that I do not know the answer.

You may say that this is not a very interesting or useful question to ask. For, if I am right in thinking that there is still a dollar problem, surely we shall have to carry on for the time being with the same sort of policy as has been followed in recent years, irrespective of whether the problem is ultimately soluble or not.

I do not agree with this argument. I believe that a view on the longer-run dollar problem is of great importance in framing policy. If we think the dollar problem is permanently insoluble, there may be a case for starting here and now to build some kind of permanent non-dollar bloc in isolation from America. If, on the other hand, we think the problem is not necessarily insoluble, there is a strong argument for patience and for avoiding a course that would inevitably be fraught with grave economic and political dangers.

In our policy during the next few years, it is not just what we do that matters, but the way we do it. There is all the difference in the world between (i) working with the United States for one multilateral world, or even one-and-a-half worlds (perhaps the sort of world outlined by Mr. Day in his recent stimulating book on *The Future of Sterling*), while explaining that it would be foolish to rush into it too quickly; and (ii) telling the Americans that they are impossible people to live with, that they are bad creditors and have a stagnating, fluctuating economy, and that we therefore propose to make our own independent arrangements.

Such a line would, incidentally, be rather tactless at a time when the Americans are pouring $20–$25 billion a year into the rest of the world, when their level of activity has been much higher and more stable since the war than anyone dared to hope, and when their barriers to imports are no higher than those of many other countries.

I therefore conclude that it is interesting and useful to ask the question: 'Is the dollar problem chronic?' I do not know the answer. I am not too optimistic. But, in view of the great improvement during the past eight years, one cannot be unduly pessimistic.

I should like to deal with the question by considering four main lines of argument that have been used in the attempt to show that the dollar problem is chronic.

First, the appeal to the experience of the last forty years.

Secondly, arguments drawn from the fact that American productivity is so much higher than productivity elsewhere.

Thirdly, arguments derived from the belief that productivity grows faster in the United States than in the rest of the world. (This type of argument is sometimes confused with the second, but is quite different.)

Fourthly, arguments based on the whole economic and political structure of the United States in relation to the rest of the world. This type of argument examines the outlook for American exports, imports and foreign investment and, taking account of political considerations, reaches gloomy conclusions.

This is not a comprehensive list of arguments, and some of them overlap. But I hope you will accept the classification for the purposes of this lecture. I propose to remind you briefly of what the arguments are, and spend a longer time on criticisms of them. This does not mean that I am necessarily optimistic. But the arguments tending to establish the chronic nature of the dollar problem have probably received more attention in this country, and I should perhaps try to do something to redress the balance.

A. THE APPEAL TO PAST EXPERIENCE

First, the appeal to past experience. It is argued that the dollar problem has been with us most of the time since 1914 — for the last forty years — and there is therefore a presumption that it will continue.

The trouble with this argument is that there was no dollar problem during the prosperous period of the 1920's (say, 1923–29), at least according to my definition and, I think, according to most authorities. And the rest of the period was abnormal. It consisted of two great wars and their aftermath and one great slump, in the 1930's.

If, then, there are no more big wars and no more big slumps, there may be no more big dollar problem. At least, it would be a bold man who would prophesy chronic dollar shortage simply on the basis of the last forty years' experience, expecially in view of the great improvement since the end of the second world war.

B. PRODUCTIVITY HIGHER IN THE UNITED STATES THAN IN THE REST OF THE WORLD

The second line of argument, in its crude form, argues that, since productivity is higher in America than it is elsewhere, all American goods will be cheaper than those produced in the rest of the world. This can, of course, be easily refuted by the theory of comparative costs.

There is, however, another form of the argument which is much more serious. It is what I call the 'films argument'. It has been well described in a recent book by Professor Nurkse, who has drawn on the so-called 'demonstration effect' of Professor Duesenberry. In simplified form the argument runs as follows:

Higher productivity in America means higher standards of living there. As a result of modern means of communication these standards are becoming better and better known in other countries, and there is more and more attempt to emulate them. This is impossible because productivity is so much lower in the rest of the world. There is thus a constant tendency for countries other than the U.S. to live beyond their means, through pressure for higher consumption today and pressure on or by governments to carry out large investment programmes to raise the standard of living tomorrow. This means inflationary pressure, a tendency to balance of payments deficit with the United States, in other words, dollar shortage.

This may well be the strongest argument for chronic dollar shortage, but I feel bound to mention some difficulties I have in accepting it fully. Drawing first on my own personal experience, the only American newspaper I read at all regularly – the *New Yorker* – is full of advertisements which seem to be largely devoted to persuading Americans to buy foreign goods, not the other way round. I sometimes wonder, too, whether there may not in time be a reaction against attempts to spread the American way of life such as that exemplified by the Coca Cola stall I saw a few years ago on the roof of Milan Cathedral.

More seriously, the argument I am discussing would lead one to expect an inverse relation between a country's standard of living and the state of its balance of payments. But this is not evident in the real world. Since the end of the war, at least, many relatively rich countries, like France, Britain and Australia, have had recurrent balance of payments difficulties, while relatively poor countries like Portugal and many of the British Colonies have had reasonably favourable balances of payments.

Nor is there any clear inverse relationship between the closeness of a country's contact with the United States and its balance of payments. The Central American republics, for example, have in general had more comfortable balances of payments since the war than many other countries with comparable standards of living but in less close contact with the United States.

We must remember, too, that Americans, as well as other people, desire a higher standard of living. They are, after all, the most exposed to high pressure salesmanship and advertisement. And we are often told that one reason for the higher American productivity is the great desire of the American worker to improve his lot, while the Briton, for example, is more content as he is.

Throughout history, moveover, the masses in most countries have been exposed to the 'demonstration effect' through the sight of the very high standards of living of the rich in their midst, standards most conspicuously displayed. One wonders why a few American films and American soldiers in their country should suddenly make so much difference.

It may be, of course, that the presence of G.I.s, for example, has shown that it is possible for the *masses* to be well off, and shaken long held fatalistic beliefs in the inevitability of poverty except for the very few. But all this is extremely vague. I am straying into the realms of sociology, about which I know even less than I know about politics. Despite the questions and difficulties I have raised, some of which are not wholly fair and most of which have answers, I think there may well be a great deal in this line of argument. But I doubt whether the evidence is really strong enough to conclude that, for this reason alone, the dollar problem is necessarily chronic.

The higher level of American productivity may, of course, have another consequence. Since it leads to a higher real income per head, it may make it easier for Americans to save, and this may make possible a higher rate of increase of productivity in America. But this takes me on to the third type of argument.

C. THE FASTER RATE OF GROWTH OF AMERICAN PRODUCTIVITY

The arguments connected with the faster rate of growth of American productivity have been well and elegantly analysed by Professor Hicks in his Inaugural Lecture as Drummond Professor of Political Economy in Oxford.

I am in general agreement with his first main proposition. This is, very simply, that, if American productivity is rising faster than productivity elsewhere, and American money incomes do not rise correspondingly faster or nearly so, there will be recurring balance of payments crises in other countries because their prices will be continuously getting out of line. The argument stated thus is, I believe, generally true (though not necessarily so). But I think the model used by Professor Hicks tends to exaggerate the difficulty because it assumes:

> *First,* that productivity in the rest of the world is stationary, whereas in fact it goes up quite a lot;
> *Secondly,* that American money wages do not normally rise as fast as American productivity, whereas in fact they often do.

Professor Hicks concludes, on the basis of these assumptions, that money wages in the rest of the world will have to fall if equilibrium is to be maintained with the United States. This would, of course, raise very difficult problems. But in fact it may not be necessary.

It is quite likely that in future American wages may rise by as much as, say, 4—5 per cent per annum in peace time. Hourly factory earnings have risen by an average of about 4 per cent per annum during this century, leaving out the years when America was at war (when the rise was accelerated) and the great depression of the 1930's (which caused wages to fall). Since the end of the last war

American wages have been rising by, on average, as much as 7 per cent per annum.

The problem for the United Kingdom, for example, may therefore be, not to reduce money wages, but to limit the rise to, say, 3—4 per cent per annum, while American wages are rising by, say, 4—5 per cent per annum. This may be very difficult indeed, but it is not necessarily an impossible task for wages policy, especially when we remember that, since the end of the war, British hourly earnings in manufacturing *in terms of sterling* have gone up no faster than American hourly earnings *in terms of dollars* despite the devaluation of 30 per cent.

Professor Hicks also analyses the consequences of different rates of growth of productivity in different industries; improvements in productivity may be what he calls 'import-biased' or 'export-biased'. That part of his argument relevant to our problem seems to be as follows. Productivity in American agriculture is increasing relatively slowly. The United States is an exporter of agricultural products. This is bad for the rest of the world and will turn the terms of trade against them.

I find it hard to apply this argument to the present situation. Since before the war, American productivity per man-hour seems to have gone up faster in agriculture than in industry, not slower. Secondly, the United States is a net importer of agricultural products, not a net exporter; only about one-fifth of her exports consists of agricultural products. Thirdly, the terms of trade — Professor Hicks' measure of the dollar problem — have moved against the United States and not in her favour.

I find certain other difficulties in Professor Hicks' analysis. For example, I am sorry that he ignores differing income elasticities of demand for his different types of goods; I think these can be very important. And he seems at times to confuse the *dollar* problem with what I call the *British* problem of paying for our imports from all parts. But I have no time to discuss these questions. I may well have misunderstood him but, though I find his analysis most stimulating, I doubt whether, in its present form, it can be applied to the problem now before us.

I now wish to be rather unorthodox and cast some doubt on the general belief that American productivity does increase so much faster than productivity in the rest of the world — at least in peace time. I think we sometimes suffer from an optical illusion here. We can easily be misled by comparing a recent pre-war year (such as 1937 or the average of 1934—38), when the United States was depressed, with a post-war year like 1949 or 1950 when the rest of the world had not fully recovered from the war. In making comparisons of Britain and America we can also be misled if we ignore the very fast growth in the American population. This is increasing by nearly one million every four months – there are one million more Americans today than there were at the beginning of last term. The American population has risen by 25 per cent since 1937, a year often used for comparisons with the present. During the same period the United Kingdom population has risen by only about 7 per cent.

I have been making some calculations about long-term trends in production – not productivity – in the United States and in the rest of the world (excluding Russia and China for which there are no good figures). Here are some preliminary and provisional results.

Raw Materials

Since 1913 production of raw materials as a whole has increased more quickly in the rest of the world than in the United States. This is true even if allowance is made for the growth of synthetic production and even if we include Canada with the United States and not with the rest of the world.

Food

United States production of food has, it is true, more than doubled since 1900. But the American population has risen very nearly as much, and there has been only a very small growth in food production per head of the population. The figures are less reliable for the rest of the world, but it seems likely that food production has gone up in roughly the same proportion as population.

Manufactures

During the last fifty years production of manufactures has increased faster in the United States – by about 3½ per cent per annum against 2½ per cent per annum in the rest of the world. But this has happened only during the two great wars, not in peace time. During the decade before the first world war it seems that manufacturing production was growing at roughly the same rate in America and in the rest of the world. During the inter-war years it was growing faster in the rest of the world – not only in the slump of the 1930's, when the U.S. was more depressed than most other countries, but also during the prosperous years of the 1920's. Since the end of the second world war production has, of course, increased much more in the rest of the world – very much faster in the early post-war period and at about the same average rate as in the U.S. in more recent years.

It is true that the United States' fast rate of growth during the wars has more than offset her slower growth in peace time. But if we try to allow for the much greater dislocation and damage caused by the wars in the rest of the world, by ruling out the years of war and only two extra years for the aftermath in each case — if we assume that these years never happened in the rest of the world — we find that the rate of growth outside America is raised from 2½ to 3½ per cent per annum, the same as in the United States.

If we take these three main forms of physical production together (raw materials, food and manufactures) it seems that physical output in the rest of the world has increased roughly as fast as in the United States, making a modest allowance for the two wars and allowing for the faster growth of the American population.

It is, of course, possible that total output of goods *and services* per *man-hour* has increased faster in the United States, even in peace time, if (i) leisure has been increasing faster in the United States, though it is by no means certain that this has been an important factor, or (ii) the output of services has been increasing faster in America — probably more significant. In general, total output per man-hour probably does increase faster in the United States than in the rest of the world, even in peace time. But the difference may not be nearly so great as is sometimes supposed.

D. THE ECONOMIC AND POLITICAL STRUCTURE OF THE UNITED STATES IN RELATION TO THE REST OF THE WORLD

The fourth line of argument is in terms of economic and political structure. Here again I shall begin by outlining briefly some arguments — mostly rather familiar — that tend to establish the chronic nature of dollar shortage. I shall consider in turn United States exports, imports, and foreign investment.

1. U.S. EXPORTS

It can be argued that there will always be a large and insistent demand for American manufactures, because the Americans always have the latest things; and for American primary products, because the United States, with her vast natural resources and large supplies of capital and technology, is the one place where primary production can be rapidly expanded whenever the rest of the world goes short. And the rest of the world may well go short, at least from time to time, especially of food.

Professor Dudley Stamp, in his stimulating book, *Our Undeveloped World,* has suggested that the main scope for increasing world food production in the foreseeable future lies in North America and Russia. (There are also possibilities of large increases, percentagewise, in such countries as Australia, New Zealand and the Argentine, but these are of much less importance in absolute terms.) Leaving out Russia — at the expense of ignoring some interesting possibilities — we are left with a picture of food production growing mainly in North America while the main increase in the population to be fed, in absolute numbers, is in the rest of the world. This suggests a tendency for the rest of the world to demand American food.

2. U.S. IMPORTS

It is argued that the United States can produce almost anything in replacement of imports, again because of her vast natural resources, her large number of technologists who are constantly discovering substitutes for imports, and her plentiful capital which makes it possible to exploit these discoveries quickly and cheaply.

There tends, moreover, to be political pressure to replace imports, not only because of the American political system, but also because there is comparatively little opposition from consumers. The extra cost to them is often hardly noticeable because imports form so small a fraction of the national income and the additional cost of home production is often not very great.

3. FOREIGN INVESTMENT

It is argued that there is no great incentive for Americans to invest abroad. This is largely, I think, because the United States is the major under-developed country in the world, and yields are therefore very high on investments within her borders. In this respect the United States today is very different from the United Kingdom in the nineteenth century.

It is also argued that the Americans have little experience of foreign investment; and since they had their fingers burnt in the inter-war years, they demand a high extra risk premium.

Lastly, if the balance on annual foreign investment and income on this investment taken together is to become more favourable for the rest of the world, American investment abroad has to increase year by year at a rate greater than the yield of foreign investments. It is argued that the latter is high, perhaps as much as 15 per cent., and the American annual investment abroad is unlikely to increase so fast. (This argument, of course, ignores the favourable effects on the rest of the world's balance of payments of American foreign investment that encourages the production of commodities which will earn or save dollars.)

COUNTER-ARGUMENTS

So much for all these rather familiar, but none the less powerful, arguments. Now may I give you some arguments on the other side — some reasons why the dollar problem may not be so difficult to solve? I wish to suggest that United States exports may be potentially vulnerable and United States imports what I call 'potentially explosive'.

First, then, the potential vulnerability of American exports, taking primary products and manufactures in turn.

The United States is an important net exporter of only four major *primary products*: grain, coal, cotton and tobacco. It may be that the very large exports of grain and coal since the war — far higher than pre-war exports — have been merely a flash in the pan, the result of temporary shortage in the rest of the world resulting from the dislocation caused by the war. U.S. exports of raw cotton are threatened by synthetic production abroad. Her tobacco exports are relatively small in dollar value and production in the rest of the world could fairly easily increase faster than consumption.

American exports of *manufactures* are vulnerable because American wages are so high. They are over three-and-a-half times the British per hour, compared with only two-and-a-half times before the war. The margin is still greater if the comparison is made with many other industrial countries. But U.S. productivity is not three-and-a-half times as high in many lines; it must always be remembered that American techniques are generally available to other countries. It may be, too, that the industrialisation of new countries will hit the United States as it has hit Britain in the past. Cars and refrigerators may prove to be the cotton textiles of tomorrow.

Now for the potentially explosive nature of American imports. This arises from the fact that many American imports are supplementary to home production and form only a marginal part of total consumption. For example, the United States draws about 5 per cent. of her iron ore supplies from abroad, 5—10 per cent. of her lumber and oil and perhaps 20 per cent. of her copper.

This means that, if the United States pursued a protectionist policy, she could easily whittle away her imports. This is one of the frightening possibilities. If, on the other hand, she pursued a reasonably liberal policy, her imports could expand greatly if consumption ran even a little ahead of production.

This is what has been happening with raw materials throughout the present century. The United States has been changing from a net exporter to a net importer of one commodity after another, and especially of oil, most of the metals and forest products. In perhaps over-simplified terms, the frontier has been reached. America has exploited her easiest mines and wells and cut down her virgin forests. The annual drain on American timber suitable for the saw-mills is now 50 per cent. in excess of the annual growth.

Taking raw materials as a whole we find that during the first half of this century American production has been increasing by roughly 1½ per cent. per annum, while her consumption has been growing by 2 per cent. per annum. Such a small difference may seem relatively unimportant but over a period of decades it can have quite striking results.

In 1900 the United States was producing about 15 per cent. more raw materials than she was consuming, the balance being 'net exported'. By 1925 consumption had nearly caught up with production. By 1950 it was 10 per cent. greater. If these trends continue, American consumption of raw materials in 1975 will be nearly 25 per cent. in excess of production. (Physically, this is not unlikely, since the United States seems to be using up her reserves of nearly all important minerals, except coal, faster than the rest of the world.)

If this does happen during the third quarter of the century, a rise in total American consumption of raw materials of two-thirds (roughly the possible increase forecast by the Paley Commision) would increase her net imports of raw materials between three and four times. This is what I mean by the 'explosive potentialities' of American imports. There is a kind of 'scissors' effect. The curve of consumption is rising more steeply than the curve of production and the difference between the two curves — net imports — rises very much faster, proportionately, than either of the two curves.

In food the same sort of thing has been happening, but to a rather less striking extent. American food imports have trebled in quantity during this century and are now about as big as our own. The United States has changed from a net exporter to a net importer of food. Fifty years ago her exports were twice the value of her imports. Now her imports are nearly twice the value of her exports. This has been a fairly steady trend interrupted only by the two world wars and their aftermath.

I would be the first to admit that American production of food can easily go up as fast as American consumption. There is great scope for increasing yields per acre, which are far lower than in N.W. Europe. But if this were done by the method recommended by

Professor Stamp — the copying of N.W. European methods, which means small-scale, mixed farming — and if this required a good deal of labour, I sometimes wonder whether American food might not become rather expensive.

But I am no agricultural expert. In practice, American food production probably will rise at least nearly as fast as consumption. I should like to emphasise, however, that even a small, temporary failure of production to keep pace with consumption could put an enormous extra demand on to world food supplies moving in international trade.

POSSIBLE EFFECTS ON THE UNITED KINGDOM

This could be a serious matter for the United Kingdom. It is a sobering thought that, roughly every seven years, Americans eat an extra amount of food equal to the whole of our food imports. This is, of course, because there are so many of them, because they multiply so rapidly, and because they eat so much.

It may be objected that the United States does not import the same kind of food as we do — that they import things like coffee. My reply would be, first, that all food, including coffee, uses agricultural resources which could usually be devoted to other purposes, at least in the long run. In the second place, the United States *is* a big importer of a good many foods which Britain also buys from abroad, such as sugar, cocoa, fish, certain vegetable oils, oilseeds and oilcake. She is even a substantial importer of beef. I was rather shocked to discover recently that, in the years 1951 and 1952, American imports of beef and veal were half as great as our own. (Admittedly, these were bad years for us because of trouble with the Argentine.) But these American imports, though large in relation to ours, were only about 4 per cent. of American consumption. If, therefore, the United States were to take 8 per cent. of her beef and veal supplies from abroad instead of 4 per cent., this could deprive us of half our own imports, at least on the 1951–52 level.

When people tell me that the United States could get meat and dairy produce from abroad at only perhaps half the price paid to her own farmers, I sometimes thank providence for American agricultural protectionism.

All this reminds us that, if the Dollar Problem were solved by a large increase in American imports of primary products, this might simply reveal in all its nakedness the British (or European) Problem of paying for imports of food and raw materials in a world where demand for these is growing rapidly. We might be out of the frying pan into the fire, and have a terms of trade problem substituted for a dollar problem.

Such an outcome is, fortunately, not inevitable. We might get the best of both worlds — and solve both our problems — if primary production abroad expanded sufficiently rapidly to meet both the growing demands of America and those of Britain and other industrial countries at a reasonable price.

There is also, however, a third and alarming possibility. We might be both in the frying pan and in the fire. This could happen if the output of primary products abroad expanded so slowly, and their prices rose so much, that they priced themselves out of the American market; the Americans might find it cheaper to produce for themselves. If this happened, we could have both a dollar problem and a terms of trade problem.

It seems then that the expansion of primary production overseas may be one of the keys to both of our problems. What are the prospects? It is impossible to say, but it is not necessary to be too gloomy, at least judging by past experience.

We have seen that since 1913 the production of raw materials has increased faster in the rest of the world than it has in the United States. At the same time, consumption of raw materials has been increasing faster in the United States than in the rest of the world. The United States has obtained about one-third of her extra needs from abroad (by importing more and exporting less). The rest of the world has used over one-quarter of its extra production to 'feed' the growing demands of American industry.

Food production has, it is true, increased rather more slowly in the rest of the world than it has increased in the United States. But it has at least roughly kept pace with population. The rest of the world has not become more dependent on United States supplies, as an analysis based on Professor Stamp's argument might have led one to expect.

THE PRICE ELASTICITY OF DEMAND FOR U.S. IMPORTS

One final point before summing up. Thinking about these problems has suggested to me that, contrary to popular belief, the price elasticity of demand for U.S. imports may be quite high, at least in the longer run, and *when American import prices rise*. For there are then great possibilities in the United States of (i) producing synthetic substitutes for imports, (ii) economising in the use of imported materials (switching from timber to steel, from sisal to wire; more intensive use of scrap; making tin cans without tin; and so on), (iii) using America's own natural resources. For example, if the price of imported oil rose 20–25 per cent. I understand that the vast American reserves of oil shale would become economic to exploit.

Similarly, if the price of foreign iron ore rose sufficiently, it would pay to use the huge low-grade reserves in the United States.

But this relatively high elasticity of demand for American imports, when import prices rise, does not unfortunately mean that the rest of the world can easily solve its dollar problem by a small reduction in the price of goods exported to America. Because I think the elasticity is much smaller in this direction. There are various reasons for this which I have not time to mention, but, for example, if import prices fall, American producers can cut their prices and run at a loss till their equipment wears out; and this takes much longer than it takes to build, say, new synthetic factories when import prices rise. I am in fact suggesting that there is a 'kinked' demand curve for American imports.

All this may, unfortunately, have a tendency to pull the American demand curve for imports over to the left. For whenever foreign prices rise — even temporarily — this may encourage a large and rapid development of substitutes and the like. But if, later, foreign prices fall, this will not restore the old demand for imports; because the new technical knowledge acquired will not be lost and the new synthetic factories take a long time to wear out. The whole comparative cost structure has in fact been altered to the disadvantage of the rest of the world.

If there is a 'kinked' demand curve for American imports, this may also mean a tendency to dollar shortage for another reason. If the rest of the world were to run into *surplus* with the United States, equilibrium could be easily and quickly restored by a fairly small rise in prices in the rest of the world. But when the rest of the world has a dollar *shortage,* it may be much more difficult to restore equilibrium because a fall in the rest of the world's prices may have only a slow and painful expansionary effect on American purchases from abroad. If, therefore, there are random fluctuations in the factors affecting trade between the United States and the rest of the world, there may be longer periods of dollar shortage than the reverse — in other words, a tendency to dollar shortage.

CONCLUSION

On the main question of whether the dollar problem is chronic I am, as I have said, an agnostic. This is because there seem to me to be strong forces working in each direction, and it is hard to say which will come out on top.

It may be that the most important factor will be a tendency of the rest of the world to live beyond its means, in the vain attempt to emulate American standards. But the factors connected with economic and political structure may be equally important. If, as many would argue, these also work against solving the dollar problem, the outlook may be bleak. But if they work favourably — and I have given some reasons for thinking that this may not be impossible — they may overcome any tendency of the rest of the world to live beyond its means.

Prophecy about the dollar problem is as difficult and dangerous as prophecy about the balance between savings and investment. Those who, before the war, claimed that a tendency to unemployment was inevitable in an advanced economy have had to eat their words. It may be that those who now foresee chronic inflation will prove to be equally wide of the mark. Likewise, in my opinion, it would require a very courageous man to forecast either chronic dollar shortage or its absence during the coming decades. I for one lack the necessary courage.

4 Notes on Professor Hicks's model of the dollar problem[1]

Professor Hicks has performed a most useful service in starting a careful discussion of these matters and by his insistence on the need to consider seperately the different types of industry in the U.S. and in the rest of the world, or in whatever two areas are being considered. The present author has certainly found his 'Lecture' one of the most stimulating treatments of this general subject. Professor Hicks's main concern is perhaps the analysis of changes in the terms of trade, and we suggested in Chapter I[2] that these may be rather unimportant, in the long run, for the U.S. and for the rest of the world as a whole (although this would not necessarily be true of other problems to which Professor Hicks's model could be applied). He also considers, in the course of his argument, changes in the balance of trade resulting from various possible changes in productivity and money incomes, but it does not seem possible to use his model as it stands as a framework for the empirical studies in this book. Some reasons are given in these notes, which are not intended to be a comprehensive critique of Professor Hicks's 'Lecture'.

I

In the first place, attention must be drawn to some of the simplifications he adopts for expository purposes. In several places he assumes certain variables to be constant while others change, and the resulting conclusions may possibly mislead some readers unless they are cautiously interpreted. These conclusions naturally had to be set out briefly in a single lecture which covered so much ground. Some examples are given below.

[1] Appendix VIC of *The World Dollar Problem* 1957, commenting on Hicks's Inaugural Lecture, *Oxford Economic Papers, June 1953*. Several of the points mentioned here are contained in a article by Mr. E. J. Mishan (*Oxford Economic Papers*, June 1955) which appeared after this Study had been prepared.
[2] Of *The World Dollar Problem*.

(*a*) When considering non-uniform improvements in productivity (import-biased or export-biased) in country A (which we shall call the U.S.), he assumes no change in relative productivities in country B (which we shall call the rest of the world). The possibility of such changes would, of course, have to be considered in any empirical study. If, for example, his conclusion is correct that import-biased improvements in the U.S. must, given his assumptions about the rest of the world, make the latter area worse off, this might presumably be offset by import-biased changes in the rest of the world.

(*b*) He assumes throughout that absolute as well as relative productivities remain unchanged in the rest of the world, whereas in practice they rise. This has the following consequences:

(*i*) It suggests, as we saw in Chapter IV, that money incomes in the rest of the world may very probably have to be reduced if trade is to remain balanced; but this will be much less likely if productivity in the rest of the world is rising.

(*ii*) It suggests that, where productivity improvements in the U.S. are import-biased, the standard of living will fall *absolutely* in the rest of the world as a result of a worsening in its terms of trade (and that this will seriously aggravate the monetary difficulties). But we have seen that long-run changes in the terms of trade are unlikely, at worst, to do more than retard slightly the growth of real income in the rest of the world, since productivity gains will by comparison be far greater.

(*iii*) It leads Professor Hicks to ignore the possibility of different income elasticities of demand for imports in the two areas. But if productivity is rising in the rest of the world these are important and can reverse his conclusions. Take his claim that, if productivity is constant in B, and rising uniformly in A, B's terms of trade will improve. He argues that, if money income is unchanged in B, and rises with productivity in A (so that all prices remain unchanged), B will demand no more of A's goods while A will demand more of B's, except in 'weird cases'. But even if we grant, for the moment, his assumption of positive income elasticities of demand for imports, his conclusion does not necessarily follow if productivity is rising in B. For the slower rise in B's productivity may be offset, or more than offset, by a higher income elasticity of demand for imports. Suppose, for example, that both productivity and money incomes rose by 5% in B and by 10% in A, so that all prices were unchanged. B's demand for A's goods might go up by, say, 7½% (income elasticity of demand for imports of 1½) while A's demand for B's goods went up by only, say, 5% (income elasticity of demand for imports of ½). B would then have a trade deficit, not a surplus. Her terms of trade would worsen, not improve.

(*c*) When analysing the effects of import-biased productivity improvements in A, he assumes that productivity rises in her import-type industries and remains constant in her export-type industries. But in practice productivity is likely to increase in the latter type of industry as well (even though more slowly) and this could reverse his conclusion that 'an improvement in A-productivity that is *import-biased* must make B worse off' (by turning the terms of trade against her), even if productivity in B remained constant. On his assumptions, and with money incomes constant in A and B, the prices of A's import-type goods fall, while all other prices are unchanged. B's demand for A's goods is unchanged, but A's demand for B's goods falls and causes a deficit in B's balance of trade, and hence a worsening in her terms of trade and real income. But supposing, to take an extreme example, that productivity in A's export-type industries rises by 9%, against 10% in her import-type industries, and that her incomes rise by 9%. The price of A's export goods is unchanged so that B's demand for them is unchanged as before. But what of A's demand for B's exports? The rise in A's incomes will tend to increase it (by 9% if we assume unit income elasticity of demand for imports), and this increase is unlikely to be offset by the 1% cheapening of A's import-type goods. A's import demand is thus quite likely to increase rather than decrease B's balance of trade, and the latter's terms of trade may well improve rather than worsen.[2]

For all these reasons, there is no very clear connection between the nature and extent of productivity improvements in the U.S. and the real income of the rest of the world. In particular, Professor Hicks's conclusion that import-biased improvements in U.S. productivity must make the rest of the world worse off has to be interpreted with caution. (i) It is obvious that any deterioration in the rest of the world's terms of trade might be outweighed by a rise in productivity which prevented any absolute reduction in real income. (ii) Even a worsening of the terms of trade might be prevented by an import-bias (or, of course, aggravated by an export-bias) in productivity changes in the rest of the world.

[2] This possibility is really implied in Professor Hicks's theory, and was no doubt omitted for reasons of space. For, if a uniform improvement in A helps B, a sufficiently slightly import-biased improvement must (for reasons of continuity) have the same effect. The extent of import-bias must pass some minimum amount before the characteristic consequences of import-bias show themselves.

(iii) Even if productivity changed uniformly in the rest of the world, its terms of trade might still improve if the unfavourable effect of import-bias in the U.S. was more than offset by the favourable effect of the faster growth of U.S. productivity generally. (iv) Finally, this favourable effect might be magnified, but equally well diminished or reversed, by differing income elasticities of demand for imports in the two areas.

We could still, however, take account of the foregoing points and reformulate Professor Hicks's conclusion somewhat as follows: *Given* the average rates of productivity increase in A and B, their income elasticities of demand for imports and the nature of productivity improvements in B (how far import-biased or export-biased), *then* the more A's productivity improvements are import-biased the less quickly will real income rise in B.[3]

II

There are, however, further problems to be considered.

First, Professor Hicks's argument seems to require that price should equal money income per unit of resources divided by productivity, so that productivity must be defined as output per unit of resources; and he deliberately lumps together changes in cost per unit resulting from shifts in supply curves and those resulting from movements along the curves. This means that if, say, the U.S. produces 100 tons of a commodity with 10 men one year, productivity will have risen by 10% in a later year if 110 tons are produced with 10 men *or* 220 tons with 20 men. But, assuming upward sloping supply curves, the effects would be very different on the demand curve for imports (if the good was import-type, or on the supply curve of exports (if it was export-type). It would thus seem necessary to look at shifts in supply curves of the two types of good rather than at changes in productivity as defined by Professor Hicks.

Secondly, even this is not enough. We must also look at shifts in the home demand curve for export-type goods and in the total demand curve for import-type goods. Only by taking differences in the shifts of the demand and supply curves for each type of good can we get the shifts in the export supply and import demand curves.

Let us see how this affects Professor Hicks's theory by taking again, as an illustration, his argument that, if productivity and money incomes remain constant in B, but both rise uniformly in the same proportion in A, so that all prices are unchanged, then B's balance of

---

[3] Professor Hicks's model also ignores population growth. As is shown in Chapter VI of the *World Dollar Problem*, this can be very important.

trade will improve. First, he argues that A's exports to B will be unchanged. But this seems to ignore possible shifts in A's export supply curve as a result of the total supply curve of exportable goods moving more or less to the right than her home demand curve for these goods. Secondly, he argues that A will demand more of B's exports (ruling out 'weird cases', by which he presumably means inferior goods). But this seems to ignore the possibility that A's home supply curve of import-type goods may have moved to the right as much as, or more than, her total demand curve for import-type goods, so that her import demand curve may be unchanged or even move to the left.

The U.S. may thus demand no more, or fewer, imports, and supply more or less exports, at the old prices. The following figures (for 'period 1' and 'period 2' (*a*)) illustrate a simple case where the balance of trade and terms of trade are *unchanged* by a uniform increase (of 10%) in U.S. productivity and incomes, while productivity and incomes elsewhere remain constant, so that all prices are unchanged.

U.S. consumption of both import-type and export-type goods also goes up by 10%, but *production,* as opposed to *productivity* (output per unit of resources), goes up rather more in the import-type industries; this is reflected in a shift of resources from export-type production. As a result, U.S. export supply and import demand both remain constant at the original prices (as do export supply and import demand in the rest of the world), so that trade remains in balance at the original terms of trade.

U.S.	Period 1		Period 2 (a)		Period 2 (b)	
	Export-type goods	Import-type goods	Export-type goods	Import-type goods	Export-type goods	Import-type goods
Resources used	50	50	49*	51*	50	50
Output	50	50	54	56	55	55
Exports	10	—	10	—	10	—
Imports	—	10	—	10	—	10
Consumption	40	60	44	66	45	65
Productivity (output per unit of resources)	1	1	1.1	1.1	1.1†	1.1†
Money income per unit of resources	1	1	1.1	1.1	1.1	1.1
Cost of production = price	1	1	1	1	1	1

*Strictly, 49.09 and 50.90.
†Whether change in productivity is measured by the change in output per unit of resources or by the shift in the supply curve.

It may be objected that there has really been an import—biased improvement in the U.S. because the supply curve of import-type goods has moved more to the right than that of export-type goods, But, even if we did measure productivity changes by shifts in supply curves (which would appear to be inconsistent with other parts of Professor Hicks's theory and would be a rather unsatisfactory measure of productivity changes for other reasons), a uniform increase in 'productivity' in the U.S. could still leave the balance of trade unchanged if U.S. demand for import-type goods went up more slowly than that for export-type goods. This is illustrated by the figures shown for 'period 2' (*b*). Both production and productivity (in both senses) go up by 10% compared with period 1 in each type of U.S. industry; there is no shift of resources. Money incomes rise by 10% and all prices remain constant. But home demand for export-type goods increases by 12½% while that for import-type goods goes up by only 8⅓%. This leaves the supply of U.S. exports and the demand for U.S. imports unchanged.

It may also be objected that imported goods are not the same as import-substitutes produced in the U.S. so that, if all prices remain constant and U.S. money incomes rise, more imports are almost sure to be demanded. But while some U.S. imports are not produced in America in any form, and the quality of others is different from that of the domestic product, there is a wide range of imports which, for all practical purposes, are more or less perfect substitutes for home production. There could be a reduction in demand for imports of the latter type which offset the increase in demand for the former type. This is illustrated in the following example which assumes, for

	Period 1			Period 2		
		Import-type goods			Import-type goods	
U.S.	Export-type goods	Perfect substi-tutes	Not pro-duced in U.S.	Export-type goods	Perfect substi-tutes	Not pro-duced in U.S.
Resources used	50	50	—	49*	51*	—
Output	50	50	—	54	56	—
Exports	10	—	—	10	—	—
Imports	—	5	5	—	4½	5½
Consumption	40	55	5	44	60½	5½
Productivity (output per unit of resources)	1	1	..	1.1	1.1	..
Money income per unit of resources	1	1	..	1.1	1.1	..
Cost of production = price	1	1	1	1	1	1

*Strictly, 49.09 and 50.90.

simplicity, that half U.S. imports are of goods not produced in the U.S. and half are perfect substitutes for home production. *Total* demand for both types of goods goes up by 10% in line with money income, but *import* demand for the latter type falls by 10%, since the supply curve of the perfect home substitutes has increased relatively faster. Total import demand is thus unchanged.

Finally, it might be thought that Professor Hicks is really assuming infinite elasticities of supply of import- and export-type goods in each area. But in this case the elasticities of demand for imports and supply of exports are also infinite, so that a uniform increase in U.S. productivity must leave the terms of trade unchanged.

III

For all these reasons, Professor Hicks's model appears to be unsuitable for our present purpose. It seems more useful to consider possible shifts in the demand and supply curves for import- and export-type goods in the U.S. and in the rest of the world.[4] This does not, of course, mean that Professor Hicks's model is of no value in a study of our problem. On the contrary his work has brought out, for example, the manner in which rising productivity in the U.S. helps as well as hinders attempts by the rest of the world to maintain a balance; and the idea of import- and export-biased improvements, when applied to the rest of the world as well as to the U.S., is of value, at least when thought of in terms of, say, shifts in supply curves.[5] But the emphasis which his 'Lecture' appears to place (no doubt unintentionally and because the need for brevity was great) on import-biased improvements in U.S. productivity as a main cause of dollar shortage is perhaps excessive. It is only part of the story and does not by any means imply, by itself, that the dollar problem is likely to be chronic. Many other factors have to be considered, some of them working in the opposite direction.

[4] This is analogous to the method used by Professor H. G. Johnson in his *Manchester School* article which was published after this Study had been prepared. He classifies the effects of expansion on production *and consumption* into three possible types — 'export-biased', 'neutral' and 'import-biased'. It should, however, be noted that he is concerned with changes in the terms of trade rather than with monetary problems.

[5] Shifts in supply curves at constant relative prices are not, of course a very good measure of *productivity* changes. Mr. Seton, in the valuable article referred to on p. 506, n. 1, of *The World Dollar Problem*, has devised a model defining the proportionate change in productivity as the proportionate change in the output of a commodity that is possible with any given collection of factors of production. He assumes a production function of the form $X = \alpha f(a, b)$, where X is output and a and b the quantities of factors employed. Changes in α over time measure changes in productivity. This definition is somewhat lacking in generality since it excludes the possibility of, for example, capital-saving or labour-saving innovations or of the exhaustion of natural resources; and these may be very important in practice. While Mr. Seton has helped to clarify the theoretical problems involved, his results are not easy to use as the framework of our empirical study.

Nor is it easy to apply his conclusions to the actual situation, at least as regards the balance of payments between the U.S. and the rest of the world (although they may well be applicable to, for example, Britain's balance with all other countries, which was also very much in Professor Hicks's mind). He appears at times to be arguing as follows. Productivity in American agriculture is increasing relatively slowly. The U.S. is an exporter of agricultural products so that her improvements in productivity are import-biased. This is bad for the rest of the world and will turn the terms of trade against it. But, first, it is by no means certain that productivity has been rising more slowly in agriculture than in other sectors of the American economy.[6] Secondly, the U.S. is a net importer of agricultural products, not a net exporter; only one-fifth to one-quarter of her exports[7] consists of agricultural products. Thirdly, the terms of trade – Professor Hicks's measure of the dollar problem – have moved substantially against the U.S. during the last twenty years and not in her favour[8] The adverse movement has been even greater, at least according to the official indices which may not be comparable, than that suffered by the U.K. It must, however, be repeated that these criticisms are not apposite in so far as Professor Hicks is identifying his country B with Britain and his country A with the whole of the world outside Britain.

---

[6] See p. 128, n. 1, of *The World Dollar Problem.*
[7] Excluding military exports.
[8] See Appendix ID of *The World Dollar Problem.* Mr. Balogh has pointed out that the adverse movement is partly the result of post-war discrimination against U.S. goods (*Oxford Economic Papers,* September 1954, p. 248).

International Investment

5 The benefits and costs of private investment from abroad: a theoretical approach[1]

I

The benefits and costs of private investment from abroad are a matter of considerable importance for Australia. This paper suggests one possible method of analysing some general aspects of the problem. It is mainly theoretical and does not attempt to reach clear-cut practical conclusions. This would require much more factual analysis and consideration of many other aspects. Some of these were discussed by Professor Arndt in 'Overseas Borrowing — the New Model' (*Economic Record*, August 1957), an article which also deals with many of the points analysed below.

The analysis is for the most part static and thereby ignores certain dynamic considerations that may be important. It attempts to assess the difference made to the real income of Australia at a given moment of time by the presence of more or less foreign-owned private capital in the country, on the assumption that the economic forces involved have had time to work themselves out (the analysis is thus a long run one). For ease of exposition this is done by starting with a given situation and then considering the effects of an increase in the foreign-owned capital stock; the analysis could equally be applied to a reduction. The moment of time may be thought of as a number of years ahead, in which case we are considering the effects on Australian income at that time of a greater or smaller inflow of capital in the intervening period.

We shall consider only relatively small changes in the stock of foreign capital. This simplifies the analysis and seems legitimate provided one is not looking too far ahead. For differences in capital

[1] *The Economic Record*, March 1960 — Essays in honour of Sir Douglas Copland. Reprinted in the *Bulletin of the Oxford University Institute of Statistics*, Vol. 22, No. 3 1960. This article was written while the author was Visiting Professor of Economics and Finance at the Australian National University. I am grateful to several economists, including Professor T. W. Swan, Mr. H. P. Brown and Dr. W. E. G. Salter, for discussing these matters with me, and especially indebted to Dr. I. F. Pearce for his help.

inflow are then unlikely to make a large proportionate difference to the foreign capital stock or, *a fortiori*, to the total stock. It will be suggested later, that, in real terms, the foreign private capital stock in Australia may have increased since the war by perhaps 6 per cent per annum on average. If this rate were increased or diminished by, say one-half, it would make a difference of only around 15 per cent in the foreign capital stock in 5 years' time, and a much smaller percentage difference in the total stock — say 1½ per cent if we make a rough guess that the foreign-owned stock is of the order of one-tenth of the total;[2] certainly the great bulk of the capital is still owned by Australians.

We start with drastic assumptions. The main ones, which will be relaxed as the analysis proceeds, are:

(1) the government maintains 'full employment without over-employment' or, more generally, a constant degree of employment of Australian resources;

(2) no taxation;

(3) the size of the labour force is independent of the stock of foreign capital;

(4) the stock of Australian-owned capital is independent of the stock of foreign capital;

(5) no external economies;

(6) constant returns to scale;

(7) perfect competition;

(8) more or less investment from abroad has no effect on the terms of trade;

(9) it creates no difficulties for the balance of payments which can be adjusted smoothly, and without cost, as required;

(10) the increase in foreign capital considered does not require changes in Australian policy that themselves may involve a loss to Australia.

II

The line *GK* in Diagram I relates the physical capital stock in Australia to the physical marginal product of capital, given the amount of other factors of production, which we shall call 'labour'.

---

[2] This is only an illustrative order of magnitude based on various 'back-of-the-envelope' calculations. For the sake of exposition it will be used on several occasions but the general arguments would be unaffected if the true figure were substantially higher, say one-fifth, and true *a fortiori* if it were less than one-tenth.

It is hard to say whether the ratio of the *flow* of new foreign investment to total new investment since the war has been greater than the ratio of the *stocks*. The ratio of the flows has been quite high in certain sectors such as manufacturing.

DIAGRAM I

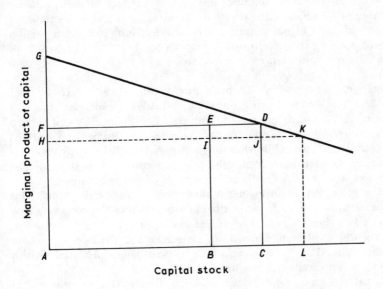

Initially, the capital stock is *AC* of which *AB* is owned by Australians and *BC* by non-Australians (called 'foreigners' hereafter). Since, on our assumptions, profits per unit of capital equal the marginal product of capital, total profits are *FEBA* on Australian capital and *EDCB* on foreign capital. Output is *GDCA* so that labour gets *GDF*.[3]

Now suppose a small increase in foreign capital from *BC* to *BL*. Foreign profits become *IKLB*. The new foreign capital earns *JKLC* and the 'old' foreign capital loses *EDJI* because the marginal product of capital, and hence the profit rate, have fallen. Total foreign profits are almost certain to rise on balance because, for reasons to be given shortly, the 'elasticity of demand for foreign capital' (as we shall call the percentage increase in the stock of foreign capital associated with a one per cent fall in its marginal product) almost certainly exceeds unity.

Australian capitalists lose *FEIH*. Labour gains *FDKH*. Australia as a whole thus gains *EDKI*. Since *DKJ* is relatively small, Australia's

---

[3] This assumes that labour could not produce any output in the absence of capital. If it could, such output should be added to the amounts shown for both total output (*GDCA*) and total real wages (*GDF*). Since the subsequent argument would be unaffected, we have retained our assumption for simplicity of exposition and to avoid the use of mathematics other than geometry. See also footnotes 9, 10, 12 of this Study.

gain is approximately *EDJI* which is the loss of income on the 'old' foreign capital. Australia does not, as is sometimes thought, gain the whole of *FDJH*, i.e., the whole of the increase in real wages resulting from labour's higher marginal productivity, but only a proportion corresponding to the ratio of foreign to total capital; the great bulk of labour's gain is merely a redistribution from Australian capitalists.

(Here, incidentally, we have one argument for restriction of foreign investment by the investing countries — which we shall call 'Britain'. Assuming no risk differential, British investors, if left to their own devices, equate the returns on home and foreign investments. But, while the marginal *national* (British) product on investment in Britain equals the private return, it falls short of this on investment in Australia to the extent of the reduction in profits on existing British investments there — *EDJI* in the diagram.[4] This loss of profits goes to Australian labour whereas the corresponding loss when there is more investment in Britain goes to British labour. If there is a difference in risk on investments in the two places — in either direction — the conclusion is unaffected provided British investors correctly evaluate the difference.)

Australia's gain (and Britain's loss) from more foreign investment in Australia is, however, unlikely to be at all large on our present assumptions. If total capital is of the order of 10 times foreign capital, the 'elasticity of demand' for foreign capital will be about 10 times that for total capital (i.e. 10 times the elasticity of the curve *GK* at *D*)[5]; and this latter elasticity is itself likely to be considerable because the substitutability of capital for labour is probably fairly high in Australia. The 'elasticity of demand' for foreign capital is thus likely to be high, so that *EDJI* will be small in relation to *JKLC*. In other words the great bulk of the extra output (approximately *JKLC*) will go to foreign capitalists; Australia's share will be small.

III

Now remove assumption (2) and allow for taxation. Suppose the rate of tax on foreign profits is t. This often approaches one-half where all profits are distributed and we shall, for simplicity, use this fraction as an illustrative order of magnitude, though it should be

---

[4] If 'Britain' is only one of a number of foreign countries with capital in Australia, and invests an additional *CL* there, the loss on her existing investments will, of course, be less than *EDJI*; part of Australia's gain will be at the expense of the other foreign countries.
[5] If a 1 per cent change in the marginal product of capital is associated with a change of *x* per cent in total capital, it will be associated with a change of 10*x* per cent in foreign capital if Australian-owned capital is constant.

borne in mind that it is on the high side.[6] Australia now gains, in addition to *EDJI*, the tax on the net increase in foreign profits and this is likely to be a considerably more important gain. Put in another way, Australia now gains $t(JKLC)$ plus, it is true, only $(1 - t) (EDJI)$ instead of *EDJI*, but this is a relatively small matter.

Taxation is not shown in the diagram to avoid complicating it. The case where the extra foreign capital is induced by lowering the tax rate will be considered in section XI; it is ruled out at present by assumption (10).

(We now have a much more important argument for restriction of investment by 'Britain'. Double taxation agreements are complicated things, but for our present purpose it is probably legitimate to assume that the British Treasury gets only the excess (if any) of the British rate of tax over the Australian rate, after the Australian Treasury has levied its tax in full. Now, if the British tax rate is the higher, British investors (ignoring differences in risk) equate the returns after the *British* rate of tax on investments in the two places, which means that they also equate the *gross* returns (before tax). But, while the marginal *national* (British) product is the gross return on investment in Britain (since Britain gets the tax), it is the net return, after Australian tax, on investment in Australia,[7] and this may be little more than half as great. If the Australian tax rate is the higher, the difference between the marginal national products equals tax at the British rate; the marginal national (British) product on investment in Australia may still be only about half that on investment in Britain.[8] These asides about 'Britain' do not, of course,

---

[6] If there is a tax on profits of 7s. 6d. in the £ plus a withholding tax of 15 per cent on dividends, the total rate of tax will be 47 per cent. In fact, something approaching this rate seems to be fairly common although some foreign profits are charged substantially less for various reasons; and if profits are undistributed the rate is also, of course, lower.

[7] For simplicity of exposition we ignore here the reduction in profits on existing British investments in Australia discussed in the last section.

[8] Let r_a and r_b be the gross returns in Australia and Britain and t_a and t_b the rates of tax. If $t_b > t_a$, British investors will make

$$r_b(1 - t_b) = r_a[1 - t_a - (t_b - t_a)] = r_a(1 - t_b)$$

i.e. $\qquad r_b = r_a = r \quad$ (say).

The marginal national (British) product is r on investment in Britain but $r(1 - t_a)$ on investment in Australia, the ratio of the latter to the former being $(1 - t_a)$.

If $t_a > t_b$, British investors will make

$$r_b(1 - t_b) = r_a(1 - t_a).$$

The marginal national (British) product is then r_b on investment in Britain but $r_a(1 - t_a) = r_b(1 - t_b)$ on investment in Australia, the ratio being $(1 - t_b)$ which is still not much over one-half for many taxpayers.

constitute a full analysis of the pros and cons of investment abroad from the point of view of investing countries.)

IV

Next remove assumption (3) and allow the size of the Australian labour force to be dependent on the amount of foreign capital. It is not unreasonable to suppose that immigration policy (and the supply of would-be immigrants) will be related in some way to the level of Australian incomes and these will be affected by the amount of foreign capital.

The gains from additional foreign capital so far described – there are more to come in later sections – will raise income per head if the labour force is not increased. It will thus be possible, if desired and if practicable, to increase population to some extent without reducing income per head below the 'initial' level, by which we mean the level it would have attained in the absence of the extra foreign capital. (This could still, of course, be consistent with a rise in income per head over time.) It is impossible to say how immigration policy might in practice be related to levels of income and thus, indirectly, to foreign investment, but some highly simplified illustrations may be helpful.

Suppose that the extra foreign capital increased total capital by 1 per cent (which would mean a 10 per cent increase in foreign capital if this were one-tenth of the total). If then the labour force were allowed to increase by 1 per cent there would, on our present assumptions, be an increase of 1 per cent in total output, total profits and total wages above the initial level; the wage rate would be reduced again to the initial level, the profit rate restored to the initial level. Assuming no taxation, and no change in the number of Australian capitalists, the average Australian worker (including the extra immigrants) and the average Australian capitalist would then be as well off as initially, i.e. as they would have been had there been no increase in foreign capital and no consequential increase in the labour force.

The new position is shown in diagram II. (This is the same as diagram I apart from the addition of the lines GN, DN, NK.) CL is 1 per cent of AC. The 1 per cent addition to the labour force has shifted the line relating the marginal product of capital to the capital stock from GK to GN. Compared with the initial position, total output is up 1 per cent, from $GDCA$ to $GNLA$; the wage bill is up 1 per cent, from GDF to GNF; total profits are up 1 per cent, from

DIAGRAM II

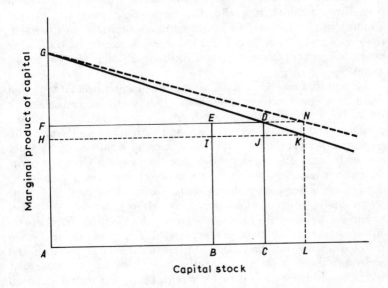

Capital stock

FDCA to *FNLA*.[9] Australian profits are *FEBA* the same as they were initially. Foreign profits are *ENLB*, higher than they were initially in proportion to the rise in foreign capital.

If we allow for taxation the outcome will depend on fiscal policy. Since we are merely giving an illustation let us make the simple, though admittedly unrealistic, assumption that only profits are taxed and that the resulting revenue is used wholly to finance social services for workers. Since tax revenue from profits (Australian and foreign) will be 1 per cent higher than it was initially, social services per worker will then be maintained at the initial level, as will profits after tax per Australian capitalist.

If the criterion for immigration were that it should vary with

[9] If labour could produce some output with no capital (see footnote 3), this output would be increased by 1 per cent. as a result of the increase in labour. The wage bill and total output would still be up by 1 per cent.

It will be noticed that the new marginal product of capital curve goes through *G*, as the old one did. This is obviously necessary for geometric reasons, if straight lines are used as in the diagram, to make the area under the curve increase by 1 per cent; and it can be shown mathematically that it is generally true, given our assumption of constant returns to scale. (With some production functions, the marginal product curve will be asymptotic to the vertical axis.)

foreign investment in such a way that variations in the latter should not affect the standard of living of workers or the average income of Australian capitalists, it would then be possible, given our present assumptions, to increase the labour force (compared with what it would otherwise have been) in the same proportion as the higher foreign investment increased total capital, i.e. by 1 per cent in our example.

This would, however, reduce average income per head. Population would be up by 1 per cent (we assume that Australian capitalists are also workers and that the labour force is a constant fraction of the population). But total income accruing to Australia would be up by less than 1 per cent since total labour income would be up by 1 per cent while total Australian profits were constant. This would be true whether we assumed (a) no taxation or (b) taxation of profits to finance social services with the latter counted as part of labour income and profits reckoned after tax. More generally, Australian income per head would be down whatever the nature of fiscal policy (provided that, as we are at present assuming, the tax rate on foreign profits is unchanged) because output would be up 1 per cent and foreign profits after tax by more than 1 per cent so that Australian income would rise by less than 1 per cent, i.e. by less than population was increased.

If the criterion for immigration were that variations in foreign investment should not affect total income per head (and it may be worth repeating that this would not preclude a rising income per head over time), it would not then be possible to increase population by as much as 1 per cent. But some smaller increase would be possible since, if there were none, income per head would be raised by the extra foreign capital.

Numerous other immigration policies are conceivable that would allow population to vary with investment from abroad. The policy actually chosen will depend on the relative importance attached to growth of population and of income per head; views on the distribution of income; fiscal policy; the supply of would-be immigrants; and so on. The question remains, however, whether more immigration resulting from more foreign capital would bring a gain of income to Australia *additional* to the gains already described in sections II and III.

While this is highly likely it is not absolutely certain. For, though the extra labour would raise output in Australia, it would also raise the marginal product of capital and so foreign profits after tax, and possibly by as much as, or more than, it raised output; there would then be no further increase in total Australian income (including the income of the extra immigrants) or even a reduction of earlier gains.

To illustrate the possibility, consider the case depicted in diagram II. Compared with the position after the increase in foreign capital but before the increase in labour (with output *GKLA*), the increase in labour raises output by *GNK* but it also increases foreign profits, after tax, by $(1-t)ENKI$, and this could conceivably be as great as, or greater than, *GNK*.[10]

That an increase in Australian income is in fact very probable can conveniently be shown with the aid of a further diagram. The line SV in diagram III shows the marginal product of *labour* corresponding to different amounts of labour, with the total capital stock fixed at the level reached *after* the increase in foreign capital. *OP* is the labour force initially. If it is now increased a little (by immigration) to *OU*, output goes up by *WVUP* (ignoring the small triangle *QVW*). The wage bill goes up from *RQPO* to *TVUO*, i.e. by *WVUP* minus *RQWT*. Total profits go up by *RQWT*, Australian profits by $(1 - c)$ *RQWT* — shown as *RXYT* — and foreigners' profits by $c(RQWT)$ — shown as *XQWY* — where *c* is the ratio of foreign to total capital. Foreigners' profits after tax go up by $c(1 - t)(RQWT)$, i.e. by $(1 - t)$ *XQWY*. Total Australian income thus changes by WVUP minus $(1 - t)$ *XQWY*, i.e. by *WVUP* minus $c(1 - t)$ *RQWT*, so that it will increase if $(WVUP/RQWT) > c(1 - t)$.

Now *WVUP/RQWT* is the 'elasticity of demand for labour' (as we shall call the elasticity of the amount of labour with respect to its marginal product, which equals the wage rate, i.e. of the line *SV* at $Q)$[11]. If we call this elasticity *e*, the condition becomes $e > c(1 - t)$. Now *e* is likely to be considerable, because the substitutability of labour for capital is probably fairly high, and almost certainly greater than $c(1 - t)$, which is of the order of $\frac{1}{10} \times \frac{1}{2} = \frac{1}{20}$. (An elasticity as low as $\frac{1}{20}$ would mean that, to employ 1 per cent more workers — say 40,000 — with a given capital stock, but allowing all the time necessary for long-run readjustments, the real wage rate would have to fall by nearly one-fifth.)

An increase in labour with capital constant is thus most likely to increase total Australian income. If extra immigration is allowed as a result of extra foreign investment it is thus most likely, on balance, to raise total Australian income beyond the level resulting from the gains described in sections II and III.

---

[10] If labour could produce some output with no capital, the increase in output would be greater than *GNK*, but it might still be less than $(1 - t)$ *ENKI*. (See footnote 9).

[11] If *L* is the quantity of labour and *M* its marginal product,

$$\frac{WVUP}{RQWT} = \frac{M\Delta L}{L\Delta M} \text{ approximately.}$$

DIAGRAM III

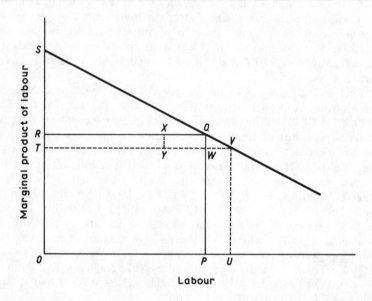

(It will be noticed that we have not relied in this section — as is sometimes done — on fixed technical coefficients, i.e. a fixed ratio of capital to labour, to show that more foreign capital will allow a larger labour force to be employed.

The assumption of flexibility seems more realistic, especially as we are concerned with the long run and with the economy as a whole. The possible applicability of the analysis to 'dual' economies in underdeveloped countries will be briefly touched on in section XII.)

V

Now remove assumption (4) that the stock of Australian-owned capital is independent of the amount of foreign capital. The higher the stock of foreign capital at some future date the higher must the inflow be between now and then and the higher is the stock likely to be at most intervening dates. The higher therefore is Australian income likely to be in most intervening years, for reasons given in previous sections, if Australian-owned capital is unaffected by the higher foreign investment.

This may suggest that Australian savings and investment are likely to be higher so that at the future date the stock of Australian-owned capital will in fact be higher. Such a conclusion, however, becomes considerably less certain when account is taken of such factors as the redistribution of income between capital and labour resulting from increased foreign investment and from any consequent increase in immigration; and it is hard to know how governmental fiscal, monetary and other policies will react to the changing circumstances — such reactions will be important. It is not inconceivable that Australian-owned capital will be lower at the future date than it would have been in the absence of the extra foreign capital. To take an extreme, and no doubt exaggerated, example, extra investment from abroad might consist of purchases of existing Australian-owned assets, and the proceeds might be spent on extra foreign consumption goods, of a type not obtainable at home, whose importation was previously prohibited but is now allowed following the improvements in the balance of payments; the extra foreign-owned capital would then be fully offset by a reduction in Australian-owned capital.

The actual outcome is hard to predict. If, as is perhaps most likely, Australian-owned capital is increased, it can be seen, using the same type of diagrammatic analysis as before, that there will be a further increase in Australian income, over and above the increases described earlier, equal to the profits on the extra Australian capital plus the reduction in foreign profits, after tax, resulting from the lower profit rate. (The reduction in profits on the 'old' Australian capital will be a gain to Australian labour.) If this higher income leads to more immigration there will be a still further increase in total Australian income for reasons given earlier.

If Australian capital is reduced, Australian income will be less than it would have been (i.e. the gain for other reasons will be diminished) by the profits on the Australian capital not created plus the increase in foreign profits, after tax, resulting from the higher profit rate; and if immigration is in consequence reduced there will be a further reduction in total Australian income.

If Australia is prodigal enough to allow the extra foreign capital to be fully offset by a reduction in Australian-owned capital (compared with what it would otherwise have been), then Australian income at the future date will, on our present assumptions, actually be lower than it would have been had the extra foreign capital not come in. For, assuming no change in immigration policy, total labour, total capital and total output will be the same as they would have been, but of this output foreigners will get an extra amount equal to the profits, after tax, on their extra capital; if, in the circumstances, immigration were reduced, there would be a further reduction in Australian income.

VI

Now remove assumption (5) and allow for possible external economies from extra foreign investment in Australia, i.e. economies external to the foreign firms investing the extra capital. If the value added to output by this capital exceeds the profits, before tax, earned on it the difference will be the value of such external economies. These will very probably bring a further gain to Australia.

We shall still assume that there are no external economies *of scale* resulting from the growth of the Australian economy generally; such economies will be considered in the next section. We shall be concerned at present only with external economies of foreign investment resulting from other factors such as (i) the breaking of bottlenecks (probably much less important now than it may have been in the early post-war years) and (ii) the introduction of 'know-how' by foreign firms.

Such know-how is presumably becoming less important as Australian technical and administrative knowledge broadens. It is perhaps hardly worth mentioning that it can bring an additional gain to Australia only if it gets outside the foreign firms. This may happen where, for example, the latter train workers who are later employed by Australian firms or where the superior techniques they bring to the country are somehow passed on to locally-owned businesses which are both made aware of them and forced to adopt them if they are to survive foreign competition. If any gain accures to Australia from this 'know-how', it does not necessarily mean that it might not have been preferable to buy or hire it without importing the capital.

While these external economies seem likely to bring an extra gain to Australia, they might conceivably reduce the gains mentioned earlier. The extra gain (which may be negative) will be equal to (a) the resulting change in the wage bill plus (b) the resulting change in profits of Australian capitalists plus (c) the tax on the resulting change in profits on the 'old' foreign capital. If the benefit of the external economies spreads to both capital and labour — and this seems *a priori* the most likely outcome — (a), (b) and (c) will all be positive and there must be a further gain to Australia. There must also be a further gain so long as labour benefits, even if capital loses; for since the external economies will presumably increase output, labour's gain must exceed capital's loss, and only part of the latter is borne by Australia. There will still be a further gain even if labour does not benefit at all, provided there is no absolute reduction in the wage bill. But if there is an absolute reduction, Australia *may* lose.

Such a reduction might occur if, for example, the presence of

DIAGRAM IV

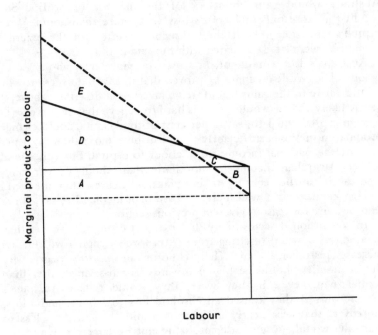

extra foreign firms spread knowledge of production methods that enabled other firms to produce the same output with their existing capital but with less labour while the marginal product of labour at full employment was reduced. There would then, as a result of the external economies, be a higher total output in Australia but a lower wage bill. Profits would go up more than the wage bill fell. This would, however, presuppose an improvement in techniques rather heavily biased towards labour-saving as opposed to capital-saving.

The possibility is illustrated in diagram IV[12]. The external economies shift the marginal product of labour curve from the full to the dotted line. Output is up by $E - C - B$, which is positive. The wage bill is down by $A + B$. Profits are up by $E + A - C$.

Australia would, however, lose only if labour's loss was nearly as large as capital's gain. For she would get the great bulk of the latter, either in profits or in taxes, actually $1 - c(1 - t)$ of capital's gain where, as before, c is the ratio of foreign to total capital and t the

---

[12] It is assumed that capital could produce no output if there were no labour. This is analogous to the assumption mentioned in footnote 3.

rate of tax on profits. Taking c and t as of the order of $\frac{1}{10}$ and $\frac{1}{2}$, Australia would gain about $\frac{19}{20}$ of the increase in profits. She would thus lose only if labour's loss were more than about $\frac{19}{20}$ of capital's gain, i.e. only if the redistributive effect of the external economies were large compared with the gain in output.

Australia's loss could not, at worst, be more than about $\frac{1}{20}$ of labour's loss. While it cannot be proved that this would necessarily be small relative to the gains from foreign investment described above, it seems likely that it would be. It is hard to believe that an increase in foreign capital equal to, say 1 per cent of total capital could change production methods sufficiently to redistribute more than say 1 per cent of the national income from labour to capital. But this would reduce Australian income by not more than about $\frac{1}{20}$ per cent, whereas it can be seen, by taking plausible figures, that the extra foreign capital might well increase Australian income by, say, $\frac{1}{2}$ per cent or more for reasons given in previous sections[13]

In conclusion it seems likely that external economies (other than economies of scale) resulting from extra foreign capital will further increase Australian income. There is no obvious *a priori* reason why the economies should be biased towards labour-saving rather than capital-saving; even if they were, they would reduce Australia's income only if they caused an absolute loss to labour, and a loss, moreover, that was nearly as large as capital's gain. Any loss to Australia would, in any case, probably not be large relative to the other gains from foreign investment.

Any gain from external economies would bring a further gain from extra immigration (given any likely criterion for immigration policy), and possibly from extra Australian capital; the reverse would be true of any loss from external economies.

VII

Now remove assumption (6) and allow for the possibility of economies of scale in the sense that, if labour and capital were both increased by 1 per cent, output would increase by more than 1 per cent, whether the extra capital were foreign or Australian. The economies of scale considered here do not, therefore, include any external economies resulting from the presence of more foreign, as distinct from Australian, capital; these latter economies could arise

[13] Of course, if the external economies benefited foreign more than Australian capitalists in relation to their respective capitals, Australia's loss could be greater; but this would be inconsistent with our present assumption of perfect competition which means that the profit rate is the same for Australian and foreign capital.

even if there were no increase in total capital or in labour, the extra foreign capital being offset by a reduction in Australian capital.

Economies of scale could be external to firms or internal; the latter type would be possible only under imperfect competition, about which more will be said in the next section. The economies could be biased in a labour-saving or in a capital-saving direction as in the case of the external economies described in the last section. They seem likely, however, to bring a further gain to Australia when foreign capital is increased. There could conceivably be a loss for reasons similar to those discussed in the last section, but this seems intuitively to be even more improbable, since a mere increase in scale seems less likely to cause drastic changes in methods of production than the presence of additional foreign capital, where the quantity of extra capital is the same in both cases.

Gains from economies of scale will, of course, allow further gains from extra immigration (and possibly from extra Australian capital), and conversely for losses.

VIII

So far we have assumed perfect competition. It might be argued that this was a reasonable assumption on the ground that, according to some post-war studies, it corresponds fairly closely to reality in the long run, or at least more closely than many pre-war theories implied. If, on the other hand we remove assumption (7), and allow for imperfect competition, the analysis becomes much more complex and it is not easy to make useful generalizations about the modifications required in our previous analysis.

Assume first that the same 'normal' rate of profits is earned everywhere. Wages plus 'normal' profits will then exhaust the total output but the reward per unit of capital or labour will be the marginal *revenue* product, which is the marginal *physical* product (assuming the firm expands) *less* this product multiplied by the reciprocal of the elasticity of demand facing the firm (where this elasticity is defined so as to be positive).[14] The *ratio* of the wage rate to the profit rate will still, however, equal the ratio of the marginal *physical* products of labour and capital.

If, now, growth took place wholly through multiplication of identical firms, and assuming no external economies, a given proportionate increase in both capital and labour would result in the

---

[14] We assume a perfectly elastic supply of labour and of capital to the firm. Units of each product are defined so as to make their prices unity. The demand curve for each firm will be tangential to its average cost curve.

same proportionate increase in the number of firms and in total output. There would thus be constant returns to scale for the economy as a whole. (The latent internal economies of scale implicit in our assumptions — according to a well-known theorem in the theory of the firm — would not be exploited.) It is intuitively plausible that each factor would then receive its marginal (national) *physical* product, even though it received less than what the marginal physical product would have been had individual firms expanded; a proof is given in the footnote.[15] On these assumptions, therefore, the preceding analysis applies. It would also seem to be a reasonable approximation even though firms are not identical, provided the new ones were representative.

If, at the other extreme, growth took place wholly within existing firms, each growing in the same proportion, the latent internal economies of scale would be exploited and capital and labour would

[15] Let the production function of each of n firms be $y = f(k, l)$, where y is output, k capital and l labour. Let Y, K, L be corresponding totals for the economy, π the profit rate and w the wage rate. Suppose an increase in total capital sufficient to allow for an extra firm producing the same output as each old one and for the maintenance of the output of each old one. Part of the extra capital will go into the new firm and part into the old firms to compensate for the labour withdrawn for use in the new one.

The increase in total output is the output of the new firm which equals that of each old one,

i.e.
$$\Delta Y = y \tag{1}$$

Rewards to the factors exhaust output in each firm,

i.e.
$$y = k\pi + lw \tag{2}$$

The increase in total capital is the capital in the new firm plus the increase in capital in all the old ones,

i.e.
$$\Delta K = (k + \Delta k) + n\Delta k \tag{3}$$

There is no change in the output of the old firms,

i.e.
$$\Delta k \frac{\partial y}{\partial k} + \Delta l \frac{\partial y}{\partial l} = 0 \tag{4}$$

The ratio of the profit rate to the wage rate equals the ratio of the marginal physical products of capital and labour (assuming firms were to expand),

i.e.
$$\frac{\partial y / \partial k}{\partial y / \partial l} = \frac{\pi}{w} \tag{5}$$

From (4) and (5),
$$\pi\Delta k + w\Delta l = 0 \tag{6}$$

From (1), (2) and (3),
$$\frac{\Delta Y}{\Delta K} = \frac{k\pi + lw}{k + (n + 1)\Delta k}$$

substituting from (6)
$$\frac{\Delta Y}{\Delta K} = \pi \left[\frac{k\pi + lw}{k\pi - (n + 1)w\Delta l} \right]$$

Now $-n\Delta l$ is the labour in the new firm (being the sum of the transfers from the old firms) and therefore also the labour in each old firm in the new situation. In the old situation their labour (l) was $-\Delta l$ greater. Therefore $-(n + 1)\Delta l = 1$.

Hence $\Delta Y / \Delta K = \pi$, i.e. the profit rate equals the marginal national physical product of capital. Similarly for labour.

get less than their marginal physical products. Extra foreign capital would then probably bring a gain to Australia as a result of the internal economies; for the profits it earned would be less than the extra output it created, the difference going to existing factors. This gain, however, is merely that resulting from economies of scale and already allowed for in the previous section.

On the above assumptions, therefore, imperfect competition does not seem to require much, if any, modification of our previous analysis. The assumptions are, of course, unrealistic. For example, in so far as the foreign capital creates new firms, these may, to get a foothold in the market, have to charge prices lower than those ruling for similar existing products that are in no way superior, simply because buyers are conservative in their habits. The new firms, if they used the same techniques, would then make a lower rate of profit than that earned elsewhere — there would no longer be the same 'normal' rate everywhere — and there would be a gain to Australia additional to those already considered. The same might be true in so far as growth was within existing firms, for extra foreign capital would probably be concentrated on a small proportion of such firms, especially those in which foreign capital was already invested.

On the other hand, the growth of foreign firms might put them in a monopolistic position in which they could exploit Australian buyers, and this might involve a loss to Australia. (Foreign investment need not, of course, foster monopoly. On the contrary, it may break down local monopolies and, by accelerating the growth of the economy and so of the Australian market, widen the scope for competition by increasing the number of firms of reasonable size possible within existing industries.)

Endless further examples could be elaborated, but this would be pointless. The present method of analysis is admittedly unsatisfactory for dealing with imperfect competition and a better method might substantially modify our earlier results. On the other hand, we have seen that, on certain assumptions, the perfect competition analysis gives a reasonable first approximation, and that the removal of these assumptions leads to modifications that do not all work in the same direction and may partly cancel each other out.

IX

Now remove assumption (8) and allow for possible effects of investment from abroad on the terms of trade. We still assume in this section that the balance of payments can be adjusted smoothly as required, so that international reserves are held constant without economic or social cost by, among other things, variations in exchange rates or in Australia's cost level relative to cost levels abroad with fixed exchange rates.

Let us start by also assuming, as is quite common in the analysis of such problems, (i) that trade barriers are not raised and lowered to correct tendencies to international deficit and surplus respectively; (ii) that an improvement in the balance of payments requires a worsening in the terms of trade, and conversely. On these assumptions, which will be critically reviewed later, extra foreign investment may affect the terms of trade in three main ways.

First, the transfer of the profits abroad will tend to require a worsening in the terms of trade to generate the necessary surplus in the other items of the balance of payments.

Secondly, the terms of trade may be affected by the increase in output and income in Australia resulting from the extra foreign investment, and by any consequent changes abroad (output abroad might, for example, be less than it would otherwise have been because there is now less capital for investment there). The outcome will depend on such factors as the pattern of changes, at home and abroad, in supply of, and demand for, different types of goods (especially export-type, import-type and other). This raises very large questions that cannot be discussed here, but it seems that the terms of trade might tend to be either worsened or improved.

Thirdly, the movements of capital across the exchanges will affect the terms of trade. An inflow will tend to improve them, by creating a tendency to surplus in the balance of payments (which, on our present assumptions, has to be corrected), provided the capital does not reflect entirely additional imports of capital goods and remembering that the government is assumed to maintain a constant degree of employment (otherwise we should have to allow for the inflationary effects of complementary Australian investment and the like). Similarly, the terms of trade will worsen if and when the foreign capital flows out again. (This may happen even with direct investment if, for example, depreciation allowances are repatriated or if foreign assets are sold to Australians.)

It is hard to say whether, on balance, these various forces will improve or worsen the terms of trade. Fortunately, however, this does not matter too much, since any change is unlikely to be very large — once more for three main reasons.

First, it is rather widely believed that terms of trade are to all intents and purposes a *datum* for Australia. The supply of imports must certainly be highly elastic since imports are such a small fraction of consumption of similar goods abroad; and, while one cannot be so confident about the elasticity of demand for exports, this too seems likely to be high, in the long run we are here considering, especially when account is taken of competition between wool and synthetic fibres.

Secondly, even if the terms of trade are not a *datum,* deficits or surpluses may in practice be prevented, in part at least, by a raising or lowering of trade barriers which limits any worsening or improvement in the terms of trade.

Thirdly, even if trade barriers are not varied in this way, tendencies to imbalance may be largely corrected by other measures so that only small changes in the terms of trade are required. Dr. I. F. Pearce, in an interesting paper not yet published,[16] has argued that, assuming 'full employment' is maintained at home and abroad, a country's balance of payments deficit, for example, can usually be removed in large part by (i) a cut in expenditure at home approximately equal to the deficit, together with a corresponding increase in other countries (which will be necessary to maintain full employment there as their surplus vanishes); (ii) a reduction, by exchange depreciation or otherwise, in the prices of non-traded goods at home relative to the prices of *both imports and exports*, and conversely abroad. These, in his view, are the important changes in relative prices necessary to restore balance. They will help to do so by stimulating production, and discouraging consumption, of both import-type and export-type goods at home, and conversely abroad. Any change in the ratio of import to export prices is, by contrast, likely to be relatively small. (He also reaches the somewhat surprising conclusion that any change in the terms of trade is equally likely to be in either direction; but whether this is a valid generalisation, and whether it applies to Australia, are questions that cannot be pursued here.)

For all these reasons any gain or loss through changes in terms of trade resulting from investment from abroad seems unlikely to be large. If there is a loss it is most unlikely to offset the gains already mentioned (this could, I think, be shown by an analysis broadly similar to one developed in another context[17]); nor does it seem likely to be as important as the losses that could arise for reasons given in the next section.

X

We now remove assumption (9) and allow for the balance of payments problems that may arise if Australia runs into substantial deficit. If exchange rates are fixed, reserves inadequate, and

[16] 'The Problem of the Balance of Payments.'
[17] MacDougall, *The World Dollar Problem*, Appendix XIIF.

emergency overseas borrowing impracticable or undesirable, there will probably have to be (a) deflationary measures that will interrupt growth and cause unemployment of resources — we are here removing assumption (1) — except in so far as the deficit can be removed by eliminating excess demand; and possibly (b) intensified import restrictions that may cause shortages, disrupt production and investment plans, create rigidities in the economy and involve more than optimum protection (this may also happen if tariffs are raised). If the currency is devalued there will be social problems and a weakening of trust in the Australian pound. Moreover, devaluation may not quickly remove the deficit because, though trade may be quite highly responsive to relative price changes in the long run, it is much less so in the short run; deflationary measures and restrictions may thus have to be maintained for some time. Nor would freely fluctuating exchange rates solve the problem; and they have various disadvantages of their own.[18]

The question is whether extra investment from abroad might contribute to these troubles. The analysis required is quite different from that of possible effects on the terms of trade.

Let us assume for the moment that there are no large and rapid fluctuations in the flow of new investment. If then, with a given flow, the Australian balance of payments tends to improve over the years ahead with fixed exchange rates, an increase in foreign investment will not cause trouble by swelling the profits that have to be remitted across the exchanges, provided the increase is not too large. If, on the other hand, the balance tends to worsen with a given flow of investment, recurring crises will in any case be likely. Extra foreign investment would not necessarily then aggravate them; it might alleviate them. The higher payments of profits abroad might be offset, or more than offset, by the higher capital inflow and by favourable effects on the balance of payments resulting from the extra production; for this might be what is sometimes called 'import-saving' or 'export-creating'.[19] Extra foreign investment might, how-

[18] For a fuller discussion by the present author see, e.g. *op. cit.,* pp. 335–42, 383–7, and 'Flexible Exchange Rates', *Westminster Bank Review,* August 1954.
[19] The correct meaning of these much-abused terms varies with the context. Here we are really combining them and postulating that, apart from the capital inflow and the additional profits payable abroad, the extra investment is 'balance-of-payments-improving', given fixed exchange rates. To determine whether this was likely, we should have to assess (a) any effects on Australia's price level relative to price levels abroad and (b) any 'structural' effects on her trade (see next paragraph); these would comprise the effects of faster growth generally (whether financed by foreign or Australian capital) and of any special twist given by the foreign capital to the pattern of development. As is well-known, such an assessment is difficult, not least because the indirect effects can be so important.

ever, aggravate the problem, especially if it were 'import-creating'or 'export-discouraging'. There could then be more serious and more frequent crises and the resulting losses would have to be debited against the gains from extra foreign investment described earlier.

One convenient method of assessing the future trend of the balance of payments, given fixed exchange rates, is to consider first the likely course of the Australian price level relative to price levels abroad (i.e. the comparative rates of inflation, if any), and secondly any 'structural' changes that might affect the balance of payments even if price levels at home and abroad moved in line. It is possible to be pessimistic or optimistic on both counts. No judgment is attempted here but, if one were only moderately optimistic, it would not seem that a continuation of something like the post-war rate of growth of private foreign investment in Australia during, say, the decade ahead would obviously cause trouble.

An uncritical interpretation of the crude figures may exaggerate the past rate of growth. They suggest that between mid-1947 and mid-1958 the value of direct foreign investments outstanding rose by an average of 15 per cent a year.[20] A more careful examination substantially alters the picture. First, the crude figures include undistributed profits of subsidiaries only since 1947; if those accumulated earlier were added, the rate of growth might be reduced to perhaps 13 per cent a year. Secondly, and much more important, it seems that a large part of the increase merely reflects the fall in the value of money (both between 1947 and 1958 and before 1947; for the fixed assets existing at mid-1947 were all installed before that date). A very rough (but complicated) calculation, based on a method used in another context,[21] suggests that the rate of increase of direct investments, in real terms, may have been only about 6 per cent per annum. While not much significance can be attached to this result, a check on its plausibility is that, in money terms, income on foreign investments in Australia (excluding public authority interest) rose from about 1.1 per cent to about 1.3 per cent of the gross national product during the same period.[22] This is not inconsistent with investments outstanding rising by 6 per cent a year in real terms and the real national product by, say, 4-5 per cent.

If, in future, foreign investments grew at 6 per cent per annum in

[20] Including undistributed profits of subsidiaries since mid-1947. Calculated from tables 5, 6, 8, 9 of *Annual Bulletin of Oversea Investment*, 1957—58.
[21] MacDougall, *op. cit.*, pp. 534—5. There is no space to describe the calculations for Australia, and little need since the result is purely illustrative.
[22] Calculated from papers on *National Income and Expenditure*; adjusted for annual fluctuations. The figures are not quite comparable with those given earlier.

real terms (one can admittedly make more startling extrapolation by taking U.S. and U.K. investments separately),[23] the growth of income on them would not obviously be embarrassingly rapid in relation to the growth of trade; for, with the real national product growing by, say, 5 per cent a year, trade may well tend to grow by, say, 4 per cent in real terms (there may be reasons why it will grow more slowly than the national product but the difference is unlikely to be very great). Since profits on foreign investments in Australia are still quite a small fraction of trade in goods and services, imports would not have to rise so very much more slowly than exports to cover the growing income payable abroad, even if we ignore the growing support to the balance of payments that would result from the rising inflow of new capital.[24]

If we now remove the assumption of no large fluctuations in this inflow, there is the possibility that these might help to cause crises, especially if a sharp reduction in the net inflow (allowing for withdrawals of foreign capital) coincided with a worsening in the balance of payments for other reasons. The higher the average flow over a period of years the more serious is this danger likely to be and this is a further cost of more rather than less investment from abroad. (The extra danger would, however, be diminished or removed if more investment resulted in an improved balance of payments, and a building up of reserves, either automatically or through deliberate policy.)

It is not obvious that the inflow of private capital will become a dangerously high fraction of the balance of payments in the foreseeable future. It has averaged only about 10 per cent of payments on current account in recent years (including undistributed profits),[25] and we have seen that it will not grow so very much faster than trade if the post-war trend continues. Nevertheless, the net inflow can contract sharply — it fell by over two-thirds between 1951–2 and 1952–3 and might even become negative — and a loss of even, say, 7–10 per cent in foreign exchange receipts can be embarrassing when reserves are low, especially if other receipts are falling at the same time.

Direct investment may be less dangerous in this respect than portfolio investment in Australian companies, since the latter is probably more volatile. (It also brings little, if any, know-how, one

[23] See Arndt., *op. cit.*, p. 258.
[24] The relationships between growth of trade, foreign investment, and income on it could be further elaborated, but this seems unnecessary for our present purpose.
[25] The balancing item is excluded; see R. J. Cameron, *Economic Record*, August 1957, pp. 263–4.

of the main gains from direct investment; and, though the rate of return on it may appear lower, this becomes less certain if allowance is made, as with direct investments, for the undistributed profits being set aside for the benefit of shareholders.)

XI

Finally let us remove assumption (10), that the increase in foreign capital considered does not require changes in Australian policy that themselves may involve a loss. The previous analysis would require no consequent modification if we were considering the effects of changing conditions abroad, say a fall in the rate of profit there that encouraged the flow of capital to Australia. But if, say, the government were considering whether to provide more information abroad about investment opportunities in Australia, the cost of so doing would have to be debited before striking a balance. Attempts to attract foreign capital by firmer guarantees on freedom to repatriate might increase the danger of future balance of payments difficulties. Higher protection, designed to encourage investment in Australia by foreign producers thereby prevented from exporting direct, might mean sacrificing some of the benefits of the international division of labour; there might also, of course, be further well-known benefits from higher protection, but some of these have already been allowed for in this paper.

Conversely, measures that might reduce capital inflow, such as insistence on a minimum Australian participation in the equity of subsidiaries of foreign firms or the outlawing of restrictions on exporting by such subsidiaries,[26] might bring other economic or political benefits.

The only case we shall consider in any detail is where investment from abroad is encouraged by a reduction in tax rates on foreign profits, whether or not this applies aqually to domestic profits. (The analysis will, of course, apply in reverse to higher tax rates.) If rates are reduced, the gain from taxation will be smaller than that described in section III. There could even be a reduction in tax revenue from foreign profits.

It can easily be shown that this will be avoided if

$$\frac{\dfrac{1}{\eta_d} + \dfrac{1}{\eta_s}}{1 + \dfrac{1}{\eta_s}} \leqslant t$$

[26] Cf. H. W. Arndt and D. R. Sherk, 'Export Franchises of Australian Companies with Overseas Affiliations', *Economic Record*, August 1959.

where t is the tax rate as before and η_d and η_s the elasticities of demand[27] for, and supply of, foreign capital; they measure the relationship between changes in the *stock* of foreign capital in Australia and in the profit rate, before tax in the case of demand, after tax in that of supply. If we took the tax rate as one-half, this would reduce to

$$\eta_s \geqslant \frac{1}{1 - \dfrac{2}{\eta_d}}$$

If, for example, η_d were infinite, 10, 4 or 2, η_s would have to be not less than 1, $1\frac{1}{4}$, 2 or ∞. We have seen that η_d is probably high, so that a fall in tax revenue might be avoided if the elasticity of supply of foreign capital were not less than, say, some figure between 1 and 2.

It might be thought that this was highly probable since foreign capital in Australia is such a tiny fraction of foreign capital abroad. But the market is very imperfect; only a very small fraction of all foreign capitalists are interested in investment in Australia. An elasticity of supply of, for example, 1½ would mean that, if the rate of profit, after tax, on foreign capital were, say, 9 per cent rather than 8 per cent, this would in the long run make a difference of nearly one-fifth, or perhaps £250 million or more, in the amount of foreign capital in Australia. Whether this is likely it is very hard to say.

It certainly seems possible that, if investment from abroad were encouraged by tax remission, there would be no gain to Australia from increased tax revenue, at least if we confine our attention to the stage of the analysis reached in section III. The reduction in tax rates might still be worth while, for the other consequences might be favourable to Australian income on balance (and might possibly convert a tax loss into a tax gain). But it should be remembered that any gains from higher immigration, and possibly more Australian capital, would now be substantially smaller than in our previous analysis, because they there depended considerably on the rise in Australian income resulting from higher tax revenue from foreign profits.

XII

The main conclusions of this analysis are fairly straightforward and obvious. The most important direct gains to Australia from more rather than less private investment from abroad seem likely to come

---

[27] Defined so as to be positive.

through higher tax revenue from foreign profits (at least if the higher investment is not induced by lower tax rates), through economies of scale and through external economies generally, especially where Australian-owned firms acquire 'know-how' or are forced by foreign competition to adopt more efficient methods.

These gains may permit higher immigration, which will further increase Australian income, if immigration policies are related in some way to the standard of living. They may also lead to higher domestically-financed investment, which will later increase Australian income still further, but this is problematical and depends considerably on government policy; if domestically-financed investment were allowed to fall when more foreign capital came in, Australian income could actually be lower at some future date than it otherwise would have been.

The effects of extra foreign investment on the terms of trade, which might be favourable or unfavourable, are unlikely to be large. The effects on the balance of payments could be more important. They could be favourable, but the danger of future balance of payments crises might be increased; for there are inevitably fluctuations in the net inflow of private capital and part at least of the foreigners' profits have to be transferred across the exchanges.

These are some of the results obtained by applying rather conventional tools of economic analysis. The assumptions used are still highly simplified even after those listed at the beginning of the article have been removed. For example, allowance is made for only two factors of production. No distinction is made between fixed interest and equity investment. No explicit account is taken of government-owned capital or of government borrowing from abroad; throughout most of the paper these are implicitly assumed to be independent of changes in private investment from abroad. The analysis, as was emphasised at the outset, is mainly static. Even if it were made more dynamic it would still fail to take account of considerations not allowed for in most economic theories and about which the economic historian, for example, might have more useful things to say. Many aspects of the problem are left uncovered, such as the relative merits of government borrowing and private investment from abroad, and little is said about short-run implications. No attempt is made to assess the political costs and benefits.

The analysis will not apply to countries other than Australia without modification, but such modification may sometimes be possible. In many underdeveloped countries, for example, there may be heavy unemployment of labour, or under-employment where the marginal product is far less than the wage rate, and marginal product, of labour in the organised sector, or perhaps even zero. The foregoing analysis might then perhaps be adapted by considering the organised sector and assuming employment in it to be as great as was feasible at a given real wage rate; more investment from abroad would then make possible more 'immigration' from the unorganised sector just as, in section IV, we allowed for the possibility that it might permit more immigration into Australia from overseas.

Despite its many limitations it is hoped that the analysis in this paper may be of some relevance, at least to Australia, and that it may provoke others to correct and improve it and to explore other aspects of the problem.

Trade and Development

6 India's balance of payments[1]

I. THE PROBLEM

It is arguable whether the balance of payments is *the* most important factor limiting the rate of India's economic development, but it will probably at least be agreed that it is *a* major limiting factor. Shortage of foreign exchange is certainly holding up production quite seriously at present and there is a danger that it will continue to restrict output and the rate of growth during the Third Plan and, looking further ahead, in the Fourth and the Fifth.[2]

THE PRESENT SITUATION

Many factories are today lying partially idle through lack of imported supplies. A glance at Table I shows unused capacity over a wide field, even on a single shift basis, and rather few industries working multiple shifts. One-third of the industries covered appear to be working at only 60 per cent of capacity or less. (The data refer to the year 1959—60, but it seems unlikely that there has since been any general improvement; output has increased, but so has capacity. The figures may sometimes overstate capacity for statistical reasons; on the other hand, the table relates production to capacity at the beginning of the year so that the percentages of capacity utilised would often be still lower if account were taken of new capacity installed during the year.)

There are, of course, many reasons other than shortage of foreign exchange for this state of affairs. New factories inevitably have teething troubles; short runs and breakdowns interrupt production even in established factories; capacity may have been installed in excess of current needs where demand is expected to increase; demand may sometimes have been over-estimated; and so on. But a substantial part of the unused capacity undoubtedly reflects shortage

---

[1] This article appeared in *The Economic Weekly*, Bombay, April 22nd and 29th, 1961, and was reproduced, with a few modifications and omissions, in the *Bulletin of the Oxford University Institute of Statistics* (May 1961). It should be borne in mind that it was addressed to an Indian audience. Rs. 1 crore=10,000,000 Rupees=£750,000

[2] The Third, Fourth and Fifth Plans cover the five-year periods beginning April 1st, 1961, 1966 and 1971.

of imported materials, components, spare parts and replacements. This is true, for example, of a good many industries using steel, non-ferrous metals, wood pulp, rubber, and intermediates for certain chemicals and drugs; factories in many fields are held up for lack of vital bottleneck items; some firms that have agreed to a 'phased programme' of reducing the import content of their production (imposed quite properly to induce progressive import-saving) have fallen behind schedule and are unable to get the imports required for full production.

Table I

Utilisation of Manufacturing Capacity. Production during year 1959—60 as per cent of installed capacity at beginning of year in 121 industries

| Production as per cent of capacity:* | Basis of capacity figures: | | |
	2 or 3 shifts†	1 shift	Total
	Number of industries		
Over 150	1	4	5
Over 100, not over 150	7	16	23
Over 90, not over 100	4	7	11
Over 80, not over 90	7	10	17
Over 70, not over 80	4	6	10
Over 60, not over 70	—	15	15
Over 50, not over 60	—	10	10
Over 40, not over 50	2	15	17
Over 0, not over 40	2	11	13
Total	27	94	121

*It is assumed that plants work 300 days in the year, or 330 in some of the three-shift industries.
†Including some industries on continuous operations, with allowance for shut-downs for normal repairs and maintenance.
Source: *Monthly Statistics of the Production of Selected Industries of India.*

It seems likely that, say, a further Rs. 100 crores per annum could usefully be imported to meet industry's requirements, given the present level of demand for industrial goods, and that this might increase industrial production by perhaps 15—20 per cent, or by several times the value of the increase in imports. Shortages of home produced goods and services, such as coal, power and transport, might limit production in certain fields, but these too could sometimes be overcome by imports, at least after a time, were foreign exchange available. Imported oil, for example, might be substituted for coal, in coastal regions, and at the same time save transport, while generating plants to be run on oil or water power might be imported to relieve the power shortage.

Industrial production might be further increased if still more foreign exchange were available for imports of materials, etc.; for effective demand might then be allowed to increase with less fear of inflation, since some extra supplies would be forthcoming to meet the extra demand.

Increased imports of fertilisers could likewise increase the value of agricultural output by a multiple of the foreign exchange cost. A still further substantial increase in national production and employment might be possible if large scale public works were undertaken, using under-employed labour and indigenous materials, and if the extra demand of the workers employed could be met by increased imports. (Mr. Andrew Shonfield recently suggested that such imports, at least of foodgrains and perhaps of cotton, might be obtained from the U.S. as a free gift, in addition to what is already being imported under Public Law 480.)

In these various ways, shortage of foreign exchange is a serious bottleneck holding up production and preventing anything like the full use of the nation's industrial capacity, land and labour. Increased aid or exports could make possible an increase in production several times as great in value and, by raising income, raise savings and investment and thus the rate of economic development.[3]

THE THIRD PLAN

Shortage of foreign exchange will continue during the Third Plan and there is a serious danger that it will make impossible the rate of development that is hoped for and is absolutely essential. Even if foreign aid is forthcoming on the large scale envisaged in the *Draft Outline* of the Third Plan (more than twice that received in the Second Plan), this may not be enough; for the import needs seem to

---

[3] The following very simple example shows how extra exports may increase savings and investment. It ignores many complications. The figures are purely illustrative.

Curtail home consumption of, say, bicycles by Rs. 100.

Increase exports of bicycles by Rs. 100.

Import Rs. 100 extra raw material.

Put Rs.75 into production of consumption goods and make an extra Rs. 300 of consumption goods.

Put Rs. 25 into production of capital goods and make an extra Rs. 100 of capital goods.

Extra income (wages and profits) is Rs. 225 in consumption goods production, Rs. 75 in capital goods production, total Rs. 300.

Say, one-third of this is taxed or saved, i.e. Rs. 100. This finances the extra output of capital goods. Consumption demand out of the extra income goes up by Rs. 200 and this is met by the extra production of consumption goods of Rs. 300, less the fall in purchases of bicycles of Rs. 100.

have been substantially under-estimated, as they were in the Second Plan.

The allowance for 'development' imports[4] implies a very rapid increase in the output of capital goods in India, and any estimate of requirements probably tends to under-state the ancillary and unforeseen types of equipment that have to be imported. The growing tendancy for aid to be tied to exports from the aid-giving country, especially the United States, will increase the cost. There is no guarantee that the prices of capital goods generally will not rise in the aid-giving countries, as they have done in the past.

The allowance for 'maintenance' imports (including capital goods for replacement) looks very low. The average for the Third Plan is put at little more than Rs. 700 crores per annum.[5] This is probably no more, and perhaps less, than the present rate of importation which is severely restricted and, as we have seen, quite insufficient for the proper maintenance of the economy. Import needs, moreover, seem likely to grow despite the large increase planned in import-saving production, if, as is contemplated, industrial output is to grow by about two-thirds over the next five years and national income by something approaching one-third.[6]

There is also the special problem of getting aid for 'maintenance' imports; aid-giving countries usually prefer to finance imports of capital goods for 'projects' that will create monuments to their generosity, though there are welcome signs that this attitude is changing. India is probably in rather an unusual position among under-developed countries in that the foreign aid required to supplement her domestic savings tends to exceed her needs for imported capital goods for new investment; for she is an important producer of capital goods. Part of the aid is thus required for maintenance imports.

There is not necessarily anything improvident about taking aid for such imports. It can help to increase investment just as much as aid to finance new capital goods. A large part of the Marshall Aid given by the U.S. to Europe was in fact used to finance imports other than of capital goods.

(Even if more aid were made free to spend on either maintenance or development imports, there would remain a problem of how much to switch to the former to 'feed' existing unused capacity. For some

---

[4] Capital goods for new investment together with components, etc. for increasing production of capital goods in India.
[5] Rs. 3570 crores over the five years. *Third Five Year Plan — A Draft Outline*, p. 53.
[6] See *Draft Outline*, p. 31 and 228.

of this would produce relatively inessential goods — a legacy of unduly liberal licensing of capacity for such goods in the past.)

India enters the Third Plan, faced with all these difficulties and uncertainties, with no cushion against unforeseen contingencies as there was at the start of the Second Plan. Foreign exchange reserves cannot be drawn upon to any significant extent — they are a small fraction of what they were five years ago — and there are few remaining inessential imports to be cut.

For all these reasons, it seems unlikely that the Plan can be achieved unless aid, or India's exports, or both, are very substantially increased above the levels contemplated in the *Draft Outline* . If more aid is not received — and I think it should certainly be asked for — exports would probably have to be increased by nearly one-half during the next five years. Even this would leave a very difficult position during the earlier years, because exports cannot be increased overnight and some of the more important import-saving investments will bear fruit only in the later years of the Plan.

THE FOURTH AND FIFTH PLANS
Even if more aid, including aid for 'maintenance imports', can be obtained in the Third Plan, this should not in any way weaken the export drive. It will still be necessary to aim at an increase approaching one-half in exports during the next five years to provide a base for the further massive increase that will be needed during the Fourth Plan if India is to achieve independence of foreign aid, and yet maintain rapid growth, in the Fifth. This would probably involve exports at the beginning of the Fifth. Plan of as much as Rs. 1500 crores per annum, more than twice the present rate of under Rs. 650 crores.

Such a very large increase may come as a shock to some readers and it requires some justification. I cannot give a detailed proof; this would require much further study, and I hope that others will attempt such a calculation. But I believe that an increase of the order mentioned can be shown to be plausible and indeed the minimum required. In brief, exports two-thirds higher are needed merely to pay for present imports; it seems inevitable that more imports will be needed in ten years to maintain the much higher activity it is hoped to achieve; heavy repayments of capital and interest will fall due on loans already received and that will be received during the next ten years.

A rather fuller justification will now be attempted. (Table II will help readers to understand some of the figures mentioned.)

'*Maintenance*' *imports*[7] at present seem to be around Rs. 700—750 crores per annum and should be nearer Rs. 850 crores to allow industrial capacity to be more fully used. If it is hoped to raise national income by over three-quarters, and to treble industrial production, by the beginning of the Fifth Plan — this would be merely a continuation of the growth rates implied in the Third Plan,[8] and an acceleration is really needed — it is hard to see how maintenance imports could be kept below, say, Rs. 1000 crores at the very least, despite a rapid development of import-saving activities. This would mean that the increase in maintenance imports (Rs. 250—300 crores) was only about 2½ per cent of the increase in national income.

I should have put down a larger increase, had it not been for the view implied in the *Draft Outline* that maintenance requirements will not rise during the Third Plan. I feel that at least some modest increase must be allowed for, considering that

(a) there have been very few examples of countries achieving rapid development without an increase in imports (although India might conceivably provide a unique example of rapid import-saving over the next decade);

(b) the present level of imports is severely restricted;

(c) a large expansion of exports will be very difficult unless special types of materials and equipment required to make goods acceptable abroad are imported;

(d) A substantial part of the expansion of exports is likely to be directed to the Soviet bloc on a bilateral basis and to some neighbouring countries on what may in effect be a bilateral basis, so that some imports may have to be accepted that would not be regarded as essential if foreign earnings were freely convertible. (In this context it is important to ensure that goods exported to Soviet bloc countries are not re-exported to other countries to replace direct exports that would have earned convertible currencies. Trade figures suggest that there may have been some diversion of this sort.)

'*Development*' *imports* in the second Plan seem to have averaged Rs. 300—400 crores per annum and are expected to exceed Rs. 400 crores per annum in the Third Plan[9]; they may well have to be nearer Rs. 450 crores for reasons mentioned earlier. It is hard to believe that

---

[7] Excluding food imported from the U.S. under P.L. 480 assistance.

[8] *Draft Outline*, pages 31 and 228. The rates of growth are over 5 per cent per annum in national income and about 10½ per cent in industrial production; these have been compounded over the eleven years 1960—61 to 1971—72.

[9] *Draft Outline*, p. 54. Development imports are at present running temporarily at a lower figure.

Table II
Trade and National Income

	1960–61 estimated	1971–72 assumed	Increase	Per cent per annum
1. National income, Rs. crores	13,700	24,700	11,000	5.5
2. Imports* Rs. crores	1,080	1,400	320	2.4
3. Imports, per cent of 1	7.9	5.7	2.9	..
4. Exports,* Rs. crores	640	1,500	860	8
5. Exports, per cent of 1	4.7	6.1	7.8	..

Year	National income (current prices) Rs. crores	Imports* c.i.f. Rs. crores	% of National Income	Exports* f.o.b. Rs. crores	% of National Income
1951–52	9,970	962.9	9.7	730.1	7.3
1952–53	9,820	633.0	6.4	601.9	6.1
1953–54	10,480	591.8	5.6	539.7	5.1
1954–55	9,610	683.8	7.1	596.6	6.2
1955–56	9,980	761.4	7.6	640.2	6.4
Average 1st Plan	9,972	726.6	7.3	621.7	6.2
1956–57	11,310	1099.5	9.7	635.2	5.6
1957–58	11,400	1233.6	10.8	594.1	5.2
1958–59	12,470	1029.6	8.3	575.9	4.6
1959–60	13,000†	923.7	7.1†	623.3	4.8†
1960–61	13,700†	1080†	7.9†	640†	4.7†
Average 2nd Plan	12,376†	1073.3†	8.7†	613.7	5.0†

*Balance of payments basis.
†Estimated.

they could be less than, say, Rs. 400 crores per annum at the beginning of the Fifth Plan if, as is hoped, investment is to be raised to over 2½ times the present level (11 per cent to 16 per cent[10] of a national income more than three-quarters higher, and a still higher investment ratio is really required). Merely to prevent an increase in the need for development imports will be difficult. Apart from the very large rise required in the output of capital goods *as a whole*, there is the problem of special types of equipment. At the stage of development that India will have reached there seem bound to be many types that she will still be unable to produce, especially as many new things will be developed in the world during the next decade. At Rs. 400 crores, development imports would be only 10 per cent of India's net investment (though a larger fraction of the capital goods required for net investment).

[10] *Draft Outline*, p. 6 and 43.

With maintenance imports at Rs. 1000 crores and development imports at Rs. 400 crores, *total imports* would be Rs. 1400 crores. This would be little more than 5½ per cent of the national income. The lowness of this figure may be appreciated when it is realised that in the United States — a large country with very diversified resources, in the van of technological progress, and with a long history of economic development behind high tariffs — imports (c.i.f.) are 4 per cent of the national income[11] (and were usually 5½ per cent or more until the 1930s). The corresponding figure for the U.S.S.R. may also be of the order of 4 per cent. Apart from China, there is virtually no other country with an import ratio anything like so low. If India's national income were valued at U.S. prices, the ratio of imports to national income assumed for the beginning of the Fifth Plan would probably be under 4 per cent.

Although I have allowed for an increase in total imports above the 1960—61 level, and thus assumed no absolute import-saving, there would have to be massive import-saving in a relative sense. Imports would have to fall from nearly 8 per cent to little more than 5½ per cent of the national income. The increase in imports would be only 3 per cent of the rise in national income. The rate of increase assumed in the quantity of imports (2½ per cent per annum) is much less than that required by the U.S. throughout the half century ending in 1929 (about 4 per cent per annum), although the planned rate of increase in India's real national income is much higher than that achieved by the U.S. during this period.

In addition to imports, the *service of public external debt* (including interest and repayments) may well be as much as Rs. 200—250 crores per annum, even if the bulk of the loans received during the next ten years are on easy terms, and especially if repayments due in the Third Plan are postponed or covered by new borrowing, as was contemplated in the *Draft Outline* (p. 55). On the other hand, *net invisible earnings* (excluding interest on the public external debt) together with net inflow of private capital may provide, say, Rs. 100—150 crores.[12] *Exports* would then have to be about Rs. 1500 crores.

It may be argued that there is no need to aim at such a high figure since foreign aid is likely to continue in the Fifth Plan. But it would

[11] 4.1 per cent in 1959. The more usually quoted figure for imports f.o.b. as a percentage of the gross national product is lower (3.2 per cent).
[12] These items at present yield under Rs. 100 crores, net, excluding also official donations. Earnings from transportation and especially tourism should rise, as should private investment from abroad. On the other hand, there may be significant extra payments of income on such investments.

seem to be rather a dangerous gamble to count on this. Political conditions can change greatly in ten years. Mr. Kennedy, for example, will no longer be President of the United States and there will be many other claimants for whatever aid is available, including many countries whose ability to use aid profitably will be much greater than it is today.

Even if it is assumed that substantial aid will be *available* to India in the Fifth Plan, this will not necessarily change the export target that should be aimed at. For if internal savings have by then been stepped up to a level that can give a satisfactory rate of growth without foreign assistance, India will presumably not wish to accept it; and it would be unfortunate if balance of payments difficulties make this necessary. If, on the other hand, internal savings are still inadequate – and it will admittedly be difficult to raise them sufficiently – it will not be hard to create a balance of payments deficit, if necessary, by stepping up the rate of investment, so that a balance of payments case for aid can still be made and the aid can be absorbed.

It is possible that there will be important discoveries of oil or other natural resources that can be used to replace imports. But it would be imprudent to count on discoveries that would have a revolutionary effect on the balance of payments until they have actually been made. In any case, such resources would take time to develop. I have, moreover, already allowed for very large scale import-saving. And a completely autarkic policy of import-saving at any cost – of producing anything that it is physically possible to produce in India – would undoubtedly slow down the rate of growth.

This is not to say that investment in import-saving should not have some preference – and perhaps quite a substantial one – over investment in production for export. I think it should, because, for example, of the greater dependence of exports on circumstances outside India's control and of the tendency for a pushing of exports to worsen the terms of trade. But the preference for import-saving should not be absolute. For example, an investment in production for export that required only, say, a 10 per cent export subsidy should normally, I suppose, be preferred to an investment in import-saving that required protection equivalent to, say, a 50 per cent import duty, after allowing a reasonable time for infant industries to grow up in either case.

THE MAGNITUDE OF THE EXPORT TASK

For all these reasons, I feel that a target of around Rs. 1500 crores per annum for exports at the beginning of the Fifth Plan is by no means too high. It would mean, very roughly, an increase of one-half during the next five years and a further increase of one-half during the following five years. There is no point, of course, in arguing about the precise figure, for in any case it will probably be agreed that the increase required is very large indeed; but I shall use the figure of Rs. 1500 crores for purposes of illustration.

The rate of increase required would be a difficult task for any country. But it is not impossible. It has been achieved over the past decade by quite a number of countries (in addition to those exporting oil), such as Yugoslavia, Israel, Japan and a good many nations in Western Europe. But how practicable is the task for India?

From the point of view of reserving a sufficient proportion of the nation's investment and additional output for exports, the task does not look unmanageable. Exports would have to rise by 8 per cent per annum compared with an increase of 5—6 per cent in the national income. Less than 8 per cent of the increase in output would have to be devoted to exports. The proportion of the national output exported would merely have to be restored to the level achieved half-a-dozen years ago.

These figures, of course, refer to output as a whole, and there will for a time be difficult problems in particular fields where home demand will have to be restrained to make room for exports. But the pattern of output can be changed considerably over a period so that, looking ten years ahead, the problem should not be too difficult, provided an appropriate pattern of investment is adopted.

When, however, one considers the problem of selling the goods abroad, the task appears much more difficult, for India's exports would have to increase faster than world trade seems likely to expand. The latter has risen in terms of quantity by about one-third in each of the last two five-year periods (and may perhaps grow more slowly in future); exports of underdeveloped countries taken as a whole have grown considerably less quickly.

Now, while world trade has been expanding quite rapidly, India's exports have been stagnant during the last ten years (at least in value, though there has been some upward trend in quantity). This is partly because her share in the world market for certain products has been falling (sometimes mainly for external reasons, sometimes in the main because Indian domestic consumption has been catching up with production). In jute manufactures, for example, Pakistan has entered the world export market, and Thailand has entered that for lac. In tea, East Africa and Ceylon have been increasing their share of the U.K. market at India's expense. India's share in the world market for manganese ore has fallen; new competitors have been entering the field. In groundnut oil, where once she had a substantial share, her exports have now virtually dried up.

Probably the more important reason, however, why India's exports have fared so much worse than world exports as a whole is that they depend rather heavily on items where world trade is expanding only slowly, if at all. Nearly one-half of India's exports still consists of the three traditional staples — tea, cotton textiles and jute manufactures. World trade in these items taken together seems unlikely to expand very rapidly in future, barring a striking increase in imports by the Soviet bloc; and the scope for increasing India's share is limited because it is already high in tea and jute manufactures, while an attempt to expand markedly her quite substantial share in cotton textiles would be likely to provoke restrictive measures abroad. Exports of the three staples must be vigorously promoted; they are far too important to be neglected. But, while quite a sizeable increase is by no means impossible, it is clear that, to achieve the total exports required, there will have to be a really striking increase in the other items; they may well have to be trebled or more.

Now among these there are some very promising exports even outside the field of the newer manufactures. There could be rapid increases in the earnings from, for example, iron ore, coffee, fish, vegetable oils and, in the field of invisible exports, tourism. These are items where world trade should expand rapidly, or where India's share is small and could be raised substantially, or both. There is also a good number of other quite promising items.

But, even on optimistic assumptions about all these and other commodities, it would seem impossible to reach anything like the level of exports required without a very substantial contribution indeed from the newer manufactures. Exports of these must be increased many times over to several hundred crores per annum. Their present share of only about five per cent of exports must be raised to a much more important fraction.

Taking account also of the rapid expansion needed in the other promising items, it is clear that an almost revolutionary change will be required in the structure of India's export trade. When this has become more heavily weighted in favour of products where world trade is growing fast, a rapid expansion of her exports will become less difficult.

I must confess that India's export task looks extremely formidable but I do not think it need be a matter for despair, for cutting down or drastically altering the fundamental nature of the Plan, or for giving up all hope of achieving rapid growth without foreign aid within a decade. In products where India's share of the market has declined, it is by no means inevitable that this must continue or that part at least of her previous share cannot be regained, provided really vigorous measures are taken to increase production, to free supplies for export, to make them competitive, and to market them. We have seen that there are a good many exports which could be rapidly increased. In the case of the newer manufactures, it is sometimes argued that the world market will not expand very rapidly in future because of the simultaneous industrialisation of a large number of under-developed countries. But, even if this is true — which is doubtful — it might still be possible for India to carve out the rather small share she needs — perhaps about 2 per cent of the world export market for the relevant products as a whole — a smaller share than that of such small countries as Sweden, Switzerland, the Netherlands or Belgium.

India, too, though poorer than the great majority of under-developed countries per head of population, is more advanced industrially than most. She should thus be able, by keeping one step ahead, to sell them manufactured products that they cannot yet produce. The trading skill of Indians and the numerous Indian traders abroad should be of assistance, as should be the selling organisations and experience built up by textile exporting firms over a long period.

It is possible, too, that more and more international firms selling all over the world will, if permitted to do so, choose India as one of their bases for production and export (as some are already doing). For, among the low-wage countries, India's claims are high. She has one of the largest home markets; the general political outlook is more secure than in many other countries (although the extent of Government control may prove a deterrent); she has a good supply of educated personnel and of industrial facilities generally.

But, while there is no need for despair, the task is certainly a very difficult one indeed. What has to be done if there is to be a chance of success?

II. CONDITIONS OF SUCCESS
I. THE ROLE OF GOVERNMENT
The first and fundamental requirement is a recognition of the vital need for a rapid and massive increase in exports if India's economic development is not to be seriously jeopardised, and acceptance of this fact as a major basis of economic policy.

While most of the actual exporting will have to be done by private business, the role of Government will be crucial. Some difficult decisions must first be made on general policy, involving much more drastic measures than have hitherto been taken. But these will be fruitless without really effective machinery, which can cut through conflicting departmental interests, to translate them rapidly into concrete measures, including schemes for each product, and then to take quick decisions on their day-to-day implementation and interpretation (for potential customers abroad, in a highly competitive world, will not wait for long while Indian officials make up their mind.)

2. EMPHASIS ON ECONOMIC EFFICIENCY

If India is to compete in world markets without prohibitive subsidies, it is essential to go all out for maximum economic efficiency, and low costs, even if this conflicts with other considerations.

Where economies of scale are important, it is vital to concentrate on large plants even if this means less regional dispersion of industry, and more concentration of economic power; competition is usually good for efficiency but the deliberate creation of several undertakings where one could produce far more cheaply is unlikely to achieve the desired result. It may be tempting to give preference to smaller firms because they employ more labour; but they may be unable to compete in world markets. Larger enterprises, even if they employ fewer people directly, may by earning foreign exchange which can be spent on scarce materials, make possible more employment in industry as a whole.

The need for exports may also conflct with the desire for fair play. For example, foreign exchange must be granted quite liberally to would-be exporters for travel and sales promotion abroad, even though this may lead to some abuse. And in so far as reliance is placed on the State Trading Corporation or other Government agencies to sell goods abroad, emoluments will have to be paid that can attract from the private sector the best experts in the various branches of trading, even if these are out of line with governmental salary scales. It will also be difficult for State traders to compete with private traders abroad if they are inhibited by the rules to which other officials, for good reasons, are subject, so that they can be called to account for each individual decision rather than for their performance as a whole.

3. RESTRAINTS ON HOME DEMAND

Consumption of exportable goods will have to be restrained where supplies are inadequate to meet both home and export demand — and even where supplies could be increased sufficiently through higher investment, if the products are not essential and the resources can be more usefully employed elsewhere. Restraint may be necessary, at least temporarily, on the consumption of such products as vegetable oils, tea, the better grades of coffee, leather and a fairly wide range of manufactures. This will seldom involve an absolute reduction in consumption or even in *per capita* consumption; a slowing down in the rate of growth will normally suffice. Restraints on home demand will normally mean that prices are higher than they otherwise would have been (though not necessarily higher absolutely). This may result from higher excise duties or from the charging of higher prices by producers who have to sell abroad at a loss.

There is a natural reluctance to restrain consumption, and especially when the goods are produced in India. But the belief that such goods must always be cheap and plentiful reveals a strange asymmetry of thought towards imports and exports respectively. If, say, 90–95 per cent of the country's needs of an article are produced in India, and the remaining 5–10 per cent imported, there will normally be little hesitation in cutting the imports drastically to *save* foreign exchange and making do with rather smaller supplies, even if this means considerably higher prices and profit margins. It thus seems a little strange that there should be opposition to a moderate slowing down in the growth of consumption of goods produced in India that could be exported and *earn* foreign exchange, especially if this is done by excise taxes which accrue to the Government.

It must be remembered that restraints on consumption will be recouped several times over in terms of production of other goods, since the extra exports will make possible the import of vital bottleneck items. In general, the public must be convinced that, without such restraints, an adequate rate of development will be impossible and that that would be a much more serious matter.

4. ADEQUATE PRODUCTION FOR EXPORT

The scope for restraining home demand is, however, limited, especially when the product meets a really essential need of the mass of the people or is a material, component or piece of equipment vital for the country's economic development. It is thus essential, particularly in these cases, that output of exportable goods is adequately expanded. It must not lag behind home demand, as has happened too often in the past. This means ensuring sufficient investment in the industries concerned, that they have adequate supplies of materials, fertilisers, etc., and that any other necessary measures are taken (for example, a modification of the legislation on cow-slaughter could increase supplies of hides and leather for export).

Since resources will remain scarce, and especially imported equipment and materials, an essential corollary is the need for severe limitation of investment in production that is not absolutely essential, and that will not yield substantial net earnings or savings of foreign exchange, and especially when continuing net foreign expenditure would be involved. Only in this way can room be found for the more vital export projects. This means that many other schemes, though desirable in themselves, will have to be postponed till conditions are more favourable, and especially when they would benefit only the higher income groups.

Care must also be taken in the allocation of investment resources *between* activities that can earn or save foreign exchange. The calculations involved are difficult. Profitability in a narrow financial sense is not a sufficient criterion since, among other things, the value to the nation of extra exports or import-substitutes is considerably greater than it appears to be at existing rates of exchange. It is certainly necessary to work out the initial foreign exchange cost of the investment, the continuing annual foreign exchange costs and the continuing annual earning or saving of foreign exchange. The *net* annual earning or saving of foreign exchange as a proportion of the initial cost will not yet, however, provide a satisfactory criterion for choosing between investments because the use of scarce domestic goods and services must also be allowed for.

Indirect effects must be taken into account as well. For instance, in deciding whether to buy additional aircraft abroad for use on internal services, credit must be taken for the extra foreign tourists who would come to the country (assuming that inadequate air transport within India is limiting their number), and not only for the fares they would pay to Indian Airlines Corporation but for their other expenditure in India as well. Though such calculations are difficult, they should be seriously attempted and perhaps done more carefully than hitherto. This might suggest ways in which a re-allocation of investment would assist the balance of payments. (For example, investment in more ships, which can recoup their foreign exchange cost in a fairly short time, might turn out to be better than investment at the margin in some other export or import-saving activities.)

5. MAKING EXPORTS COMPETITIVE

Even if sufficient supplies are made available for export, they cannot be sold unless prices are competitive. Measures to reduce costs will take time to bear fruit. In the meantime, if India is to achieve the large and rapid expansion in exports that is necessary, it seems essential that a good many exports should be sold below the domestic price and some below cost of production. This will be necessary over a fairly wide range of manufactures and for a rather small number of primary commodities, sugar being an outstanding example.

To make the best use of the nation's resources, preference should normally be given to products requiring a smaller rather than a larger rate of subsidy. (On this criterion sugar looks a bad bet, at least as a continuing export in the long run unless costs can be very substantially reduced, either through a geographical redistribution of Indian production or in other ways. But in the shorter run India clearly cannot afford not to sell the substantial surpluses that have arisen.)

Direct or indirect export subsidies will arouse some antagonism abroad. The rules of G.A.T.T. are somewhat strict on this matter (and suprisingly more strict than on import restrictions) but India has reserved her position. Trouble may, however, arise with producers both in rival exporting countries and in the importing nations.

India can, however, make a good case for at least temporary subsidies. The urgent need for increased export earnings is apparent. It can also be reasonably claimed that the 'infant industry' argument for protection of import-competing industries applies, *mutatis mutandis*, to infant export industries, of which there are many in India. Moreover, many Governments subsidise exports in various ways; and the sale by industrial firms of exports at prices lower than those charged at home is a very common phenomenon.

(With some commodities, that do not need a subsidy, stable prices are as important as low ones. When prices fluctuate so widely as, for example, those of jute goods, buyers abroad will switch to substitutes with more stable prices; and every sharp rise in price will encourage substitutions and economies which will not be wholly reversed when prices fall again. Measures to reduce fluctuations in such prices are thus necessary.)

6. INVESTMENT IN SELLING

The selling of vast additional amounts of exports, especially of the new manufactures, is bound to be an expensive business, in terms both of rupees and, more particularly, of foreign currencies. Such expenditure must be regarded as essential investment designed to earn foreign exchange and must not be skimped any more than investment in say, steel works to save foreign exchange. Expenditure of foreign currency, both public and private, that can properly be attributed to export promotion probably does not exceed a very few crores. Even a large proportionate increase, say a doubling, though apparently difficult to afford in present circumstances, would be small in relation to the extra exports it might yield.

More Government money will have to be spent on, for example, trade fairs and missions; on trade representatives abroad (who will have to supply much more detailed and expert market information than has hitherto been available, for use both by Government and by business); and perhaps on export credit guarantees (the terms must be fully competitive with those offered by competitors abroad and this may require Government subsidisation of the Export Risks Insurance Corporation).

Foreign exchange must also be granted quite liberally to business firms, including those not yet well established, and to Government agencies engaged in export trade, not only for travel abroad but also for advertising, for building up stocks abroad and for the other needs of marketing; some firms or industries may need offices, showrooms or even foreign subsidiaries. Nor can India afford not to grant credits as long as those offered by other exporting nations, even if this sometimes involves waiting several years for the foreign exchange; this will still be a well worth while investment.

7. THE ROLE OF THE ADVANCED NATIONS

The advanced, aid-giving nations can do much to help or to obstruct India's export drive. They must be convinced that, without a massive increase in exports, India can never achieve independence of foreign aid, while maintaining rapid growth, and at the same time repay the large loans she is receiving. The slogan at the moment must be 'aid *and* trade' if it is ever to be 'trade *not* aid'. In particular, the advanced nations must be convinced of the need for much more competition from the new Indian manufactures, not only in third markets but even in their own home markets. If restrictions are imposed on goods produced with 'cheap' or 'sweated' labour, as with cotton textiles, India's chances of achieving the exports she needs will be considerably reduced.

Merely to refrain from imposing such restrictions will not, however, be enough. More positive action to *encourage* imports from India (and other under-developed countries) is required. The analogy of the Marshall Plan is relevant. The U.S., while giving massive aid to Europe, embarked in effect on an *import* drive to help sales of European goods to the U.S. (while tolerating severe discriminatory restrictions against her own exports to Europe). For example, U.S. officials abroad actively sought out European products that might be saleable in the U.S.; American tourists were allowed to bring back as much as $500 worth of goods purchased abroad without paying duty; local purchases by American military forces in Europe were encouraged in various ways. (These measures have now, quite rightly, been reversed, as Europe's balance of payments has become much stronger.) The advanced nations could also help by persuading firms with interests in factories in India to waive agreements limiting exports from these factories.

III. EXPORTS OF THE NEWER MANUFACTURES
I cannot discuss here the measures required to promote exports of each individual item of India's trade, but it may be useful to explore in a little more detail the special case of the newer manufactures, which will have to play such a vital role in the expansion of India's exports. During the Third Plan their contribution, though important, may not be a major one, but it must be during the Fourth.

HOW COMPETITIVE ARE THEY?
There are various reasons why a significant range of these newer industries seems likely to be capable of exporting at competitive prices and why the range is likely to widen steadily:

(*a*) With very high grade iron ore, India should be able to produce cheap steel, although at present the prices charged by Indian steel works seem to be higher than those charged by many foreign producers, at least for steel to be made into exports.

(*b*) Indian wages per worker are a very small fraction of wages in the main exporting countries of Western Europe and North America (and probably less than half of wages in Japan). Even if output per worker in manufacturing as a whole were a still smaller fraction, so that labour costs per unit of output were in general higher in India, one would expect to find a fair number of industries in which Indian labour costs were lower. For international comparisons show that the relationship between output per worker in one country and another usually varies widely from industry to industry, and one would thus expect to find industries in which India's lower output per worker was more than offset by her lower wages.

In fact, I have found quite a number of firms in which this is so and even some where output per worker appears to be higher than it is abroad, although allowance must sometimes be made for higher costs resulting from lower efficiency of labour that are not reflected

Table III

Fair Ex-works Price as per cent of C.I.F. Import price, excluding duty, for 62 manufactures *

	No. of items	Per cent of total	Per cent Cumulative
% %			
60 and under 70	1	2	2
70 and under 80	7	11	13
80 and under 90	8	13	26
90 and under 100	7	11	37
100 and under 110	5	8	45
110 and under 120	7	11	56
120 and under 130	6	10	66
130 and under 140	5	8	74
140 and under 150	3	5	79
150 and under 200	8	13	92
200 and over	5	8	100
	62	100	

*See Table IV for details.

in figures of output per man, for example, where tools are used up more quickly. The quality of some Indian products may also be lower than that of foreign goods but again I have found quite a number of cases where users of Indian products have no complaints on this score.

(c) The reports of the Tariff Commission suggest that, while the ratio between costs at home and abroad varies greatly, a significant proportion of India's industries may, in fact, be competitive. The 'fair ex-works price' of Indian products was found to be lower than the c.i.f. price of imports, excluding duty, in more than one-third of sixty-two cases studied (see Tables III and IV). Conclusions about individual products cannot be drawn without further study — for comparisons of this sort are fraught with many difficulties[13] — but the general picture shown may be correct, unless the list is seriously unrepresentative of industry generally. The 'fair ex-works price' refers, not to the most efficient undertakings in each industry, but to a representative firm, and allowance is made for a reasonable profit.

To get a fair picture of India's competitive position in third markets, allowance should, however, be made for the cost of transporting manufactures from Indian factories to overseas

[13] While most products where the Indian price is lower are exported, there are also some exports of a fair number of products where the Indian price is shown to be higher and sometimes substantially higher.

countries — perhaps 5—10 per cent of the ex-works price *on average*, including handling, insurance and miscellaneous charges. (To assess India's ability to sell to countries now exporting to her, it would be necessary to make a further allowance for the cost of transporting their exports to her.) If appropriate allowances could be made, it might show that India was competitive in only perhaps one-quarter or less of the products.

(*d*) A wide range of manufactured products (in addition to cotton and jute manufactures) is in fact already being exported, though usually in very small quantities. It is not difficult to draw up a list of around fifty such products, or groups of products. Some may admittedly, however, be sold at prices that do not cover costs, for example, to secure import licences for machinery under export incentive schemes, to fulfil undertakings to export entered into when the plant was licensed, or to relieve temporary shortages abroad when a foreign collaborator cannot meet the demand in full.

(*e*) India's manufacturing costs should progressively decline, and the quality of her products improve, as the scale of production is increased, as managements acquire greater experience, as labour is trained and as better equipment is installed. The process should be faster than it is in the advanced countries since the rise in scale of production should be more rapid in India, since the advanced nations have largely exploited the economies of mass production in many industries, and since India can benefit greatly merely by taking over techniques they are already using, while they must rely much more for further cost reductions on new technological discoveries.

The growth in India's relative advantage, or the decline in her relative disadvantage, will however, be retarded by the need to rely more and more on materials, components and equipment produced in the country which, initially at least, may often be more expensive than the imported product. Much will depend, too, on the rate of increase of wages, but despondency on this score can be overdone. What figures are available suggest that, in the engineering industries for example, labour earnings have risen substantially less quickly than labour productivity over the past decade; if true, this compares favourably with the experience of many other countries.

For these various reasons, it seems likely that Indian industry is capable of competing in export markets over a significant range of products, and that the range will widen. Even where industries are not yet competitive, the margin of disadvantage is often not very large. India is thus more favourably placed than a good many under-developed countries where the great bulk of manufacturing industries is sometimes still hopelessly uncompetitive.

PROMOTING THE NEW MANUFACTURED EXPORTS

The range of competitive industries does not yet seem wide enough, however, to make possible the rapid expansion of exports required, and to induce sufficient firms to enter foreign markets, even in a small way, early in the Third Plan, so that they can gain experience of marketing which will enable them to achieve the really massive expansion of exports that must come during the Fourth. Concentration on a narrow range of products will not be enough, especially as this would mean securing more substantial shares of markets for individual products and so increase the danger of protective reactions abroad.

In the U.S.A., which still relies substantially on exports of primary products, probably nearly half the manufacturing industries can produce more cheaply than their competitors abroad. In countries like the U.K. and Germany, which rely mainly on manufactured exports, the fraction is probably substantially higher. It would seem that, if India is to achieve the rapid expansion of exports she needs, something approaching one-half of her industries must now be made competitive, especially as her manufacturers will often have to sell below ruling prices to get an entry into new markets. Some measure of subsidy is thus necessary until costs have been sufficiently reduced.

In addition, even where Indian producers are competitive, the pull of the sellers' market at home, with its strong demand and good prices, seriously weakens any incentive to export. In countries like the U.K., Germany, Belgium, Sweden or Japan, where a substantial fraction of output is traditionally exported by many manufacturing industries, producers will continue to make efforts and sacrifices in the export market even when home demand is strong. But in India there is no such tradition of exporting manufactures on a large scale outside the cotton and jute industries. Powerful measures to make the home market relatively less attractive are thus necessary.

It may be that a change in the relative profitability of home and export sales by as much as would result from a devaluation of about 25 per cent is required, and that the measures taken should include direct and indirect export subsidies of more than half this amount. These guesses are based partly on evidence given above and in Tables III and IV, partly on general experience of the degree of devaluation required in the past by countries needing a large expansion of exports. A twisting of the relative cost and price structure of this order through *general* measures seems necessary to provide the background against which *specific* measures can be effectively operated to bribe, bully or cajole individual producers or industries, export houses, etc., to sell more abroad.

Such specific measures will also be essential, but it would be unwise to rely on them alone, if only because of the time required to put them into operation on a sufficient scale, since so many industries and firms are concerned. The administrative problems, too, are formidable and the dangers of abuse probably greater than with general measures. Moreover, while business men may be persuaded to export provided any financial sacrifice is not too great, they are much less easily persuaded, and much more likely to find ways of getting round a directive, if the sacrifice is substantial.

General measures may, it is true, give a few exporters more subsidy than they need; but they will normally be the ones with greatest comparative advantage who should be encouraged most. In any case, any resulting inequities, and any demoralising effects of subsidies generally, would seem to be a much less serious matter than a failure to expand exports sufficiently.

The choice of general measures will depend on administrative and political considerations and on how far a particular method of, in effect, subsidising exports is likely to provoke unfavourable reactions abroad. Whatever methods are chosen, it is essential that, taken together, they give an incentive to export of the required magnitude. Five possible types of general measures may be mentioned (and others are conceivable) together with some illustrative orders of magnitude.

(i) Drawbacks of customs and excise duties on materials used are already given to some exporters (as are certain rebates on railway freights), but the field covered is limited and the procedure often complicated and prolonged; and while an exporter is waiting for refunds, he may be short of working capital. Drawbacks might be simplified, consolidated, applied to more products, and perhaps to materials contained in components bought by exporting firms. They might also be made more generous and to cover more taxes. I do not suppose, however, that the assistance to exports would much exceed, say, 5 per cent on average.

(ii) A difference of, say, 20 per cent between the prices of steel for the manufacture of home and export goods (obtained partly by raising the former prices, partly by lowering the latter) would reduce the relative costs of engineering products for export by around 5 per cent, assuming that steel accounts for about one-quarter of the cost on average. In some engineering industries the effect would, however, be smaller — it seems, for example, that iron and steel accounts for only about one-eighth of the cost of electric fans and bicycles and about one-sixteenth of the cost of sewing machines — and the effect would be negligible in most non-engineering industries. Similar schemes might thus be introduced for other materials.

(iii) Additional excise or purchase taxes on an appropriate range of manufactures would help to restrain the growth of consumption, release supplies for export and force manufacturers to seek out export markets. They would also tend to reduce the price to the manufacturer of sales in the home market and thus the gap which often exists between home and export prices; but a tax of, say, 10 per cent would not usually reduce the home price to the producer by as much as 10 per cent since part at least of the tax would be passed on to the consumer. Taxes on manufactures seem to be moderate and not very widespread, at least in comparison with a country like the United Kingdom.

(iv) Exporters of manufactures could be given a remission of tax on profits. Ideally one would like to reward only those making *additional* exports but the danger of collusion might rule this out. (For example, two exporters might agree that one would increase the exports made under his name while the other reduced his by an equal amount, and that the gain from tax remission would be shared between them.) Since, however, exports of the newer manufactures are at present small but should grow rapidly, tax remission on *all* such exports would come to more or less the same thing, and involve only a small loss to the revenue for some time to come. Any danger of over-invoicing could presumably be largely avoided if the tax-payer were given credit only for foreign exchange turned in to the authorities.

If, say, 20 per cent of export proceeds were allowed to be deducted from taxable income, this would be equivalent to an export subsidy of nearly 10 per cent. The loss of revenue (together with that on the drawbacks mentioned earlier) could be financed many times over by the indirect taxes proposed above or, alternatively, by a somewhat higher rate of tax on profits generally, so that the profit-earning class as a whole would not benefit while the general public was making sacrifices as a result of higher excise taxes and in other ways. (It should also be remembered that the additional exports resulting from the tax remission would make possible extra imports of scarce materials which would in turn allow an increase several times as great in production and incomes; and taxes on these might go far to offset the initial loss of revenue.)

Schemes of this type are in operation in some other countries, including Japan and Ireland. Ireland has been able to administer a scheme applying to *additional* exports of manufactures and, incidentally, nearly doubled her industrial exports between 1958 and 1960, although the tax relief cannot, of course, be given full credit.

(v) Exporters could be allowed, in effect, to retain a fraction of their foreign exchange earnings and use this to buy imports which could be sold at a substantial profit, as has been done with success in, for example, Pakistan. If any article, including a luxury, could be imported, this would, besides raising social problems, add to the import bill, which tax remission would not. Exporters might, of course, only be given import licences that were then taken away from other importers; but this would not be easy to administer and the extent of the effective subsidy would vary greatly from time to time. Measures of this sort cannot be ruled out but it might prove better to reserve them for specific incentive schemes, including those where, as at present, the exporter is allowed to import supplies for use in his own factory.

Against a background of general measures such as these, specific measures would have much more chance of success. Individual industries or firms might more easily be induced, for example, to export an agreed, and rising, fraction of their output as a condition for permission to buy vital components, etc. (It would hardly seem practicable to use a financial sanction since this would in effect be a tax and it would be difficult to define with sufficient precision the conditions under which it would be imposed.) In some industries a single firm might be selected to concentrate largely on export and in return receive preferential allocations of foreign exchange for machinery, materials, foreign travel, etc.; such a firm could achieve economies of scale in foreign marketing and concentrate on types and qualities demanded abroad. In some industries, levies on home sales might be necessary to finance export subsidies, despite the general measures; in other it would be sufficient for individual firms to finance any losses on exports by higher profits on home sales.

If, moreover, the general cost and price structure had been substantially shifted in favour of exports, expenditure on trade fairs and missions, more liberal allocation of foreign exchange to would-be exporters and all the other paraphernalia of an export drive would be likely to yield much higher returns.

SELECTING THE NEW MANUFACTURES
The proportion of India's total output of the newer manufactures that has to be exported in the Fifth Plan seems likely to be less than 10 per cent. But, since this ratio will not be uniform, some industries may have to export 20 per cent, 30 per cent or more of their output. These are substantial fractions and it is thus important to get some idea of what the industries are likely to be, so that provision can be made for them in the Third as well as in the Fourth Plans. A number of promising candidates could already be selected with some confidence and these should be given every facility and

encouragement to expand, especially where rapidly growing supplies are vital for the domestic market as well, so that home demand cannot be significantly restrained.

Unfortunately, however, it is often hard to forecast an industry's export potential, certainly much more difficult than demand for the home market; for so much depends on developments abroad and it is very hard to tell which infant industries will mature most quickly into adults capable of exporting. A great deal of flexibility will thus have to be maintained.

MARKETING THE NEW MANUFACTURES

Providing capacity to export and making prices competitive will not be enough. The exports have to be sold, and getting into foreign markets for manufactures can be a slow, difficult and expensive business, quite different from that of selling primary products in highly organised world markets (although the marketing of some primary products admittedly requires a high degree of skill and experience). Markets for manufactures are imperfect. Success in selling depends not only on price – though this is very important – but on quality, attention to local needs and preferences, quick delivery, effective advertising, employment of the right agents, facilities for after-sales service, the provision of spare parts, etc.; and competitors will often fight hard to preserve their share of the market. Exporting manufactures is a tough and competitive business. It is quite a different matter from producing for a highly protected home market, often with few competitors.

It is thus necessary to start now an intensified export drive. Such a drive may well take five years to bear much fruit. This was, I believe, broadly the experience of Western Europe and Japan in their attempts to raise exports of manufactures to the U.S. after the war to help fill the dollar gap.

The export drives of most of these countries hardly began until, say, 1949 (previously too they mostly had few goods to export and their currencies were often over-valued until the 1949 devaluations). Many people were rather sceptical about the possibilities, just as some are sceptical in India today. 'How,' they asked, 'can you possibly export large quantities of manufactures to the U.S. when her productivity is so high, when she always has the latest things and when her industry is so flexible? Moreover, whenever you start doing well, the American Government will impose protective measures or American industry will find other ways of driving you out of the market.'

But, despite these forebodings, European Governments embarked on export drives and European business men went to the U.S. to explore the market and begin selling. They made plenty of mistakes but they learned by experience. During the five years 1950–54 progress was slow and often frustrating, but the ground was being well prepared. And during the following five years – 1955–59 – the harvest was reaped. Exports of manufactures to the U.S. were trebled; and the success was achieved by a wide variety of industries. (It was not simply a matter of small cars, as is sometimes thought; these accounted for only about one-quarter of the increase.)

As I see it, the Third Plan period should correspond to 1950–54 and the Fourth Plan to 1955–59. Hand in hand with the development of capacity, and reduction of costs, during the Third Plan should go preparations for a massive expansion of export sales all over the world in the Fourth; and one of the essential requirements is for producers in many fields to start exporting *now*, if only in a small way. The 'infant industry' argument can be applied not only to exports as well as to import-replacement, but also to selling as well as to producing.

In deciding whether to grant licences to schemes involving the collaboration of foreign firms, it is important to remember the advantages that could accrue to India's export trade from the use of their selling organisations abroad. Any attempt to impose restrictive agreements limiting the right to export from India would naturally have to be resisted. Where such agreements already exist and exports seem possible, foreign firms may be prepared to waive them if they are shown that, unless foreign exchange can be earned by exporting, it will be difficult to grant them import licences for components, machinery, etc.

IV. IMPORT ECONOMY

Until recently, there has been much more emphasis on import saving than on export promotion in the strategy of India's economic development. This has quite rightly led to large investments in the production of goods that were previously imported and the process will continue; without it India's development could not proceed very far. It is now necessary, however, to ensure that the imports required to maintain this rapidly growing production are forthcoming and this means far higher exports to pay for them.

The greater emphasis required on investment in exports must not be at the expense of import-saving, for both are needed in a big way; it is not a question of 'either/or'. It must be at the expense of activities that are not essential and that would not help the balance of payments.

scarce for many years and it must be husbanded with great care. Though this paper is more concerned with export promotion, it may be worth mentioning some ways in which import economies might be made.

I doubt, for example, whether imported equipment is always used as sparingly as it should be. There is often a good deal more flexibility then is sometimes thought in the extent to which capital may be substituted for labour, and *vise versa*, in the large number of processes of production, handling, etc., that takes place in a modern enterprise. Licensing authorities cannot possibly check every detail in a proposed investment and a private business naturally tends to choose the methods that are cheapest at ruling prices. But ruling prices substantially understate the scarcity and cost to the nation of imported equipment (and indeed of capital equipment generally, but that is a problem in itself).

An increase in taxes on such equipment even above the levels to which they were raised in the last Budget — which was a step in the right direction — would induce more economy and lead to some substitution of India's plentiful labour. Such taxes should also apply to equipment used by public enterprises; ideally they could be told to use high 'shadow' prices for equipment when choosing their methods of production but I am doubtful whether this would be effective in practice. These taxes might lead to higher prices for the finished product but any increase would usually be rather small. Where the product was exportable, a rather larger export subsidy could be given if necessary.

The planned increases of production could also be achieved with smaller imports of capital equipment if more industries worked double or even treble shifts. Table I illustrated the rather suprising lack of multiple shift working in India. It may even be less common than in an advanced country like the U.S., an extraordinary state of affairs in a country so short of capital as India. The marginal capital — output ratio could be greatly reduced by more multiple shift working, especially while it was being extended, but later, too, when it was fully in operation. It would also help to spread the electricity load throughout the twenty-four hours of the day and so alleviate the power shortage.

Single shift working may often appear more economical, for multiple shifts raise a number of problems, but the advantage may be more apparent than real, at least from a national point of view. It would probably pay some firms to introduce multiple shifts if the prices of capital equipment and power were brought nearer to their cost to the nation, say by a tax on equipment as suggested above, and if electricity charges for industry were made higher during the day than at night. Multiple shifts would be further encouraged if firms that work them were given, for example, preferential allocation of materials and higher income tax allowances for depreciation than at present. Shift working could be enforced by stricter policies towards the licensing of new capacity in industries until double or treble shift working was in operation, even at the risk of limiting competition.

V. WHY NOT TO DEVALUE

It may be argued that the measures proposed in this paper, and particularly the taxes on imports and subsidies to exports, are rather similar in their effect to devaluation and that this would be a much simpler and more straightforward alternative. I have no space to discuss this complicated matter in any detail but a few brief comments may be made.

Table IV

Fair Ex-works price as per cent of C.I.F. Import Price, excluding duty [1]
(Based on Reports of Tariff Commission)

		Year of Tariff Commission's Report
Under 70%	Cotton belting	1957
70% and under 80%	Diesel fuel injection equipment—pump—Kirloskar	1959
	Transformers 750 K.V.A.	1960
	Fluted rollers	1960
	Sewing machines	1954
	Oil pressure lamps	1957
	Plastic shirt buttons	1959
	Sodium bichromate	1958
80% and under 90%	Automobile leaf springs	1959
	Piston rings	1960
	Automobile hand tyre inflator (pump)	1960
	Wood screws	1960
	Machine screws, ¼ in. x 2 in. [2]	1959
	Aluminium circles	1960
	Phenol formaldehyde moulding powder [3]	1959
	Potassium bichromate	1958
90% and under 100%	Hair belting	1959
	Aluminium sheets	1960
	Brass sheets	1959
	Bare copper conductors	1960
	Bleaching powder	1958
	Calcium lactate	1960
	Plastic bush coat buttons	1959

		Year of Tariff Commission's Report
100% and under 110%	Electric motors (squirrel cage) 3 and 10 h.p.	1958
	A.C.S.R. conductors, 30/7/0.118 in.	1960
	Oleic acid	1959
	Teachest plywood	1960
	Pears in syrup	1957
110% and under 120%	Transformers, 3000 K.V.A.	1960
	Aluminium ingots	1960
	Copper sheets	1959
	A.C.S.R. conductors, 6/1/0.083 in.	1960
	Hydroquinone	1959
	Plastic pant buttons	1959
	Dry cells[4]	1953
120% and under 130%	Piston assembly (Fiat)	1960
	Electric motors (squirrel cage) 50 h.p.	1958
	Transformers, 25 K.V.A.	1960
	Automatic looms	1960
	Grinding wheels	1959
	Stearic acid	1959
130% and under 140%	Spinning ring frames	1960
	Copper tubes	1959
	Brass tubes	1959
	A.C.S.R. conductors, 7/0.1379 in.	1960
	Caustic soda	1958
140% and under 150%	Acid dyes	1954
	Commercial plywood	1960
	Raspberry jam	1957
150% and under 200%	Diesel fuel injection equipment – Nozzle holders Kirloskar	1959
	Automobile sparking plugs	1960
	Bicycles[5]	1960
	Machine screws, $\frac{3}{16}$ in. x $\frac{1}{2}$ in.[2]	1959
	Zinc sheets	1959
	Calcium Carbide	1958
	Direct dyes	1954
	Sheet glass	1960
200% and over	Ball bearings	1960
	Ball bearings adapter	1960
	Soda ash	1958
	Congo red dyes	1954
	Sulphur black dyes	1954

[1] The 'fair ex-works price' is a slightly smaller percentage of the landed costs, ex duty.
[2] Compared with imports from Japan. If a comparison is made with imports from Sweden, the fair ex-works price is less than 80% of the c.i.f. price for machine screws of ¼ in. x 2 in., and less that 110% for screws of $\frac{3}{16}$ in. x ½ in.
[3] Exclusive of duty on phenol formaldehyde and hexamine.
[4] Compared with imports from Hong Kong. If comparison is made with imports from the U.S., the fair ex-works price is less than 70% of the c.i.f. price.
[5] Lowest Indian price compared with price of imports from Japan. British bicycles are more expensive.

The import taxes would apply to only a fraction of imports and the export subsidies to only a fraction of exports. Devaluation would have much more widespread effects. It may prove necessary at some later date, if detailed controls become quite unworkable and ineffective because the gains from evasion become so great. But this time has not yet arrived and it may never come. It may eventually prove possible to achieve a balance, at existing rates of exchange and without too many controls or special taxes and subsidies, when infant export and import-saving industries have grown up and when sufficient investment has been made in export and import-saving activities generally.

If this is so, there is a strong case against a drastic measure that would have inflationary tendencies, reduce confidence in the currency, weaken a powerful argument for cost reduction and be fraught with other dangers and uncertainties. It might well, moreover, actually worsen the balance of payments, at least in the short run, because the foreign exchange earnings from exports might well be reduced while the foreign exchange cost of imports, which are severely restricted, would not fall.

Britain and Europe

7 Western European economic co-operation[1]

This brief note can merely sketch some aspects of Western European economic co-operation. It does not deal, except indirectly, with the political or military aspects, with Western Europe's dollar problem, or with co-operation outside the O.E.E.C. Only brief references are made to the "Schuman Plan"; the information available at the time of writing seems inadequate for a balanced appraisal of its economic implications.

THE REASONS FOR CO-OPERATION

It will be well to distinguish at the start some of the main reasons for which co-operation has been advocated. First there was the need for mutual help during the period of Marshall Aid so that the U.S. should not be asked to finance dollar supplies where similar goods were available in Western Europe but prevented from crossing national frontiers. Secondly, there was the need to maintain trade between Western European countries, despite the dollar shortage, by discriminatory trade and payment agreements. But such measures cannot necessarily be justified as a permanent arrangement. Nor is there any obvious economic reason why they should not be extended to other countries suffering from dollar shortage, or, for that matter, include certain hard currency countries in Western Europe.

Economic co-operation has, however, been advocated for more deep-seated reasons, both economic and political. The economic argument compares the large U.S. market with the numerous national markets of Western Europe. If only the latter could be unified, would this not go far to narrow the formidable gap between European and American productivity? There is some truth in this argument, but it has become increasingly realised that progress towards a single Western European market must be slow, and that even its achievement would not raise productivity to anything like the American level. Merely to keep pace with the rise in American

[1] *London and Cambridge Economic Service Bulletin*, **August 1950**.

productivity will be a major task. It is also recognised that, while freer trade in Europe will be of great importance for her future prosperity, when the necessary adjustments and investments have been made, it cannot notably ease the dollar problem during the period of Marshall Aid. It may, by stimulating competition and so reducing unnecessary costs and profits, make European products more competitive, even in the short run. But it will not appreciably reduce the demand for dollar imports, which are in general different from the additional goods likely to move in European trade. It may, moreover, divert export goods from the dollar area, investment from dollar-earning industries, and exporters from the vital task of winning dollar markets. And if it proceeds too quickly, the losses through dislocation may outweigh the gains.

In the political field the case for closer association is well known and it has often been argued that, if only progress could be made in economic co-operation, political co-operation would easily follow. This is partly true. In the frequent meetings of O.E.E.C. in Paris,[2] Ministers and officials have learned much of other countries' problems, and acquired the habit of working with other Europeans. There are now in most national administrations high officials concerned primarily with the work of O.E.E.C. They or their colleagues in Paris have to defend national policies before other countries' representatives, and they will naturally try to ensure that in the innumerable decisions taken by their governments the European point of view is not forgotten. The existence of an international secretariat, with several years of practical experience and a tradition of loyalty to Western Europe, might be of value if more ambitious forms of co-operation were attempted. But while economic co-operation may help to pave the way for political, it has become clear that a strong desire for political co-operation is indispensable for economic co-operation, which can make little real progress without a readiness to sacrifice national interests.

In some recent proposals for economic co-operation the primary motives appear to have been non-economic. Examples are the "Schuman Plan" for co-ordinating coal and steel, and perhaps the proposals christened Ukiscan and Finebel.[3] In other fields, notably the attempts of O.E.E.C. to free trade and payments, the tendency has been rather to concentrate on economic measures which, while

---

[2] O.E.E.C. has been described as an international conference in permanent session. During 1949 there were over 2,000 meetings of committees, sub-committees, etc., not counting informal meetings.

[3] These provided for closer associations between (a) Britain and Scandinavia, (b) France, Italy and the Benelux countries. The former led to a limited freeing of transactions between member countries, the latter to few, if any, results.

not spectacular, are obviously desirable in themselves and also practicable. The line of reasoning has been less: "It is desirable politically to co-operate economically; what shall we co-operate about?" and more on the following lines: "There has been a large growth of barriers to trade throughout the world. Here in O.E.E.C. is an existing organisation including many of those countries worst affected by the stifling of international competition. Let us try to stop the continued trend to autarky apparent in national programmes, and reduce the barriers between members. Let us start with those that have grown most in the last ten of twenty years, quantitive trade restrictions and exchange controls. Let us leave for the moment the problem of tariffs which would raise in more acute form the question of permanent discrimination and the desirability of a permanent Western European bloc."

FORMS OF CO-OPERATION

Various forms of co-operation have been proposed and four of these will be briefly discussed: customs unions, co-ordination of investment plans, "liberalisation" of trade, and payments arrangements.

CUSTOMS UNIONS

Customs unions between some or all of the Western European countries were the most striking form of co-operation advocated in 1947, and a Study Group representing most of the governments was set up to study the problem.[4] It may seem strange that such a drastic proposal, involving complete freeing of trade between members should have been so enthusiastically received, in view of the great difficulties then being experienced in securing even minor relaxations of trade barriers and of the serious problems that had arisen in the past (when barriers were much lower) when even two countries had attempted to form a customs union. Apart from an understandable tendency to embrace a new (or even a resuscitated) idea in times of crisis, the main reason was probably that customs unions were not regarded as discriminatory.[5]

[4] This Study Group, which is still working in Brussels, has collected much useful information about tariff structures, etc.

[5] Customs unions have in the past been a recognised exception to the M.F.N. rule, and they are now a recognised exception to the rule of non-discrimination in the Havana Charter. The reasons why this extreme form of discrimination has been regarded as non-discriminatory may be (1) that it is less likely to reduce total world trade than mere preferential arrangements — the latter may be achieved largely by raising barriers against non-members, while the customs union must at least mean a major reduction of barriers between members; (2) that a customs union is unlikely to be achieved without political union, in which case it becomes no more discriminatory than national tariffs applied equally to all foreigners.

It was, however quite impracticable for governments with low foreign exchange reserves, and pledged to maintain employment, to run the risks involved in rapid progress towards a customs union. The ultimate implications of customs unions, even if long postponed, were also realised. Historical experience cast grave doubts on the possibility of forming and maintaining customs unions without a degree of economic and political union to which many governments felt they could not commit their peoples; apart from customs unions between one major and one minor country (e.g., France and Monaco) none except the *Zollverein* had hitherto been achieved and maintained without political union.[6] If a Western European Customs Union meant virtually complete economic union this might, moreover, imperil living standards in the richer member countries. Free migration, a federal budget, and the like, might reduce their share in Western Europe's total output by more than the latter was increased through greater specialisation; it is noteworthy that geographical differences in living standards are considerably smaller in the U.S. than they are in Western Europe. It was hard to see also how a European Customs Union of which Britain was a member could be reconciled with Imperial Preference, although the latter might, of course, be consistent with a less drastic European system. In the event, apart from the Benelux agreement, which had first been made as early as 1944, no new accord was reached, even to work in principle towards a customs union, except that between France and Italy in March, 1948. Benelux, though making progress, is encountering difficulties, and advance towards a Franco-Italian Customs Union is still largely on paper.

CO-ORDINATION OF INVESTMENT PLANS

In the autumn of 1948, the O.E.E.C. turned to the co-ordination of investment plans. Large-scale investment was proceeding in each country with little regard to what was happening in others. It was clearly desirable, if only to ensure the best use of Marshall Aid, to avoid both over-investment and under-investment in particular industries, and within each industry to stop the trend to autarky revealed in national investment plans. The difficulties of reducing barriers to trade in goods produced from existing capacity were apparent; this would affect businesses and workers already producing. But it was thought that co-ordination of investment might achieve the economies of specialisation, without affecting existing interests, at least in respect of production from new capacity. The idea of

---

[6] See *Customs Unions*, U.N. 1947 and J. Viner, *The Customs Union Issue*, for useful surveys.

"co-ordination," involving direct control, was also more in line with some current ideas of economic planning than the reduction of trade barriers and reliance on the price mechanism, which, in any case, would not necessarily secure the optimum distribution of investment in Europe if those responsible for investment were not fully aware of plans in other countries.

The O.E.E.C. accordingly decided to attempt co-ordination of investment plans, and in 1949 the fields of oil-refining, steel and electrical generation were selected for special study, while studies were also made in many other industries as part of the normal work of the technical committees. The difficulties in this approach, many of which had been recognised in advance, became apparent during 1949.

(*a*) In the first place, governments may experience difficulty in *obtaining the necessary information* from private businesses, which may not have it or may be reluctant to reveal it, and governments themselves may be unwilling to release information of value to foreign competitors.

(*b*) If the information can be obtained — and O.E.E.C. has been in general succesful — the next step is to *estimate the total future supply and demand*. This is notoriously difficult. There have been many examples of bewilderingly rapid changes in demand/supply relationships recently. Estimates of future demand involve forecasts of export markets, of rates of exchange and of developments in other sectors of the economy. The demand for fertilisers depends on agricultural policy, that for steel and coal, in substitution for timber and oil, on future rates of exchange. There is a danger that the conclusions reached, which are bound to be influenced by the views of producers, may err on the side of under-estimating demand and lead to undesirable restriction of investment. It is significant that countries have often been most anxious for co-ordination when they wished to stop investment in a rival country.

(*c*) Even if the overall demand and supply can be correctly estimated, it is still necessary to ensure the *best location of investment* — to decide, when there is a danger of over-investment, which plans should be abandoned, and, when under-investment seems likely, where additional investment should be made. Even where the total investment planned seems about right, the location may be far from ideal. Each country might be planning to cover the whole of its needs, whereas the full economies of speculation required concentration in a few countries.

To determine the best location is no easy matter. It is seldom sufficient to assemble merely technical information without figures of monetary cost. Output per man-hour is an unsatisfactory criterion since wage-levels vary greatly; different technical methods, such as the use of hydro-electric power and coal, cannot be usefully compared without knowledge of costs.

But the relevant costs of production are very hard to establish. Even if accounting problems can be overcome, the figures obtained may be irrelevant. Allowance must be made for future changes in costs and for artificial price and cost structures and rates of exchange. There is the problem of prime and capital costs; new copper refineries should presumably be built in Austria to replace existing and serviceable refineries in Belgium only if the total cost of the former is less than the prime cost of the latter. There is the problem of the less developed countries which might, on the evidence of existing costs, be debarred from investments that would prove economical in the long run. There is the problem of countries suffering from heavy unemployment in which investment may be desirable though the money cost is higher than elsewhere. In the work of O.E.E.C. the problems of establishing monetary costs, and of making allowance for all these factors, and possibly for preference to poorer members with a view to reducing international inequality, have not yet been solved.

(*d*) Even if the best location can be established, it may be hard to *persuade governments to abandon their plans*. This will often run counter to their interests and perhaps upset their balance of payments. Such a sacrifice can hardly be expected unless corresponding advantages are offered in return. This is an argument for simultaneous co-ordination of a number of industries. Countries asked to restrict investment in one field might then be shown opportunities of expansion in others where fellow-members had agreed to restrict investment. But it is doubtful whether co-ordination is practicable in a sufficient number of industries for such compensatory arrangements to be worked out. In this respect co-ordination of investment is inferior to trade negotiations, where there is a much wider range of possible reciprocal concessions. A European fund might possibly be established to compensate countries asked to forego investment and to help them to adjust their economy. Dr. Stikker, the Chairman of the Council of O.E.E.C., recently proposed such a fund to help countries adversely affected by liberalisation of trade. The principle of providing financial compensation to private industry for losses resulting from freer trade might, however, be a dangerous one for governments to accept, although international financing of modernisation or alternative investment might be useful.

(*e*) Even if the best location can be established and agreed, there remains the problem of *enforcement*. Some governments may be unwilling to interfere with private enterprise and many have no direct powers to control investment.

The co-ordination of investment thus raises most of the difficulties involved in reducing trade barriers. It reveals the same clashes of interest. But it also involves many additional difficulties, including that of ensuring mutual advantage. It raises most of the problems met with by governments in the national sphere when planning the economy in detail without reference to relative prices. These problems are greatly magnified when the attempt is made on an international scale.

It is not surprising that the attempt at co-ordination in the full sense, which would involve international planning of investment from Paris, has achieved only limited success. In steel and oil-refining the existing investment plans were, by and large, accepted, although the steel study revealed a danger of over-investment. It is far from clear that there is no trend to autarky in both industries but without figures of monetary cost this is hard to establish in detail.

Despite all the difficulties, the *confrontation* of investment plans can be of value. First, investment decisions can be made in full knowledge of plans in other countries, and of the best possible estimates of future demand; studies in O.E.E.C. have, for example, revealed a danger of over-investment in certain chemical industries, and extreme caution has been recommended in planning new investment. Better knowledge of the plans of others will not necessarily, however, ensure the best location so long as protective barriers remain; the result may simply be that the most efficient countries, finding their neighbours intent on self-sufficiency, give up their plans for export. Secondly, the studies may bring to light industries with acute and harmful autarkic tendencies on which the efforts of O.E.E.C. to reduce trade barriers can be especially concentrated. A list of products is now being prepared on which countries are to concentrate in their further efforts to remove quantitative trade restrictions, and Dr. Stikker has even suggested that completely free trade, including the abolition of tariffs, should be sought in a number of selected industries. Thirdly, the studies may reveal a danger of under-investment and O.E.E.C. may then attempt to stimulate further investment. But while confrontation may be generally useful, full co-ordination is likely to be possible in only a limited number of industries. An example is the building of hydro-electric stations in the Alps, where international planning is often desirable, and has proved practicable, while trade negotiations are inadequate.

During 1949 the O.E.E.C. turned more and more to liberalisation of trade and payments as a more practicable way of achieving specialisation and competition in Western Europe. The Schuman Plan has now, however, raised once again the question of direct co-ordination. It raises the problem of co-ordinating not only investment but also current production when there is danger of surplus capacity. There is, however, no room to discuss here the difficult problems of concentrating production in the most efficient plants, of arranging alternative employment for workers displaced, and of dealing with private cartel arrangements that threaten to frustrate governmental attempts to free trade.

LIBERALISATION OF TRADE

The 1947 proposals for customs unions, involving complete removal of trade barriers, had little relevance to immediate action. The attempt, begun in 1949, to remove quantitative trade restrictions, after the difficulties of co-ordinating investment had been learned, was a much less ambitious, but more practicable, attack on trade barriers. It was an attempt, by adopting a limited objective and an empirical approach, to get concrete results, not in 1960 or 1970, but in 1949 and 1950.

There was realistic appreciation of the underlying difficulties. First, there were obvious currency difficulties, and arrangements, discussed below, were sought to ease them. Another main difficulty was the need to maintain employment. It used to be thought that full employment provided the ideal atmosphere for reducing trade barriers. But while it is true that trade barriers have in general risen most in times of slump, and that in times of high employment workers displaced by foreign competition can more easily be absorbed elsewhere, the need to maintain very high employment can also inhibit attempts to free trade. Governments may feel they must avoid even transitional pockets of unemployment that may result from freer imports. They realise that freer trade will mean less diversification of their industries and greater vulnerability to changes in demand. The maintenance of very full employment may prove inconsistent with the abolition of quantitative trade restrictions unless the degree of inflationary pressure is approximately the same in each country, which is hardly possible. If, moreover, governments faced with balance of payments difficulties feel unable to adopt monetary or budgetary policies involving even a risk of unemployment, and if they are also reluctant to devalue their currency for fear of an inflationary spiral, they will almost certainly be forced to restrict their trade. The desire to avoid any unemployment may thus make it hard for governments to forswear quantitative trade restrictions.

It was with difficulties such as these in mind that O.E.E.C. started its attempt to liberalise intra-European trade. The procedure adopted, largely by trial and error, is of some interest. There are three main ways in which international bodies can attempt to reduce trade barriers. First, they can exhort their members to take unilateral action. With a keen desire to co-operate, the results may be substantial but they are bound to be limited since countries will wish to know what others are doing in return. Secondly, countries can be exhorted to undertake bilateral negotiations. These may take longer but the results may be more substantial since mutual concessions can be arranged. But so long as measures of liberalisation are bilaterally negotiated, even though they are extended to all other members, the full possibilities of freeing trade cannot be exploited. A point will be reached where further concessions by A benefiting mainly B could only be compensated by concessions from C benefiting mainly A, while B granted concessions benefiting mainly C. The third method is thus to organise multilateral negotiations, but these in turn tend to be slow and complicated.

The procedure adopted by O.E.E.C. secured many of the advantages of these three methods. In the summer of 1949 countries were asked to submit by October 1st a list of articles which they would immediately, and without *quid pro quo*, import without quantitative restriction from other members. The lists submitted covered about one-third of all private trade between participants. They included items previously freed, but even this was useful since the freedom could now be less easily withdrawn and since the lists helped to establish the facts. Countries were also asked to submit lists on which they were prepared to negotiate. These covered perhaps a further one-fifth of private trade. To have advanced from this stage by purely bilateral or purely multilateral negotiations might well have been slow and tedious. It was therefore decided that all countries should bring their proportion of "liberalised" trade up to 50% by December 15th, or show good reasons why this was impossible. Bilateral negotiations were permitted, and the advantages of this method thus retained. And while the slowness of multilateral negotiations was avoided, some of their advantages were secured, for countries were prepared in bilateral negotiations to give more concessions than they received; they knew that these would count towards their 50% commitment, and that they stood to gain roughly equal concessions from member countries *as a whole* (although there was still, of course, an incentive to secure the maximum concessions in bilateral negotiations).

The removal of quantitive restrictions on 50% of the trade was a good start, but its importance must not be exaggerated. 30—40% of a country's imports from other participants may often be goods which it scarcely produces itself (including non-European goods bought as re-exports from other members or directly from their colonies), and a further fraction may be goods which it does produce but of which it could, were supplies available, import more from Western Europe in place of dollar imports without affecting domestic producers.[7] It is the liberalisation of the second 50% of a country's imports that significantly affects domestic producers and is most important for international specialisation. The O.E.E.C. did in fact set a harder task than the removal of restrictions on the easiest 50% of trade, for the 50% rule applied to food, raw materials and manufactures counted separately; this meant that a low percentage in manufactures, which was significantly common in the lists originally submitted, could not be offset against a high percentage in raw materials, which was also common. In the event, the 50% target was reached in food and feeding-stuffs and exceeded by most countries in raw materials. In manufactures, the proportions "liberalised" ranged from about 25% to virtually 100%. It has now been decided to raise the 50% to 60% at the latest 15 days after signature of the European Payments Union, and to 75% as soon as possible thereafter; all discrimination against other member countries will, moreover, be removed by the end of 1950.

The percentages refer to private trade and exclude government importing. Since about one-third of Britain's total imports from other members, and over half her food imports, are bought by the Government, this is of great importance. Three possible ways of dealing with government importing were considered. (*a*) It could be counted as non-liberalised trade; this was unacceptable to Britain who could not then have reached her target in foodstuffs. (*b*) It could be counted as free; this could hardly have been accepted by other countries. (*c*) It could be excluded from the calculations; this was the alternative chosen.[8]

---

[7] The percentage of actual imports represented by goods freed from control also tends to exaggerate the degree of liberalisation because imports effectively restricted form a small percentage of the total. A country that prohibited a wide range of imports but allowed the rest in freely could claim 100% liberalisation!

[8] One odd result is that a country could, in theory, fulfil its obligation by transferring items from private to government account, *e.g.*, if its trade were wholly private with 40% free and 60% restricted, by transferring one-third of the restricted trade to government account.

A fourth alternative would have been to determine for which items government importing was equivalent to free private importing, but this would have raised formidable problems.

In the freeing of invisible trade, O.E.E.C. has also made considerable progress and a comprehensive agreement was reached in May 1950.

PAYMENTS ARRANGEMENTS

It is difficult to liberalise trade in Western Europe unless each country has (1) adequate current earnings to pay for its imports, (2) adequate reserves to finance unforeseen deficits resulting from liberalisation, and (3) the ability to use a surplus with one member country to finance a deficit with another; otherwise it may be hard to grant concessions equally to all members.[9] The first two Payments Agreements made by O.E.E.C. (for 1948/49 and 1949/50) did much to fulfil the first condition, but not the second or third. It is with these last two that the European Payments Union is mainly concerned. This necessarily brief section discusses in the simplest possible terms the main features of these three exceedingly complicated agreements.[10]

Under the *Agreement for 1948/49* members granted each other "drawing rights" to finance expected balances between each pair of countries. These drawing rights (63 in all) were "bilateral" in the sense that France, for example, could use those granted her by Britain to finance only her sterling deficit and not her deficit with, say, Belgium. In return for drawing rights granted, countries received a part of their dollar aid; this was in theory to be forfeited to the extent that drawings rights were not used, but the provision was not enforced. (Unused drawing rights were mostly cancelled or carried forward to 1949/50.)

The agreement (signed in October 1948) had the great merit of maintaining, and indeed of allowing a continued expansion in, intra-European trade at a time when many countries, having exhausted credit margins under bilateral payments agreements, would otherwise have had to curtail imports to protect their reserves.[11] The disadvantages were probably inevitable. First, the

[9] Britain and certain other countries felt unable to extend their liberalisation measures of 1949 to Belgium, Germany and Switzerland. When E.P.U. restores transferability of currencies, such discrimination will in general cease.

[10] An earlier agreement between a number of Western European countries had dealt with compensations only. This, and the first two O.E.E.C. agreements, are well described in the 18th, 19th and 20th Annual Reports of the Bank for International Settlements, which acted as agent for all the agreements.

[11] The volume of trade between Western European Countries (1938 = 100) moved roughly as follows:

Quarters	1937	1938	1947	1948	1949	1950
I				67	87	114
II	100	100	66	78	93	
III				79	93	
IV				91	107	

estimates of balances, usually a small fraction of the total turnover, were necessarily inaccurate, the more so as they were made on a bilateral basis. Italy, for example, proved a creditor of the U.K., not a debtor as forecast. Where the estimates did prove reasonably accurate, this may simply have meant that debtors finding their drawing rights being too quickly exhausted restricted imports, while debtors in the opposite situation encouraged them or made little effort to expand exports.

A second disadvantage of the scheme was thus that it put little pressure on debtors to restore equilibrium, by appropriate monetary or financial policy or in other ways. If they did better than the forecast, they wasted their drawing rights and might also find it harder to claim large ones for the following year. This illustrates a major problem that recurs in all discussions on payments agreements: the attempt to maintain trade, by providing credits or grants which obviate dollar settlements, conflicts with the attempt to restore an equilibrium where no country has to subsidise another.

A third disadvantage was the bilateral nature of the scheme.[12] Apart from increasing the inaccuracy this reduced the power of countries to buy in the cheapest European market and restricted competition between exporting countries. Transferable drawing rights, spendable in countries other than those granting them, were opposed largely on grounds of equity. France, for example, might have used her sterling drawing rights to finance a deficit with Belgium (thereby causing a loss of British gold to Belgium), simply because Belgium had been less generous than Britain in granting drawing rights.

The *Agreement for 1949/50* did little or nothing to reduce the inaccuracy of the earlier scheme or to increase the pressure on debtors, but it made, in general, 25% of the drawing rights received "multilateral." These could, under certain conditions, be used in any member country; if more were used in a country than had been forecast, its dollar allocation was correspondingly supplemented, if less were used, it was correspondingly docked. These multilateral

---

[12] There were, it is true, some multilateral elements in the scheme. Drawing rights up to a point obviated the need for strict bilateral balancing. They were granted by, for example, Britain to Italy, by Italy to Belgium, and by Belgium to Britain. The compensation arrangements also allowed for some automatic multilateral reductions in accumulated balances, but only when, for example, Britain owed Belgium, Belgium owed Denmark, and Denmark owed Britain, so that debts could be scaled down all round (so-called "first category compensations"). In the more common type of situation, where Britain owed Belgium and was owed by Denmark, but Denmark also owed Belgium, a cancelling of Britain's debt and credit would have *increased* Denmark's debt to Belgium, and such "second category compensations" required the consent of all parties which was seldom given.

drawing rights (equivalent to only a few per cent. of trade between participants) were confined to such narrow limits for fear that creditors might otherwise (*a*) feel obliged to limit imports from debtors to make sure of their vital Marshall dollars or (*b*) lose an undue proportion of their dollar aid to other creditors, not because their goods were less competitive, but because the other creditors made their currency scarce by restricting imports, by allowing heavy unemployment or by granting less generous drawing rights.

A particular problem here was Belgium who, with an estimated dollar deficit (and therefore E.R.P. allocation) of only $200 Mn., was naturally reluctant to give drawing rights equal to her estimated European surplus of $400 Mn. without some *quid pro quo*. But if she granted only $200 Mn. drawing rights, other creditors would almost certainly lose dollars to her. If, on the other hand, dollars were subtracted from the allocations of all other countries to finance additional Belgian drawing rights, this might force Norway, for example, to forego dollar imports vital for reconstruction so that Belgium could buy Packards or put dollars to reserve. The resulting wrangle, which was essentially over who should get the dollars, absorbed much time in the hot Paris summer of 1949 before a compromise settlement was reached.[13]

The *European Payments Union* suffers from few of the drawbacks of the earlier schemes. It is infinitely more multilateral; there is less room for inaccuracy since estimates of future deficits play a much smaller role; there is pressure on the debtors, but this is made gradual to avoid undue restriction of trade. But comparison with the earlier schemes is of little value since the E.P.U. is so very different. It aims far more at increasing international liquidity and at transferability of currencies and far less at the provision of "emergency" finance to cover *expected* deficits during the coming year. Instead, countries are given overdraft facilities at E.P.U., roughly in proportion to their transactions with other members, to cover *unforeseen* deficits with the group as a whole. They also pledge a corresponding amount of credit should they be in surplus. Each member's international liquidity is thus increased,[14] while monthly compensations[15]

---

[13] The estimated gap of $200 Mn. was filled as follows: Belgium gave an extra $112½ Mn. multilateral drawing rights (against which Marshall dollars were set aside, subtracted from the allocations of all other countries) and a further $87½ Mn. in lines of credit to France, the Netherlands and Britain. In fact, Belgium's European surplus has been far less than $400 Mn., partly as a result of the revaluations of September 1949 and of the loosening of the market for steel and capital goods.

[14] The sum of the credits available to all countries is about $2,400 Mn. (This is 60% of the sum of the quotas.) Purely to illustrate the order of magnitude, the gold and foreign exchange reserves of members totalled approximately $7,000 Mn. at the end of 1949.

[15] Every two months for the first six months.

provide transferability, i.e., they offset surpluses with some countries against deficits with others.

These major changes have been made possible by the much closer approach to balance in transactions between participants during the past year. It is thought that there are now no European currencies so obviously "scarce" that transferability will threaten severe restriction of trade.[16] Nor are there any longer many obvious debtors requiring large-scale "emergency" finance. Six prospective debtors start off with an initial credit at E.P.U. (and three prospective creditors with an initial debit), but the net deficits foreseen are much smaller in total than those allowed for in the 1949/50 Agreement. It is assumed that most countries are near enough a balance to do without drawing rights and the general feeling is that in the sixth year of peace it is high time countries began, wherever possible, to stand on their own feet (either by earning enough with the group as a whole to meet their payments or by settling any difference in gold or dollars). Why should Italy continue to subsidise the Netherlands, a much richer country?[17] In any case the dwindling of Marshall Aid will reduce more and more the possibility of persuading countries to give drawing rights; more and more cases like Belgium in 1949/50 would arise if it were attempted to continue the old scheme.

But the pressure put on debtors to restore a balance is gradual. A first tranche of their overdraft facilities can be drawn freely to cover deficits. Thereafter they must make simultaneous gold payments to E.P.U. to cover a steadily rising proportion of their deficits until, when their quota is exhausted, they must pay 100% gold to cover any further deficits. Creditors must give their first tranche of credit to E.P.U. without demanding gold, and thereafter have to give $1 of credit for every $1 of gold received. They have thus some incentive to reduce their surplus. No decision has been taken about what happens when creditors' quotas are exhausted. Many countries hope they will then receive 100% gold in settlement of further surpluses; any incentive would then disappear.[18] But they will probably, during the next two or three years, have to continue giving 50% credit if they wish to remain in E.P.U. and to continue to receive non-discriminatory treatment from other members.

---

[16] If, for example, the Belgian franc were very scarce, the possibility of paying for a deficit with Belgium through a surplus elsewhere might lead countries unnecessarily to restrict imports from each other as severely as imports from Belgium.
[17] The Netherlands received no drawing rights from Italy in 1949/50, but she was a net receiver from the group while Italy granted drawing rights and received none.
[18] It might disappear earlier if creditors expected their quota to be exhausted in the fairly near future.

It would be wrong to force each country into exact balance with the group as a whole. In a satisfactory system some countries should have net surpluses, some net deficits with the group, offset by deficits or surpluses elsewhere. The assumption underlying E.P.U. seems to be that such countries would gradually move towards the 100% gold points and that the desirable multilateral pattern would thus emerge. This may be so, but many difficult questions spring to mind. For example, if the dollar shortage persists, will countries that "should" be debtors to the group sufficiently liberalise their trade; and is there not a distinction to be drawn between countries that "should" be creditors in the long run and those that acquire a surplus by insufficient liberalisation or by allowing heavy unemployment?

Time alone will tell whether the numerous and ingenious provisions of the scheme are well founded. Is there the right balance between pressure on debtors and justice for creditors on the one hand and the need for finance to permit freer trading on the other? Do the rules sufficiently cater for extreme creditors and extreme debtors? Are the credit margins wide enough? Shall we rapidly reach the position where 100% gold is payable or receivable by most countries? Will this happen before the dollar shortage is sufficiently overcome, or freer trade arrangements sufficiently established, to prevent 100% gold payments causing severe restriction of intra-European trade? Will the special arrangements made at Britain's request safeguard sterling and its use as an international currency? Complicated and automatic schemes seldom cater for all the contingencies that arise and it is well that, in the tradition of O.E.E.C., the E.P.U. will be completely reviewed in June, 1951, and in March, 1952, and any necessary amendments made.

OTHER FORMS OF CO-OPERATION

The achievements of O.E.E.C. in freeing trade and payments have been considerable. But these have not been the only forms of successful co-operation. On two occasions agreement has been reached on recommendations for the division of Marshall Aid — a stern test for co-operation.[19] There has been much exchange of information hitherto considered confidential. Countries have been prepared to discuss their internal financial policies and to allow publication of joint reports critical of them. Two agreed reports have

[19] This absorbed much of the Organisation's time during its first 18 months, but for the last two years of Marshall Aid the division will be made by E.C.A., in principle in the same proportions as in 1949/50.

diagnosed Western Europe's economic problems and drawn morals for policy. These have been partly based on, but have not necessarily accepted, national forecasts for future years. A similar inquiry is now in train, looking ahead to 1955, and it is hoped that this can be closely related to the inquiry into the American balance of payments now proceeding in Washington under the direction of Mr. Gordon Gray.[20]

There has been much unspectacular but useful co-operation on detailed practical problems. These include such widely divergent matters as joint publicity in America to encourage travel to Europe, a common code of customs procedure for tourists and the abolition of visas; a new research unit at Cambridge to study Western European national income statistics; joint showing of European products at an American Trade Fair; co-operative research on matters ranging from oxygen utilisation to windmills as a source of power; standardisation; grassland improvement and technical advice to farmers; transport in Africa south of the Sahara; combined missions to the U.S. (financed by E.C.A.) to study problems of electrical generation, paper and pulp, inland transport, timber, chemicals hybrid maize, hotels, the measurement of productivity; periodical publications showing availability and delivery dates of new machinery in member countries.

PROSPECTS AND PROBLEMS

For an international organisation little more than two years old, O.E.E.C.'s record of co-operation is not unimpressive. But sterner tests lie ahead. With the end of Marshall Aid countries will no longer feel that their dollar receipts may depend on their record of co-operation. Only if there survives a strong European financial institution, such as a Payments Union or an Investment Bank (as suggested by M. Petsche on behalf of France), with power to grant or withhold funds, will the financial inducements to co-operation remain.

The second half of the quantitative trade restrictions will be much

---

[20] It has been argued that the failure of O.E.E.C. to make a "master plan" for Western Europe in 1952/53 out of the national forecasts submitted in 1948 proves the futility of such long-term analyses. But a "master plan" would have given quite a misleading impression of accuracy and perhaps a false impression that the problem was solved just because the figures added up, although in fact the "plan" could not be implemented. Instead, the O.E.E.C.'s *Interim Report* drew attention to the inconsistencies and impossibilities in the national programmes and pointed the way to policy. Though it said little not already contained in, for example, the earlier E.C.E. Survey, it had the advantages (a) of being an official statement of governments (in which every word was carefully weighed), and (b) of showing that national governmental plans were incapable of fulfilment. If approached in this way an analysis of national long-term programmes can be of considerable value.

harder to remove than the first, and, as the process continues, tariffs will assume greater importance. These are already being examined by O.E.E.C., where they clearly vitiate the removal of quantitative restrictions. Low tariff countries, like Denmark and the Netherlands, are, moreover, naturally reluctant to remove further quantitative restrictions so long as other countries have high tariffs. But tariff reduction will raise in more acute form questions of national protection and defence, of Imperial Preference and of discrimination against the U.S.; M. Pella has already suggested, on behalf of the Italian Government, preferential tariff reductions between Western European countries. It remains to be seen how far trade can be freed between countries with independent internal policies, and with this problem in mind O.E.E.C. is studying the possibilities of "harmonising" the "financial, economic, social, tariff and investment policies" of member governments.

A severe dollar shortage after Marshall Aid ends would provide a searching test for co-operation; how far would debtors in Europe, paying gold to their neighbours, accept harsh restriction of their dollar imports to maintain a liberal import policy, and transferability of their currency, in Europe? Full co-operation in the face of dollar shortage might be held to require a pooling of gross dollar receipts and their distribution according to some criterion of equity.

The urgent problem of reducing Italian and German unemployment may require not only a change in the internal policies of these countries, but also substantial help from other countries to alleviate any resulting balance of payments difficulties, and possibly to assist migration. Perhaps most important of all, the growing desire for co-operation between the whole Atlantic Community will require fundamental reconsideration of the philosophy and machinery of Western European economic co-operation. Agreement has already

O.E.E.C. = *Organisation for European Economic Co-operation*, comprising Austria, Belgium, Denmark, France, Greece, Iceland, Ireland, Italy, Luxembourg, Netherlands, Norway, Portugal, Sweden, Switzerland, Turkey, United Kingdom, Western Germany and Trieste, established by Convention of 16th April, 1948 (see *Cmd* 7388).

E.R.P. = *European Recovery Programme* ("Marshall Aid"), financed under the United States Economic Co-operation Act (Title I of the Foreign Assistance Act of 1948).

E.C.A. = United States *Economic Co-operation Administration*, the American body set up under the Economic Co-operation Act to administer E.R.P., with headquarters in Washington, a United States Special Representative in Europe, of ambassadorial rank, to keep in contact with the O.E.E.C. in Paris, and E.C.A. Missions in each of the participating countries.

E.C.E. = *Economic Commission for Europe*, under the Economic and Social Council of United Nations, comprising countries of both Western and Eastern Europe (including the U.S.S.R.) who are members of United Nations; of the O.E.E.C. countries, Austria, Western Germany and Switzerland are not included.

been reached on the closer association of the U.S. and Canadian governments with the work of O.E.E.C.

The problems to be faced are not easy. But if the countries of Western Europe, and others that may be associated with them, have a real desire for cooperation, if they make full use of the experience gained, the contacts made and the traditions established during the last few years, if they continue to set limited objectives and adopt a practical, empirical approach with their motto *solvitur ambulando*, the problems may not be insoluble.

8 Britain and the Common Market[1]

I have been asked to write about the special problems facing the United Kingdom in connection with her desire to join the European Economic Community. I shall say nothing about the special problems facing the Six in accepting British membership. This does not mean that I regard them as unimportant; but they are outside my terms of reference.

Three special British problems are well known and frequently emphasised by British spokesmen: those related to the Commonwealth, to agriculture and food prices, and to the European Free Trade Association. I shall consider these in due course, but it is important to remember that there are other considerable difficulties, both political and economic.

GENERAL POLITICAL CONSIDERATIONS

The most important arguments for and against Britain joining the Community are, in my view, political rather than economic. The main arguments in favour are that a growing split in Western Europe would be injurious to the Western alliance; that the peoples of this small peninsula at the end of the Eurasian continent, so often divided in war, must stick together in view of the growing might of Russia — and of China — and of the rapid growth of population, and it is hoped of economic power, in the under-developed world generally. In addition, some would argue that we must build a firmly knit group that will compare in strength and influence with the United States, although others would prefer an Atlantic Community of which, sooner or later, the U.S. was a full member. From a more narrowly British point of view there is a fear that, standing alone, and with leadership of the Commonwealth a steadily dwindling asset in the eyes of other powers, our influence in the world will rapidly decline; that, in particular, the Six will take our place as the United States' major ally.

[1] Rotterdamsche Bank Review (December 1961).

Now whether or not such considerations on the grand scale are conclusive, they will not necessarily convince a majority of the British people. It is true that opinion is changing swiftly. There has been a Grand Debate on the subject this year. The Government has applied for membership of the Community. Their policy has been endorsed by an overwhelming majority of the Conservative Party Conference. The Labour Party has not opposed the Government's decision to enter into negotiations. The Trade Union Congress has commented quite favourably on the idea of British membership. Leaders of industry have spoken strongly in support. Nonetheless, there is still a good deal of doubt and apprehension.

Apart from the Commonwealth question, to be discussed later, it can be argued that it is preferable to be a small independent power, like Sweden or Switzerland, without much say in world affairs, rather than only a part of a large powerful group. Moreover, apart from a certain amount of irrational British prejudice against foreigners in general, there are some doubts about the political stability of the Six, some dislike of their Colonial and military records, and some fear among socialists that they are in general too right wing and *laissez-faire*. There are, of course, counter-arguments. For example, the British political, colonial and military records are not blameless; we may have much to learn from the way in which continental nations manage their affairs; the French have a Plan (though it may be more difficult to operate under a Common Market), the EEC will have a controlled agriculture, and many British Labour M.P.s favour our joining the Common Market.

Nevertheless, British people are bound to feel qualms about pooling with our European neighbours more and more of our sovereignty on political as well as economic matters — and on economic and social policy that goes far beyond the comparatively narrow field of tariffs and trade. If we go in we must be prepared, in the words of the preamble to the Rome Treaty, for 'an ever closer union', and work wholeheartedly with our fellow members to that end. If a true picture could be painted of the extent to which we might have given up our freedom of action in, say, ten years' time, the revulsion of a good many British people might now be extreme (even though they might accept the situation quite happily when the time came).

Such an attitude may be hard for those on the Continent to understand. But we have not been defeated, ravaged and occupied in war. And the instinctive longing for close and irrevocable union that seized many Europeans a decade and a half ago largely passed us by.

It is only quite recently, as we have realised that our relative strength is declining and that of the Six mounting rapidly, that we have felt a growing desire not to be left out in the cold.

GENERAL ECONOMIC ARGUMENTS

Many of the arguments used in favour of joining the Community have been in economic terms. But none, in my opinion, is compelling. We can, I believe, prosper and grow more rapidly than in the past whether or not we take this decisive step. It is even possible that entry might aggravate our economic difficulties. Let us run through some of the arguments.

First, it is undoubtedly true that membership of a European market would make possible larger scale production, larger expenditure on research and development, and more rapid introduction of new products and processes. The potential gains, particularly those of a dynamic character, may be important in a good many fields, and they may become increasingly important as a result of modern technological developments. But they are impossible to quantify, and they can be exaggerated. The British market of over 50 million people, living at a high standard, together with our large export markets throughout the world, already make possible most of the economies of scale in most industries. Our failure to exploit some of these potential economies through lack of standardisation could, in principle at least, be remedied by measures other than entry into the Common Market.

Secondly, quite apart from economies of scale, there are the gains from international specialisation that would result if we concentrated more on the production of goods in which we have a comparative advantage and exported these to pay for goods in which our European neighbours have a comparative advantage. This is the traditional argument for free trade. But this type of gain from free trade with the Six, though desirable, could hardly have a very appreciable effect on British real incomes.

Our trade in each direction with the EEC is under 3% of our national product. Even if this percentage were greatly expanded — and in some lines, such as cars, it might be multiplied several times over — the increase would still be only a small fraction of our total income; and the gain to real income would be quite a small fraction of this increase in trade. Moreover, there would be losses resulting from the diversion of British imports from cheaper overseas sources to more expensive sources in Europe. On balance, it seems unlikely that any net gain would be as much as 1% of the British national income. Over a period of, say, five to ten years, this would be unimportant compared with the growth of the national product.

Thirdly, there are the possible gains from greater competition from the Continent. It is hoped that this would eliminate inefficient producers, force others to become more efficient, and generally help to remove the lethargy which is thought to have gripped British industry. Many in Britain now think that this would be the main economic advantage of entry into the Common Market. This may well be true, but a number of observations may be made.

It is implicitly assumed that British industry would respond to the challenge. I believe that it would. But it is not inevitable. The winds of competition do not necessarily stimulate a country's industry; they could cause it to wither away. Weak areas can go the wall in a common market.

Even if greater foreign competition had a favourable effect — and I think that it would do — it might be equally possible to achieve greater efficiency and faster growth without joining the EEC. More competition could be provided by a unilateral reduction in tariffs, or, preferably, by reductions matched by concessions by other countries, negotiated through the GATT. This could be accompanied by some or all of the following: measures to prevent restrictive practices, both by business and by trade unions; changes in the structure of taxation that would provide greater rewards for the efficient, greater penalties for the inefficient, and a greater incentive for labour-saving investment; the devotion of a higher proportion of the national income to investment; possibly "planning" on the lines of the French model. In addition, to prevent our costs from rising faster than those of our competitions, and the resulting need for measures to safeguard the balance of payments, which have caused recurring periods of stagnation in the past, we must devise a policy for incomes that will prevent wages and profits from rising faster than productivity.

Measures such as these will be required in any case, whether we join the Common Market or not. The argument for joining is, in part, that we need this external stimulus to force us to make the necessary changes. If this is not the case, the economic argument for joining is considerably weaker, although the gains that could be obtained in no other way may certainly be substantial.

The mere fact of joining a group of nations whose production has been growing fast will not automatically make us grow fast as well, as is sometimes thought. The Six as a whole were growing much faster than Britain before the inception of the Community, so that other causes must have been responsible. Even if the Common Market speeds up the growth of the Six — and there is no clear evidence that it has yet done so[2] — it will not necessary lead to rapid growth of every member, including Britain if she joins. The relatively slow growth of Belgium in recent years is suggestive in this context.

THE BALANCE OF PAYMENTS

So far I have hardly mentioned the effects of joining the Community on Britain's balance of payments. If these were unfavourable they could, by necessitating restrictive measures that retarded growth, offset any favourable effects.

In the first place, if joining speeds the growth of our productivity and if money incomes do not rise correspondingly faster, any tendency for our cost and price levels to rise will be checked, thus helping the balance of payments. The balance will also benefit if the pace of innovation in British industry is improved, as well as the standard of design, of service, and so on. On the other hand, we have seen that faster growth and innovation, and all the rest, might be achieved, at least to a considerable extent, without joining the Community. In any case, faster growth is also likely to increase the demand for imports, as incomes and the need for raw materials rise.

The general consequences for our balance of payments of joining the Common Market are thus hard to forecast, although, in the longer run at least, they might well be favourable. What of the more specific effects of changes in tariffs and preferences?

On the export side, we should gain duty free entry into the markets of the Six and, moreover, a preference over exporters in all other countries except those that joined the Community with us, or became associated with it. At present, the main industrial competitors at whose expense we should gain are the United States and Japan. Other serious competitors will doubtless emerge later as their manufacturing industry develops, but, if we became a member of the EEC, we should presumably press for liberal treatment of their exports, especially if they are under-developed countries and members of the Commonwealth.

On the other hand, we should presumably lose the preferences we at present enjoy on exports to Commonwealth countries, both because their retention would be inconsistent with our membership of the EEC and because many Commonwealth countries would be reluctant to continue the preferences they give to our exports if we were removing the preferences we now give to imports from them. Moreover, our preferences in Commonwealth markets might

---

[2] See A. Lamfalussy, 'Europe's Progress: Due to Common Market?', *Lloyd's Bank Review*, October, 1961.

well be removed more by the raising of duties on British goods than be a lowering of duties on goods from other countries; for most Commonwealth countries are anxious to protect their growing industries and they might well feel, rightly or wrongly, that their trading position had been worsened by Britain's entry into the Common Market. Some might also feel obliged to enter into closer, preferential arrangements with other countries.

We should also lose our preferences in EFTA countries, at present rather small but potentially important. In the case of EFTA countries that joined the Community, or became associated with it, we should have to share these preferences with the Six, although they would be retained against outside competitors. In the case of any EFTA country that stayed outside we should presumably lose the preference altogether, and, moreover, have to pay import duty, whereas if the EFTA had remained in being we should ultimately have enjoyed free entry.

The balance of gain and loss resulting from these complicated changes is impossible to estimate but a few broad orders of magnitude may be suggestive. At present about 16% of our exports go to the Six, and the average Common Market tariff on them will probably be about 10-15% (allowing for the reduction of one-fifth provisionally made on the average rates prevailing in January 1957). About 13% of our exports go to the EFTA countries (including Finland, which is an associate member) and the average potential preference on these is probably of the order of 10%. About 45% of our exports go to the Commonwealth (including former members who still give us preference) and of these about one-half, or rather more than 20% of our total exports, receive preferences probably averaging around 10%.

Entry into the Common Market would thus involve a preferential abolition of duties averaging 10-15% on about one-sixth of our present exports (those to the Six), and a loss of preferences, or potential preferences, averaging around 10% on about one-third of our present exports (those to the Commonwealth and EFTA). These figures suggest that the losses on British exports might outweigh the gains. While such a crude calculation cannot prove that this is probable, it at least seems doubtful, in view of the many uncertainties, whether a more elaborate one could establish that the reverse was true, that the gains were likely to exceed the losses.

It is true that in such calculations one should use, not the present proportions of our exports to the various groups of countries, but the proportions that would be likely to obtain in, say, five or ten years' time if we did not join the Common Market. It may be thought that this would show a much higher proportion of our exports to the rapidly growing Six and a lower proportion to the Commonwealth and EFTA countries taken together. But this is not certain when one allows for the growing discrimination against British goods that would occur in the EEC and the growing discrimination in their favour in the EFTA. It may also be that Commonwealth preferences would wither away even if we did not join the Common Market. But, if they did, we should be able to secure some commercial concessions in return.

So far as exports are concerned, it is thus at least not clear that the direct effects of the changes in tariffs and preferences that would result from our joining the Common Market would be advantageous. But it is virtually certain that our imports, particularly of manufactures, would increase — and probably very substantially — as a result of the abolition of duties on imports from the Six. (There might be some increases in duties on imports from the Commonwealth, but it would presumably be our endeavour to limit these as far as possible; and adherence to the common external tariff of an enlarged EEC would, on average, involve lowering our duties on imports of manufactures from non-Commonwealth countries.)

Looked at as a purely commercial deal, and ignoring the indirect cosequences, it is thus by no means obvious that entry into the Common Market would be a good proposition for Britain. It might well tend to worsen the balance of trade.

Even if it is thought that the indirect economic consequences, and the political ones, would be decidedly advantageous, this danger is bound to be a matter of concern to a country like the United Kingdom, whose balance of payments has repeatedly run into difficulties since the war, and may have become even more unsatisfactory in recent years. This is especially true since the full favourable indirect consequences of joining the common Market would be likely to emerge only after a number of years. Adverse effects on the balance of payments could, by contrast, emerge quickly. A recent study of the prospects for British cars,[3] for example, concluded that, while in the longer run entry into the Common Market might force the industry to become more competitive, the immediate effect would almost certainly be to reduce Britain's share in the world market for cars (including the British market) below what it would otherwise have been.

In little more than a couple of years from now, Britain's tariffs against imports from the Six might have to be reduced by as much as 60%, a much sharper reduction than was made by the Six on their imports from each other in the first two years of the Common

[3] *National Institute Economic Review*, September 1961, p. 31.

Market. This, together of course with the corresponding reduction in duties on our exports to the Six, would bring changes which, in the aggregate, would be important in relation to our balance of trade, even though, as we saw, the gain from more trade would be a very small fraction of our national income. Even uncertainty about the direction in which our balance of payments woud be affected must be worrying in our present position, and even though our rather exigous reserves of gold and foreign exchange might be buttressed by firm promises of support from the Six with their much stronger reserve positions.

It is true that France joined the Common Market when her balance of payments was unsatisfactory. But, in the first place, she was faced with a more gradual reduction in tariffs. Secondly, she radically improved her competitive position by devaluing her currency not long before the first tariff rductions, and such a course would be much more difficult for a country with a major international currency.

THE BALANCE OF ADVANTAGE
It is true that the economic gains from joining the Community, particularly the imponderable benefits of membership of a group of dynamic nations, which would bring a more intensive interchange of people and ideas, might turn out to be very considerable, at least in the long run. But, if the foregoing analysis is correct, there is no really *compelling* economic argument for Britain's joining, unless it is thought that, without being exposed to the blast of competition from the Continent, she will never put her house in order. If one does not take this rather defeatist view,— although it is quite possibly a realistic one — there seems to be no reason why exclusion from the Community should prevent Britain from achieving a perfectly satisfactory economic performance in the future, and a very considerably better one than she has achieved since the war.

On the other hand, while there are economic risks in joining, especially perhaps in the short run, these are not sufficiently important to stand in the way of our entering if the political arguments for such a course are strong. It is not impossible that joining would necessitate a devaluation of the pound. But it is not inconceivable that this would prove necessary at some stage even if we did not join. If one looked back after ten years in the Community, and weighed up the costs and benefits of membership, it might be that balance of payments difficulties, and even devaluation, in the early years would appear to be a rather minor cost.

The whole issue should, in my opinion, be decided mainly in terms of long run political considerations. But this does not mean that, in practice, short run economic and political exigencies, and the need to satisfy vested interests, may not be of importance. Moreover, as I mentioned at the beginning, there are a good many fears and hesitations, some based on prejudice but some honest and well-founded, about the political wisdom of joining the Community. If we are to join, the agreement reached must be satisfactory to a majority of the wide variety of opinions and interests represented in Parliament, and presumably be judged acceptable to a majority of the electorate.

It is now time to say something about the three well-known political problems: EFTA, agriculture and food prices, the Commonwealth. Of these, the first causes least concern to British people. We certainly have obligations to our EFTA partners, and difficulties may arise in the negotiations, particularly perhaps in relation to the association of the 'neutral' countries; but the Six have as much interest as Britain does in finding a solution, and it is hard to believe that this problem would be allowed to prove the decisive obstacle to Britain's joining the Community.

BRITISH AGRICULTURE AND FOOD PRICES

The problem of British agriculture and food prices is more important politically in Britain, and it may cause difficulties, but it seems to be a rather minor one in relation to the wider issues involved, and far less important than the problem of the Commonwealth.

Both Britain and the EEC support the prices received by their farmers above the world level, but a problem arises because this is done in different ways. In the Community the farmer will generally be protected from foreign competition by tariffs and import levies and restrictions; he will, in fact, be assisted at the expense of the consumer, through the higher prices he pays for his food. In Britain, while there are tariffs on fruit and vegetables, an import levy on sugar, and a monopolistic marketing board which maintains the price of liquid milk at a high level, a large part of the farmers' output is subsidised by the Government. The taxpayer rather than the consumer of food bears the burden, and we thus reconcile protection for agriculture with a long-standing tradition of cheap food.

If Britain joined the Community, it seems likely that, to a very large extent, we should have to accept the Continental system; this is an essential aspect of the Treaty of Rome, and for the Six to adopt the British system would involve serious budgetary problems.

This means, in the first place, that the prices paid for food by the

British consumer would rise. Some prices, such as those of milk, fruit and vegetables, might fall, but others, such as those of meat, bread and butter, might rise. It is impossible to say how important the net effects would be: target prices for food in the Community have not yet been agreed; they may be influenced by the entry of Britain and other new members; the treatment that would be accorded to Commonwealth products is not known. Various illustrative estimates that have been made suggest that the wholesale price of food might rise by 6—20%. But, as nearly half the retail price represents the costs of processing and distribution, the cost to the consumer might rise by only perhaps 3—10% (although the practice of percentage mark-ups might raise this figure). Since the cost of food accounts for only about one-third of the cost of living index, the latter might be raised by only about 1—3%.

Spread over the transitional period of six years at present envisaged under EEC, the average rise would be unlikely to exceed about ½% per annum. Moreover, there would be a drop in the price of some manufactures imported from the Continent (although a good many of these might be luxuries and the price of some British manufactures for which the export demand was stimulated might rise). In addition, the Government might use the money saved on agricultural subsidies (less any loss of customs revenue) to reduce indirect taxes on other commodities (or to augment pensions or family allowances so as to mitigate the regressive effects of a relative rise in food prices).

Even a slow rise in the cost of living, with its consequences for wages, could have inflationary effects that would be worrying in the context of Britain's balance of payments position. But, on a longer view, this does not seem to be a very serious matter.

Acceptance of the Community's agricultural policy could also have important consequences for the British farmer. Here again one cannot make precise forecasts until more progress has been made in the negotiations among the Six, and between the Six and prospective new members. But it is certain that the *method* by which British farmers receive their assistance would be changed, and a good many of them feel that the present system gives them greater security (although this system may admittedly be changed even if we do not join the Community). Moreover, while some branches of farming, such as wheat and cattle, might gain, others might lose. The producers of fruit and vegetables would certainly suffer from Italian and Dutch competition, and others, such as egg and milk producers, might suffer from lower prices and a higher cost of feeding stuffs.

Considerable adjustments might thus be necessary in British

farming. But, in the aggregate, it is not obvious that farmers would suffer. Taking a longer view, they would have a formidable ally, in seeking a fair deal for agriculture, in the farming community on the Continent – a powerful political force that constitutes a far higher proportion of the population than it does in Britain. It is true that the efficiency of Continental farmers may grow rapidly, but this seems as likely to be reflected in a rise in their incomes as in a fall in agricultural prices.

The problems of British agriculture and of food prices do not thus appear to be too serious, although some concessions by the Six will no doubt be necessary to secure political acceptance in Britain of the agricultural aspects of the EEC.

THE COMMONWEALTH

The problem of the Commonwealth is of a different order. I am not thinking of the effects on British exports, which I have already discussed, but of the effects on the rest of the Commonwealth. It may be that Commonwealth political and economic ties are in any case loosening rapidly, and some would argue that in ten years' time there will be little left of them whether or not we join the Community. But, whether this is true or not, we have definite obligations to peoples who have unhesitatingly come to our aid in two world wars. We have long-standing ties both with our kith and kin in Canada, Australia and New Zealand, and with the poorer members for whose economic development we feel a special responsibility. We must not enter the Community on terms that would suggest that we are joining a "rich man's club".

Many in Britain feel less at home with Europeans than they do with some inhabitants of the Commonwealth, of all races, with whom they share a common language, a common cultural, legal and sporting tradition, and sometimes a common education. The idea of allowing freer immigration from Europe than from the Commonwealth is repugnant to many Britons. Apart from feelings of emotion and a sense of moral obligation, there is a strong belief that our multi-racial Commonwealth still has an important contribution to make to the world. Joining the EEC is bound to be, to some extent at least, a parting of the ways. It may be that the Commonwealth will wish to keep closer to a Britain strengthened by membership of the Community, and with a larger influence on world political developments, than to a Britain standing alone and declining in relative power. But in other ways our special relationship with the Commonwealth seems bound to be weakened, and there is no desire to speed the process by entering the Community on terms that seem unfair to them.

For all these reasons, it will be difficult for Britain to accept membership unless it can be shown that reasonable safeguards have been secured for the interests of Commonwealth countries. Even if it were in our own interest to join without making some special arrangements for them, it is hard to believe that we should in fact do so.

In general economic terms it is argued that a Britain growing faster as a result of membership of the EEC would provide a better market for Commonwealth countries and be better able to assist them through aid and foreign investment; also that, by going in, we can get better terms for their exports to the rapidly expanding Continental market, and more aid and capital for them from the Six. On the other hand, some British investment might be diverted from the Commonwealth to Europe, and we have seen that Britain's economy might be strengthened without joining the Six. Moreover, if we do join, our treatment of imports from the Commonwealth is bound to become less favourable.

The British market is of great importance to many Commonwealth countries. At present, about one quarter of their total exports go the U.K. For some countries, such as New Zealand, Nigeria, Sierra Leone, Mauritius, Fiji and several of the Caribbean territories, the proportion is over one-half and sometimes as much as four-fifths.

The great bulk of Britain's imports from the Commonwealth enter free of duty, and what duties are levied are mostly of a revenue nature; hardly any are protective. Moreover, through the imposition of duties on non-Commonwealth products, nearly half of Britain's imports from the Commonwealth are granted a preference, averaging rather less than 10%, so that the average preference on *all* imports from the Commonwealth is 4–5%.

If Britain entered the Common Market without special arrangements being made, these preferences would disappear, *vis-à-vis* the Community and associated territories, since British imports from these sources would then become duty free. Moreover, they would often be turned into 'negative preferences', since Britain would have to impose the Community's common external tariffs and import levies against the produce of the Commonwealth. These might often be quite high, perhaps some 20–25% on, for example, wheat, meat, butter and cheese.

Even where such a reversal of preference might be rather unimportant in the longer run for the economy of a Commonwealth country taken as a whole, it might seriously affect groups of producers (such as fruit growers in Australia) and lead to internal political difficulties; and even quite a small loss of export earnings would be worrying for the numerous Commonwealth countries that are concerned about their balance of payments.

Troublesome problems would arise, both for the less developed Commonwealth countries, and for Canada, Australia and, particularly, New Zealand. The last three, being situated in temperate zones, export foodstuffs that compete directly with the produce of European farmers. They also export some of the few raw materials on which significant import duties are levied by the Community, such as aluminium, lead, zinc, newsprint, woodpulp; Canada's actual and potential exports of manufactures would also suffer.

The agricultural exports of these countries would be restricted, not only by tariffs, but by import levies and import licensing, the severity of which would vary and could not be predicted. With agricultural production rising rapidly on the Continent, and with France, the Netherlands and Italy anxious to sell actual or potential surpluses to Britain, these Commonwealth countries must naturally be apprehensive. Their exports could fall sharply since they form a much less important proportion of total consumption in the Community, including Britain, than they do of British consumption alone. (Britain's total consumption might also be reduced somewhat through the higher prices that would, as we have seen, be charged to consumers.)

It is not easy to say how these difficulties and dangers might be alleviated. So far as raw materials are concerned, the Six might perhaps agree to admit some duty free under the Common Tariff. For a few commodities, and at least temporarily, Britain might be allowed to admit a certain quota duty free from the Commonwealth. But it seems doubtful whether this would be an acceptable longer term arrangement for the bulk of the temperate zone foodstuffs, since it would be inconsistent with a common level of prices in the EEC, including Britain, and this is an essential aspect of the Community's agricultural policy.

Another possibility would be the granting by the Community of long term contracts to traditional exporters (including, presumably, those outside the Commonwealth), with guaranteed export quotas to each. This could provide some security to Commonwealth producers and give them the benefit of the higher Common Market prices, while allowing a common price policy within the Community, and avoiding the imposition by Britain of import levies against Commonwealth foodstuffs. It is questionable, however, whether such measures could satisfy the desire of these countries for steadily *rising* exports to Britain.

The Commonwealth countries in the tropical and sub-tropical regions — which are also the poorer members — are in a rather different situation. They would lose what preferences they have in Britain, but a wide range of their raw material exports would continue to enter duty free, since the Common Market tariff is zero. On some tropical foodstuffs and beverages, though the Six are not competitors, there are duties designed primarily for revenue. Britain would have to ensure that these were not excessive. If no special arrangements were made, Commonwealth exports of certain tropical foodstuffs, such as cocoa, coffee, oils, fats and fruit, would be at a disadvantage compared with those of the associated territories of the EEC (mainly former French Colonies), since the latter are to be granted entry into the Community free of protective duties. This problem could be overcome if British Colonies and ex-Colonies were granted similar status. Some of these, however, seem at present reluctant to accept this status, for political reasons, despite the commercial benefits and the additional advantage it would bring of access to financial and technical assistance from the Six. It is doubtful, moreover, whether the status would be appropriate to older Commonwealth members such as India, Pakistan, and Ceylon.

Perhaps the best way in which Britain could help the poorer members of the Commonwealth, and prevent them losing from our entry into the Common Market, is by pressing on the Six (and on other advanced countries) the need for the most liberal possible treatment of imports from the under-developed countries generally. 'Trade *and* aid' is now necessary if 'trade *not* aid' is ever to become a reality; and the diversion of purchases by mature nations away from developing countries and towards other mature nations is against the general trend of thinking on world economic problems.

Liberal treatment should be given, not only to foodstuffs and raw materials, but also to manufactures. These are already of importance in the exports of India and Hong Kong in particular. I am convinced that, in the case of India at least, they can become rapidly more important, and cover a much wider range than the traditional cotton and jute textiles; and that this *must* happen if India is to balance her international accounts and become independent of foreign aid within a reasonable time. I also believe that the same developments will ultimately be necessary in the trade of many other under-developed countries.

The problem of safeguarding the interests of the Commonwealth is a highly complex one. It bristles with difficulties. But it is to be hoped that the Six will recognise the value of keeping the

Commonwealth together, and approach the negotiations with this as one of the objectives. Unless there is a good deal of give and take on this matter, and in view of the other economic and political problems discussed earlier, it will not be easy for Britain to join the Community.

Part Two: Domestic Economic Policy

9 Inflation in the United Kingdom[1]

I

Most Australians, though not all, seem to have a robust attitude towards inflation — an attitude with which I have some sympathy. They think it does not matter too much provided it is not too rapid. Growth, full employment and high output are more important than price stability. There are, however, other countries, including some important customers of Australia, where people appear to think differently. Whether they are right or wrong I have no time to discuss, but it is a sociological fact that has to be reckoned with.

One of these countries is, I think, the United Kingdom, where I believe that both major political parties take inflation seriously. A couple of years ago the British Government decided to take drastic action to stop it and so did several other governments at about the same time. They largely succeeded — at least for the time being — but only at the expense of considerable loss of employment, output and growth; and the resulting stagnation had a good deal to do with the fall in world commodity prices which Australians know all about.

Recovery is now well under way in the industrial nations, but the 64,000 dollar question is whether this will bring on a renewed threat of inflation which leads governments once more to clamp down on demand, thereby nipping recovery in the bud while there are still plenty of unused resources. This seems to be an important question both for the countries directly concerned and for other countries, including Australia.

There are really two questions. First, will it prove possible in future to have full employment without inflation? Some might answer 'yes' on the grounds that inflation since the war has been caused, not by full but by overfull employment, and by certain special factors, which it is hoped will not recur, arising out of the second world war and the Korean war. The second question is

[1] *The Economic Record*, December, 1959. This is a lecture given in Australia in September and October, 1959. References have been kept to a minimum.

whether, if this proves over-optimistic (as I personally fear it will), a way can nevertheless be found of reconciling full employment with price stability through some changes in our economic and political organization, for example in the field of wage negotiations.

There was a good deal of heated controversy in Britain in 1957 and 1958 about the rather drastic measures taken by the Government to restrict demand. This controversy reflected in part different social and political attitudes on the relative importance of price stability on the one hand and of high employment, output and growth on the other. But it also reflected different views on economic relationships: on for example how sensitive prices are, in a country like Britain, to demand and to deflationary policies, and on the related but distinct question of how much if any sacrifice of employment, output and growth is necessary to stop inflation.

The controversy was so heated partly because surprisingly little careful work had been done on these matters so that protagonists on both sides were able to throw rather dubious statistics and arguments into the ring. In the last few years, however, more careful work has been done, and a good deal more has been started, so that in a few years time I am hopeful that we may know much more about the economic relationships involved — and not only because of the research now in progress but also because the events of the next few years seem likely to be revealing.

I propose in this talk to say something about the work that has been done and the controveries we have been having — of necessity in a highly simplified form because my time is so limited. I do not know whether any of this will be directly relevant to Australian problems but I hope that some of it may be. So far most of the work that has yielded interesting results has been based on statistics — of prices, wages, unemployment and so on — for Britain as a whole. Some work has also been done, and more started, on case studies of particular industries and firms, and on the institutional background of wage negotiations, price fixing, etc., but so far these studies have not, I believe, yielded very useful general results.

II

The Figures show some of the basic information used. Fig. 1 merely shows the well known history of retail prices in Britain since 1914, including the continuous, quarter-of-a-century rise since the mid-1930's that has got people so worried.

Fig. 2 shows in more detail the rise in retail prices since the second world war and also the course of wage rates and import prices. A study of the diagram shows that the *pace* of inflation has varied — it

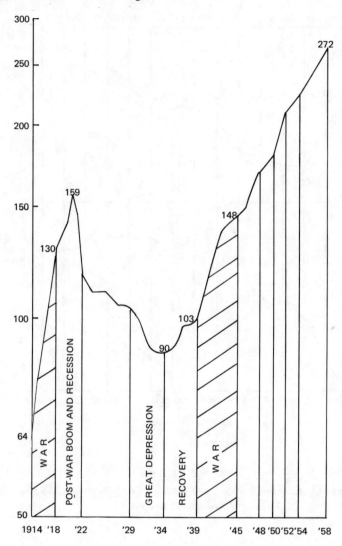

FIGURE 1
Index of U.K. Retail Prices, 1914–1958
1938 = 100 (Semi-logarithmic scale)

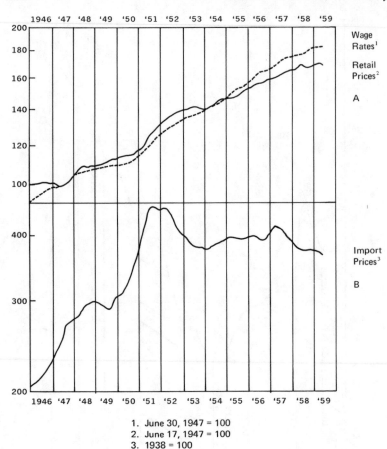

1. June 30, 1947 = 100
2. June 17, 1947 = 100
3. 1938 = 100

FIGURE 2

Indices of U.K. retail prices, wage rates and import prices, 1946–1959
(Semi-logarithmic scale)

has gone in waves – and these variations form the basis of a good many of the statistical inquiries.

1. Until the summer of 1947 (I shall refer throughout to Northern Hemisphere seasons) the curve of retail prices suggests virtual stability. I have, however, used the official index which was 'phoney'; the true cost of living rose significantly.

2. There was then a sharp rise until the spring of 1948. This was partly because the government introduced a more accurate index but mainly because it placed a ceiling on food subsidies and stopped stabilizing the index. The rapid rise in import prices during 1947 — the result of world shortages and the abandonment of controls in the U.S. — was thus bound, after a time, to work its way through to the cost of living.

3. There followed a couple of years or so of comparative stability in retail prices. This was the period of Sir Stafford Cripps' 'wage freeze' which was helped by the relative stability of import prices in 1948 and 1949, the result in part of a recession in the U.S.

4. The 'wage freeze' broke down in the autumn of 1950. Wages went up sharply and there was a rapid rise in retail prices again, the whole process being stimulated by the jump in import prices resulting from recovery in the U.S., the devaluation of sterling and, later, the Korean war.

5. This sharp inflation gave way once more to a period of more gently rising retail prices which lasted until the spring of 1954. Two important reasons were the fall in import prices after the Korean boom broke, and the recession and rising unemployment in Britain in 1952 which weakened the bargaining power of the trade unions and slowed down the rise in wages. This period is rather uncomfortably like the period of comparative price stability we have had during the last year or so especially as it was followed by a renewed rise in retail prices.

6. This rise, which began in 1954, lasted for several years. Not much blame can be attached to import prices which did not rise very fast. Rather must we look for an explanation to the rapid rise in wages.

7. Finally, during the last year or so, retail prices have once more been comparatively stable, aided by a fall in import prices and by the recession of 1958, which raised unemployment to the highest level since the fuel crisis of 1947[2] and once more reduced the bargaining power of the unions.

Fig. 3 shows more clearly the variations in the pace of inflation. Part A shows, for each quarter of the year, the percentage increase in retail prices over the same quarter a year earlier. The rest of the diagram shows some possible explanatory variables. Parts B and C show the rates of change of import prices and of wage rates. Part D

---

[2] In Part D of Fig. 3 the figure for unemployment in the first quarter of 1947 has been adjusted for the fuel crisis; the actual level of unemployment was much higher.

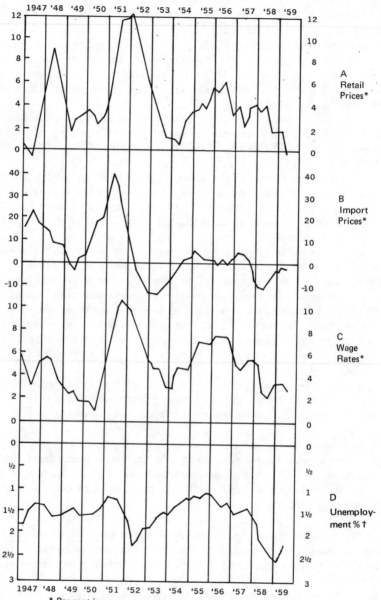

* Per cent increase over same quarter in previous year
† Inverted scale, seasonally adjusted

FIGURE 3

shows the movements in the unemployment percentage;[3] the scale is inverted so that the line can serve as a rough indicator of the demand for labour. The scale used for import prices is one-fifth that used for retail prices. This is partly because the fluctuations are so great that they would otherwise have filled the page and partly because a reduction of the scale in this way gives a very rough indication of the direct contribution of changes in import prices to changes in the cost of living.

III

One of the first things one notices is the importance of import prices. In the very unscientific account just given of the varying pace of inflation I brought in import prices as a partial explanation of most phases. Now it can be seen, by comparing parts A and B of Fig. 3, that the rates of change of import prices and of retail prices have moved fairly closely together, with changes in retail prices usually lagging some nine to twelve months behind changes in import prices. (This is rather what one would expect, at least if final prices are based on the historical, rather than on the replacement cost of imported materials and foodstuffs — which they probably are.)

It is, therefore, perhaps not surprising that Mr. Christopher Dow, in a celebrated article published some three years ago,[4] presented a plausible model of post-war inflation in Britain in which import prices were the primary independent factor. Wages were also in the model but they were largely passive, their rate of increase being mainly determined by previous increases in the cost of living (and not much influenced by the demand for labour). Mr. Dow's model, if I may simplify it greatly, was somewhat as follows. Suppose there is an increase in import prices. This directly raises costs of production which leads businesses to raise the prices of finished goods, such prices being largely determined by the addition of a fairly constant mark-up to costs. The resultant increase in the cost of living leads to a rise in wages; and so on.

This model suggested, among other things, that inflation in Britain was largely an imported phenomenon so that, if import prices stopped rising, there was a good chance that inflation would also, after a time, come to an end. It also suggested that, since the rate of increase of wages, and profit margins, were not very sensitive to

[3] These seasonally adjusted figures are taken from Dow and Dicks-Mireaux, 'Excess Demand for Labour', *Oxford Economic Papers*, February 1958, and the *National Institute Economic Review*.

[4] 'Analysis of the Generation of Price Inflation: A Study of Cost and Price Changes in the U.K., 1946–54', *Oxford Economic Papers*, October 1956.

demand, there was little point in restrictive measures to reduce demand as a means of fighting inflation.

Dow's model seemed a plausible explanation of inflation up to 1954, where it stopped. But as time went on it became doubtful whether it would really do; for, although import prices remained fairly stable, the cost of living continued to go up, at least until rather recently. People began to ask whether the main cause of inflation was not now the very rapid rise in wages and whether this was not in turn caused by the high demand for labour — whether wages were not in fact rather sensitive to demand after all.

A comparison of parts C and D of Fig. 3 suggests that they may be because the rate of increase of wages does seem to vary, to some extent at least, with the demand for labour, after a certain time lag. One trouble is that the rate of increase of wages (C in Fig. 3) also varies with the rate of increase of the cost of living (A), which Dow had thought to be the main determining factor. It is therefore difficult to disentangle the relative effects of the demand for labour and of previous changes in the cost of living on the rate of increase of wages.

However, Mr. Dow, this time in collaboration with Mr. Dicks-Mireaux, worked away at this problem at the National Institute of Economic and Social Research in London. After much careful and ingenious analysis they thought they could disentangle cause and effect and presented their results to the Royal Statistical Society just before Christmas 1958.[5] They concluded that the demand for labour[6] does, after all, have an important influence on the rate of increase of wages. They still believe that previous changes in the cost of living are of considerable importance, but they are no longer all-important, as in Dow's previous analysis. They also introduced a third possible determinant of wage increases, but this is a joker which I shall keep up my sleeve for the moment.

Round about the same time, Professors Paish and Phillips, of the London School of Economics, reached rather similar conclusions.[7] Professor Paish gave no very elaborate statistical analysis but Professor Phillips analysed the experience of the last hundred years and concluded that the rate of increase of wages depended almost wholly on the demand for labour and that the cost of living was

[5] L. A. Dicks-Mireaux and J. C. R. Dow, 'The Determinants of Wage Inflation', to be published in the *Journal of the Royal Statistical Society*.
[6] Their index of the demand for labour brought in unfilled vacancies as well as unemployment but this does not significantly affect the argument.
[7] F. W. Paish, 'Inflation in the United Kingdom, 1948–57', *Economica*, May 1958. A. W. Phillips, 'The Relation between Unemployment and the Rate of Change of Money Wages in the United Kingdom, 1861–1957', *Economica*, November 1958.

important only on rare occasions when there was a particularly sharp jump in import prices. Mr. Klein, working with others in the Institute of Statistics at Oxford, has also found that wages are rather sensitive to the demand for labour (as well as to price changes).[8]

Moreover, the results both of Phillips and of Dow and Dicks-Mireaux seemed to imply that only rather a moderate amount of unemployment, 2½% or less, was necessary to stop wages rising faster than productivity seems likely to rise, thus causing inflation.[9]

All this seems, at first sight, to justify those who supported the restrictive measures of 1957. It appears to suggest that deflationary fiscal and monetary policies are a potent weapon for fighting inflation, because wages are quite sensitive to demand, at least when unemployment is low; that such policies can stop inflation without very much sacrifice of employment (at least if import prices are fairly stable); and that any wages policy, or attempt to change the attitude of the trade unions, is therefore unnecessary, and moreover rather pointless because the rate of increase of wages seems to be determined to a large extent by the level of unemployment as though by an iron law that the unions cannot do much about.

IV

If, however, one considers the matter rather more carefully, these preliminary conclusions seem open to considerable doubt.

1. First, it is hard to be entirely convinced by the statistical calculations. All the variables seem, at first sight at least, to be correlated with all the others so that it is difficult to disentangle the relative importance of the various factors. The introduction of different variables can yield substantially different results; a comparison of the two models on which Dow worked provides an example.[10] Then again Phillips' analysis of the last hundred years used unemployment figures for various periods that are not comparable; if they had been adjusted the results might have been different. Finally, wages never have gone up as slowly as productivity for any prolonged period since the war, apart from the Cripps 'wage freeze', so that any conclusion that this will happen if unemployment is at a particular level is largely a theoretical extrapolation.

[8] L. R. Klein, R. J. Ball and A. Hazlewood, in 'Econometric Forecasts for 1959', *Bulletin of the Oxford Institute of Statistics*, February 1959, give a summary of the work, which is a general econometric study of the United Kingdom. The full results have not yet been published.
[9] Dow and Dicks-Mireaux did, however, warn against extrapolation, arguing that the relation between unemployment and the rate of increase of wages was almost certainly non-linear.
[10] The first model was, however, not supported by correlation analysis.

2. A second reason for doubt is the joker of Dow and Dicks-Mireaux, their third possible determinant of the rate of wage increase (in addition to the demand for labour and previous changes in the cost of living). This is what they called trade union 'pushfulness'. They distinguished five degrees of pushfulness, ranging from 'marked restraint' to 'marked pushfulness', and gave these values. They then decided (largely subjectively of course) what the degree of pushfulness had been at various times since the war. When they put pushfulness into their equations as a third explanatory variable they got just as good an explanation of wage increases since 1951 as before; and the idea of varying pushfulness was *essential* to explain the earlier period, which included the Cripps 'wage freeze'. Phillips, too, really needs something like 'pushfulness', or rather the absence of it, to explain this period; and Klein's model contains a 'political' factor, which is rather similar.

It seems then that the statistical facts are at least consistent with the attitude or mood of the trade unions having been important. Indeed Dow and Dicks-Mireaux found that the effect of varying trade union pushfulness was very important. For example, a change from 'marked pushfulness' to 'marked restraint' could make a difference of nearly five per cent per annum in the rate of wage increase. In other words, if wages were going up by say 7 per cent a year at a time when the unions were 'markedly pushful' and they could somehow be persuaded to be 'markedly restrained', then the annual rate of increase of wages would be reduced to little more than 2 per cent, without the level of employment having to be reduced at all.

3. A third reason for doubting the preliminary conclusions mentioned above is that even if the rate of increase of *wages* is sensitive to the demand for labour, it does not follow that the *prices of goods* are anything like so sensitive. When demand is reduced this usually reduces productivity, and the rate of growth of productivity, which may partly or wholly offset any reduction in the rate of increase of wages so that *labour costs per unit of output* may be little, if at all, affected, at least for a time; and it is labour costs that will largely determine prices, except in so far as deflation may lead to some squeezing of profit margins.

In fact, if one compares the period of expansion between 1952 and 1955, when output was rising rapidly, with the following three years of stagnation (1956—58), when output hardly rose at all, it appears that labour costs per unit of output actually rose faster in the second period taken as a whole, the slower rise in wages being more than offset by the slower rise in productivity. Nor was there any significant reduction in average profit margins.[11] More recently, however, there has been a notable change. Over the past year or so labour costs per unit of output have levelled off, and even begun to fall as economic recovery has accelerated the pace of productivity increase while wage rates have remained fairly stable.

4. A fourth reason for doubt is as follows. Even if prices were fairly sensitive to changes in the level of *unemployment* so that, for example, an increase in unemployment from 1½% to 2½% would stop inflation, this would be likely to involve a much bigger proportionate drop in output. This is because deflationary policies, as has just been mentioned, usually reduce productivity, and because they usually lower employment more than they raise unemployment; older people and married women in particular tend to leave the labour force. Judging by what happened in Britain in 1958 this might mean that if, say, 2½% unemployment were required to stop price rising, there would be a loss of anything up to 10 per cent of potential national output, at least for a time; and that is a lot.

For all these reasons I am not convinced that, in future, price stability will prove compatible with full employment, high output and rapid growth — at least if we keep our present methods of wage bargaining. Nor am I convinced that the pace of inflation is so sensitive to demand as recent empirical studies might suggest at first glance.

V

Very few, however, would deny that there is some sensitivity, and it is now therefore necessary to discuss the *manner* in which the level of demand affects the rate of increase of wages and prices. There has been a good deal of controversy on this too, and it also is important for policy.

First, there is the possibility that the prices of goods and services are directly affected by demand. This idea of 'too much money chasing too few goods' and directly pulling up prices has now, however, become rather outmoded. Most people, on all sides of the controversy, now take the view that prices charged by British manufacturers and shopkeepers are rather sticky and that they are usually raised only when costs go up. There is need for further empirical study here and it may tend to rehabilitate the old theory a little. But the fashionable view nowadays — rightly or wrongly, and I think probably rightly — is certainly that variations in the demand for goods and services affect the prices of goods *indirectly* by

---

[11] *National Institute Economic Review*, No. 3, May 1959, p. 21.

affecting the demand for labour and so wages, which in turn leads businesses to change the prices of their goods because their costs have changed, at least if the change is in an upward direction. (The apparent reluctance of many firms to reduce prices when costs fall may prove a stumbling block in any attempt to stop inflation because a stable general price level must involve falling prices in industries where productivity is growing particularly fast to offset rising prices in industries were it is growing more slowly than the average.)

The question remains of how the demand for *labour* affects the rate of increase of *wages*. Here there are divergent views. Let me give you two extreme ones.

The first extreme view is that, when the demand for labour is high in relation to supply, individual employers have to offer higher rewards to get, or even to keep, the labour they need. They do this by payments above negotiated rates, by inventing special bonuses, by unjustified upgrading, and so on. Then, when the nationally agreed rates are increased at the next negotiations between trade unions and employers' organizations, this simply recognizes a *fait accompli*. According to this view, the unions have no effect at all. They are merely engaged in shadow-boxing.

The other extreme view is that, when the demand for labour is high, individual employers do not bid up earnings much. What happens is that, when the next negotiations come round, the increase in rates will be high because the bargaining power of the unions is strong and the resistance of the employers weak.

The difference between these two views may not seem very important for policy but in fact it is. For if the first extreme view is correct, if the unions are merely engaged in shadow-boxing, then there is no point in urging them to be restrained or in trying to make a deal with them. Any restraint on their part would be frustrated by employers bidding up earnings. The only way, according to this view, to reduce the rate of increase of wages is to damp down demand; and if stopping inflation in this manner means less than full employment, that is just too bad.

If, on the other hand, the second extreme view is correct, that trade unions matter, then there may still be some point in cutting demand to reduce the rate of wage increase. But there may also be considerable point in trying to persuade the trade unions to be more moderate (provided, of course, that wage increases are not wholly determined by the demand for labour — and I have suggested that they are not). For if an appeal to the unions is successful it may be necessary to cut demand less, or perhaps not at all, in order to stop inflation; and this may be a considerable gain in terms of output and employment.

What then is the truth as between these two extremes? Unfortunately, there have so far been few case studies of individual firms and negotiations, certainly too few to allow generalizations to be made. Most of the discussion has related to the so-called 'earnings drift' in industry as a whole.

It is well known that actual weekly earnings are normally far above nationally agreed rates for various occupations and grades — perhaps one-third higher on average. The more interesting fact, however, is that earnings for a long time went up faster than rates — about 1% a year faster on average — and this is what is known as 'earnings drift'. It is illustrated in Fig. 4.[1 2] Part A shows an index of weekly earnings drawing away fairly steadily from an index of weekly wage rates. Part B shows the earnings index as a percentage of the rates index. It is, in fact, an index of earnings drift.

It is sometimes argued that this drift shows that individual employers have been bidding up earnings, with trade union negotiations tagging along behind. But in fact the phenomenon might easily be explicable in other ways, for example by a rising proportion of skilled workers or by increasing earnings on piece rates.

There is, however, a more formidable argument based on the fact that the *pace* of earnings drift has varied from time to time. This can be seen with some difficulty in part B of Fig. 4 and more clearly in part C which shows the percentage change in B over the preceding 12 months or, in other words, the rate of earnings drift per annum. Some of the supporters of the first extreme view have pointed out that the rate of earnings drift has varied with the demand for labour, at least since 1952. (This can be seen by comparing parts C and F[1 3] of Fig. 4). They have gone on to claim that this shows how employers have bid up earnings when demand was high and not when it was low.

Their argument is not, however, very convincing. First, the correlation is not apparent before 1952. Secondly, a great deal of the variation in the pace of earnings drift has nothing at all to do with employers bidding up earnings but is simply due to variations in overtime and short-time. When demand rises, more overtime and less short-time are worked, so that weekly earnings naturally rise faster

[1 2] This Figure is based mainly on estimates given in the *National Institute Economic Review* and in articles by Messrs. Penrice, Dicks-Mireaux and Dow (*London and Cambridge Economic Bulletin*, December 1955 and September 1958, *Oxford Economic Papers*, February 1958).

[1 3] Part F is the same as Part D of Fig. 3 except that it covers a rather shorter period.

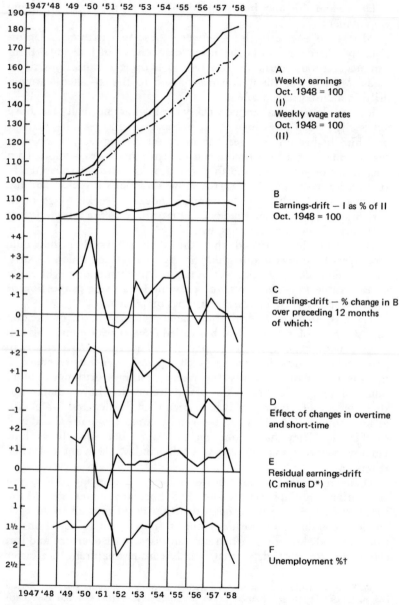

FIGURE 4
Earnings-drift

*Also allowing for changes in age, sex and industrial pattern of labour force.
†Seasonally adjusted. Inverted scale.

than rates for a normal week, both because more hours are worked and because overtime attracts higher pay per hour.[14] Part D of Fig. 4 shows the estimated effect of changes in overtime and short-time on the pace of earnings drift (C). It will be seen that it explains a large part of the variations in C. Part E shows the 'residual earnings drift' after allowing for changes in overtime and short-time (and for certain other factors that have been of minor importance). It is not correlated at all with the demand for labour (F).

Even if it were, this would not necessarily show that employers were bidding up earnings when demand was high. It might simply mean that higher demand led to higher output per man-hour (because, for example, there was less hanging around in factories waiting for work to come through) and that this brought higher earnings per hour for workers paid by results.

For all these reasons the study of earnings drift does not get us very far. It certainly does not prove that higher demand for labour leads to a higher rate of wage increase *merely* because employers are bidding up earnings. This may be of some importance when demand is high. But even if it had been the main cause of rising wages since the war (which I very much doubt) it would not follow that if, in future, demand were reduced enough to stop it, trade union pressure would not then become the main factor and push up wages faster than productivity, thus causing inflation. The evidence on earnings drift is certainly still consistent with trade union pressure at negotiations being the important thing, even when demand is high. This pressure, as we saw, depends on the demand for labour to some extent, but it is also partly independent of it and related to, among other things, cost of living increases since the last negotiations and the mood of the trade unions. This mood in turn depends on such things as government economic policy generally and the size of the annual increase in money wages that has come to be regarded as reasonable for trade union leaders to obtain for their members.

This is all relevant, incidentally, to a problem we have had on several occasions in Britain since the war: whether an increase in indirect taxes, or a cut in food subsidies, would help to restrain wage increases. If one takes the view that the level of demand is all-important then the deflationary effects of such changes would certainly help. If, on the other hand, one believes that trade union pressure may be greatly influenced by the cost of living and by the general tenor of government policy, the net effect might be to

---

[14] Some of the increase in overtime may admittedly, however, be unnecessary and merely a concealed form of 'bidding up' by employers.

accelerate, rather than to decelerate, the rate of increase of wages. (I have several times in the past taken the view that, when a round of wage negotiations was in the offing, the deflationary effect of cutting subsidies or increasing indirect taxes might be swamped by the 'pinprick' effect on trade union attitudes.)

VI

In the light of the evidence from the past, what conclusions can be drawn about the future? The first is that, while inflation in the United Kingdom was to some extent — perhaps to a large extent — imported through rising world prices in the earlier postwar period, this can hardly be an explanation of inflation in the later years. There is, therefore, no guarantee that, even if import prices are fairly stable in the future, inflation can necessarily be avoided, although stable import prices would certainly help considerably.

Secondly, if inflation threatens again we certainly can stop it by restricting demand sufficiently, through fiscal and monetary policy. For, though wages and prices may be much less sensitive to demand than has sometimes been argued, they are certainly not wholly insensitive. If, however, we rely entirely on such measures, this may be pretty expensive in terms of employment, output and growth; for there is no guarantee at all that the level of demand that gives full employment and all the other good things will also stop prices rising.

It follows, in the third place, that action to influence the attitude of the trade unions may be an indispensable part of any policy that attempts to achieve price stability without sacrificing employment, output and growth. Such action is certainly not pointless, as some have tended to argue on the grounds that the rate of increase of wages is almost wholly dependent on the demand for labour, as through an iron law, or on the grounds that it depends largely on employers bidding up earnings with trade unions merely engaged in shadow-boxing.

The fundamental problem is how to reduce the level of unemployment required to stop prices rising. So far I may have seemed to imply that the only way is to change the attitude of the trade unions, so that they are prepared to accept an increase in wages no greater than the increase in national productivity when unemployment is, say 1–1½%, instead of having to increase unemployment to, say, 3–4% in order to curb their bargaining power sufficiently. There are, however, at least two other possible ways which I shall say a word about before considering how trade union attitudes might be changed.

First, it would probably help if we could make productivity grow faster, because wages might not grow correspondingly faster. If we could raise the rate of productivity increase, we could bring it up towards the rate of increase of money wages that trade unionists have come to expect instead of having to reduce this rate to the present rate of productivity growth. Now we might be able to accelerate the growth of productivity to some extent by a better distribution of our present volume of investment (including under investment such things as expenditure on education and research). But any major acceleration would probably involve saving and investing a higher fraction of the national income, and whether this should be done is an important question that should, I think, be decided largely independently of the fight against inflation. If we can get productivity to grow faster, any resulting help on the inflation front should be regarded as no more than a welcome by-product.

Secondly, measures to reduce frictional and structural unemployment would lower the critical level of total unemployment at which labour shortages become serious and lead to rapid increases in wages. Such measures would include, for example, the steering of demand to depressed areas where there are pockets of heavy unemployment and anything that would improve the mobility of labour (between regions, industries and occupations), such as retraining grants, help with moving expenses and so on. A good deal has, however, already been done in these fields and I doubt whether a great deal more can be hoped for from measures of this sort.

VII

We come then to measures to change the attitude of the trade unions. I should like to distinguish three general types of policy which appear possible. I shall call them:

(a) 'shock tactics';
(b) 'showdown with the unions', or 'calling their bluff';
(c) agreement with the unions to exercise restraint.

These might be regarded as alternative policies or combined in various ways.

(a) By shock tactics I mean temporary but sharp measures to reduce demand, such as were adopted two years ago, in the hope that this will reduce the size of the annual money wage increase that workers have come to expect. Such tactics, however, as we know to our cost, mean a substantial loss of employment, output and growth. Of course, if the shock we have had proves to have reduced the expected annual wage increase from the 6—8% that seemed to have become normal to only, say, 2½%, even when employment is really full, then it will have done the trick. But, in the light of all I have said, I am not very hopeful.

(b) The second policy of a 'showdown with the unions' might also take the form of shock tactics but it could be pursued continuously. It would consist of firmer action by the government in negotiations with its own employees, government pressure on local authorities and nationalized industries to be firmer in their negotiations, and government encouragement of private industry to be firmer. It is often claimed that, in the past, the government has been much too weak in all these respects; for example that in the engineering dispute of 1957 it first encouraged employers to be firm, then panicked and completely let them down.

It is argued that, even if firmer action led to strikes, the loss of output would be only temporary and far less than the continuous loss involved in keeping down the bargaining power of the trade unions by depressing demand. This might mean keeping unemployment continuously several per cent higher than it need be. By contrast, in no year since the war has the direct loss of working days through strikes been more than a tiny fraction of one per cent of the total. One must also, of course, allow for the indirect losses resulting from strikes and for the possibility of much more serious ones if a tougher policy were followed. But against this it is claimed that the strike funds of the unions are low (their total funds probably average only £10 a head or less, though the finances of some unions are, of course, much stronger) so that their power to stage really serious and prolonged strikes may have been exaggerated. Whatever the merits of such a policy if pursued within limits it is, however, clear that, if carried to extremes, it would at best hardly provide a happy solution. After all, strikes are unpleasant things and industrial peace is an end in itself.

(c) Finally then there is the possibility of agreement with the trade unions to exercise restraint. I have left little time to discuss this partly because I thought it more interesting and useful to try to establish the need for it and partly because discussion of this problem in Britain is at a very early stage. The Cohen Council on Prices, Productivity and Incomes has, however, thrown some ideas into the ring in its latest report (the third).

Agreement could take various forms. A least ambitious first aim would be simply to persuade trade union leaders to give their general support to restraint in wage negotiations; this might not be so pointless as it may sound. It might perhaps be possible to go further and to persuade the union leaders to agree, after discussions with employers' organizations and the government, to state publicly some figure, such as 2½% per annum, as a reasonable average wage increase, either for the current year or over a period of years. I understand that something on these lines is done in Sweden. One obvious danger is, of course, that any average figure would come to be regarded as a minimum for each industry, but ways might be found of overcoming this difficulty.

We might, I suppose, conceivably go further and have a more closely regulated system. Anything approaching the Australian system would, of course, be alien to the traditions that have developed in the United Kingdom. But I think that more and more people are at least coming to realize that absolute freedom of collective bargaining is not an indispensable feature of democracy, and that it is really a matter of degree because already the existence of trade unions and of collective bargaining themselves limit the freedom of the individual and of smaller groups than are covered by the main negotiations.

It is often argued in Britain that, in countries that have had some kind of wages policy, this has not stopped them having inflation at more or less the same rate as elsewhere, at least over a fairly long period. But I think that such countries have on several occasions been able to stop, or slow down, the rate of increase of wages for a time, when this was important and useful and when drastic deflation would have been a much more costly method. We did this ourselves in Britain during the 'wage freeze' of 1948–50. I hope, too, that I may have convinced you that changes in the attitude of the unions would be useful, and any of the possibilities I have mentioned would involve a change in their attitude.

How to persuade the trade union leaders to change their attitudes is, of course, a political problem. One possible method that I have heard suggested is somewhat as follows. The government would say in effect to the trade unions: 'We are determined to prevent inflation. If you exercise restraint on the wages front, we shall be able to do this while preserving a high level of employment. If, on the other hand, you insist on being aggressive, we shall have to cut down demand to whatever level is necessary to curb your bargaining power sufficiently. Therefore, it is up to you.' One trouble with this approach is that it contains an important element of bluff. For I do not believe that any government is going to give absolute priority to price stability. If it does, and this involves heavy unemployment, it may not remain in office.

There might well then have to be some *quid pro quo*. The government might, for example, have to give an undertaking that the cost of living would not rise by more than a certain amount (or that, if it did, wage restraint would lapse) in order to convince the trade unions that restraint on their part would not lead to a fall in real wages. For the government to give such an undertaking it would have to be fairly confident that wage restraint would itself largely stop inflation or be prepared to control prices or to stabilize the cost of living by changes in subsidies and indirect taxes.

The trade unions might, however, want more. In return for wage restraint they might demand some form of restraint of dividends (as during the Cripps 'wage freeze'), or of profits, or perhaps a capital gains tax. Apart from questions of social justice and fairness they might well point out that, as we have seen, it will be impossible to achieve a stable general price level if firms whose costs are falling fail to reduce their prices.

Even if the trade union leaders were prepared to co-operate there would remain the very great problem of convincing, and securing the co-operation of, the rank and file; individual unions, acting by themselves, have nothing to gain from restraint, and there will always be some who regard their wages as unreasonably low in relation to those of others. In general, any kind of 'wages policy' for Britain simply bristles with economic, political and administrative difficulties which I have no time to discuss. Despite this, however, I am not entirely unhopeful that we shall in time be able to do something. If we cannot, I fear that we may have to put up with either some inflation, or less than full employment and less growth than we are capable of, or perhaps a bit of both.

10 The distribution of income in Venezuela[1]

INTRODUCTION
In studying the tax structure of any country it is essential to form some idea, in quantitative terms, of the distribution of income. So far as we are aware no comprehensive study of this problem has been made in Venezuela. We have therefore had to make for ourselves the best estimates we could in the time available and with the limited material at our disposal.

We have relied mainly on material collected by the Banco Central in connection with its estimates of national income and expenditure; on the results of various sample surveys carried out by 'Datos', a market research organization, in the course of which certain information on incomes was obtained; on statistics of the Ministerio de Hacienda arising out of the collection of income tax; on the results of the National Agricultural Inquiry (Encuesta Agropecuaria Nacional) of 1956, carried out by the Ministerio de Agricultura y Cría with the assistance of a technical staff provided by the Food and Agriculture Organization; on details of payrolls in a number of establishments shown to us by the Ministerio del Trabajo; on the results of an inquiry into the conditions of 'The Venezuelan Peasant Farmer' recently carried out by Dr. George W. Hill and some of his students in the Central University, Caracas;[2] and on conversations with numerous people in various parts of the country.

While our estimates are inevitably subject to a margin of error it is reassuring that, when the problem is approached from various angles, and independent sources are used, the same general picture emerges.

The income of Venezuela is unevenly distributed — between town and countryside, between regions of the country, between sectors of the economy, and between the individual members of the population — to an extent that inevitably impresses a visitor from the United States or the United Kingdom.

[1] Chapter 1 of *The Fiscal System of Venezuela*, by Carl Shoup, John Due, Lyle Fitch, Donald MacDougall, Oliver Oldman and Stanley Surrey.
[2] Some preliminary findings were presented to the 8th Annual Convention of the Venezuelan Association for the Advancement of Science at Caracas, 28 May 1958.

A. TOWN AND COUNTRY

Income is heavily concentrated in Caracas and, to a lesser extent, in the other larger towns. In general, the larger the town the larger the average income tends to be; and it is lowest of all in the rural areas. According to our estimates, presented in Table I.1, the average income in Caracas per income earner (not *per capita*) is Bs. 14,000–15,000 a year. In other towns of more than 20,000 it probably approaches Bs.9,000. And so on down the scale until we come to people living outside towns of over 500 inhabitants; they have an estimated average income of only Bs.1,500 a year, one-tenth of that in Caracas.

Table I.1

Estimated Distribution of Private Incomes: Rural and Urban, by Size of Towns, 1957

Population of town or area	Number of incomes (thousands)	Average income (Bs. per annum)	Total income (Bs. million)	Per cent of number of incomes	Per cent of total income
Over 1,000,000 (Caracas)	350	14,500	5,100	17	40
20,000–1,000,000	470	8,750	4,100	22	32
5,000–20,000	210	6,250	1,300	10	10
500–5,000	280	4,000	1,100	13	9
Under 500 (rural areas)	800	1,500	1,200	38	9
Total	2,110	6,000	12,800	100	100

Sources: Information obtained in the course of constructing Tables I.5 and I.6. The item 'Profits, etc. not reported in survey' in Table I.6 was mainly, but not wholly, attributed to the larger towns.

Looking at the matter in another way we find that Caracas, with only one-sixth of the country's population, has about two-fifths of the income (and this does not, of course, include the Government's income from oil; we are considering only private incomes). Adding in the other larger towns we find that about two-fifths of the population live in the twenty to twenty-five towns of over 20,000 people; yet they have nearly three-quarters of the income. At the other extreme we find nearly two-fifths of the population living in rural areas; yet they have only about one-tenth of the income.

It is true that prices are higher in Caracas, and to a lesser extent in the other larger towns, than they are in the small towns and in the countryside, so that the differences in *real* incomes tend to be less marked than our figures suggest. But, apart from rents, the differences in prices are perhaps not so great as is sometimes thought; many branded goods, for example, have a uniform price throughout the country. Moreover, Government expenditure on such things as roads and schools has probably brought greater benefits to the larger towns than to the rural areas. These greater benefits, which are not reflected in money incomes, may quite possibly offset the higher prices. If so, the figures in our table may, after all, give a fair indication of relative real incomes in towns of various sizes and in the countryside.

B. REGIONAL DIFFERENCES

The size of a town is not, of course, the sole determinant of the average income of its inhabitants. Much depends on the region of the country in which it is situated. Thus, for example, in the group of towns with a population of between 20,000 and 1,000,000, those connected with the petroleum industry — such as Maracaibo, Cabimas-Lagunillas, Punto Fijo — have an average income between two-thirds and four-fifths of that in Caracas,[3] while in those situated in relatively depressed agricultural areas — such as Valera, Mérida, and San Cristóbal in the Andes — the average income is well under half that in Caracas; in Cumaná, in the Sucre fishing region, it is only one-quarter. (This is a depressed region in which, in a large fish-processing factory, the commonest wage is Bs.6 a day for women and B.6—7 for men.)

Similarly, among the smaller towns and in the rural areas there are patches of prosperity: for example, around the oil fields (in small towns such as Valle de la Pascua) or at Calabozo, the site of a large irrigation and flood control scheme where farmers, many with considerable experience, are being settled on specially prepared farms of about 200 hectares.

C. INDUSTRIAL DISTRIBUTION OF INCOME

The level of income generated per head varies greatly from one sector of the economy to another. In particular, there is a marked contrast between the two extremes: agriculture (which is taken to include animal husbandry throughout this chapter) and petroleum. Agriculture, as is shown in Table I-2, may employ over two-fifths of the economically active population but generates only one-tenth of the national income. The petroleum industry employs only 2% of the

---

[3] The figures quoted in this paragraph are based on data provided by 'Datos.'

Table 1.2
Industrial Origin of National Income, 1957

| | | Income generated Bs. | | Active population | |
		thousand million	%	Thousands	%
Agriculture		1.5	10	900	43
Petroleum:					
Remuneration of labor	0.9				
Government taxes and royalties (ex. new concessions)	2.9[1]	3.8	24	46	2
Other private activities[2]		10.4	66	1164	55
Total		15.7[2]	100	2110	100

[1] 4.1 Government income from oil *accruing* during year (this is more than the income received) less 1.2 new concessions. Banco Central.
[2] Excludes Government income from property other than petroleum.
Sources: Table I.3 and notes above.

country's labor force but generates one-quarter of the national income, if we include the taxes and royalties paid to the Government (other than payments for new concessions, which we have excluded as they are of a non-recurrent nature).

These comparisons are less striking if we exclude the oil industry's payments to the Government, as we should do in an analysis of private income. But even then we find incomes in agriculture to be only 12% of the national total and the earnings of oil workers alone to be 7% although they comprise only 2% of the labor force. (In addition, of course, the oil industry has important effects on private incomes in other sectors of the economy. It provides a market for contracting work and supplies generally; the oil workers provide a market for consumer goods; and the large sums turned over to the Government enable it to employ many Venezuelan firms and workers on public works and the like.)

D. A MORE DETAILED ANALYSIS

We shall now look in more detail at the way in which private income is distributed between various classes of the population, using figures calculated by the Banco Central for the purpose of estimating the national income. (*Private* income falls short of the total national income by the amount of Government income from the oil companies and from various forms of Government property.)

The last column of Table I.3 gives estimates of the income of various classes of the community. These correspond to figures given

Table I.3
Analysis of Private Income, 1957
(Round figures are used throughout)

	Number of incomes (thousands)	Average income (Bs.)	Total income (Bs. thousand million)
1. Independent professionals[1][2]	4.5	80,000	0.35
2. Petroleum workers[2]	46	20,000	0.9
3. Industry, commerce, mining, services, construction[2][3]:			
a. Salary earners: Federal Dist.	60 ⎫	16,000	1.0 ⎫
b. Salary earners: Interior	150 ⎬ 850	8,000	1.2 ⎬ 5.1
c. Wage earners: Federal Dist.	180 ⎪	7,000	1.3 ⎪
d. Wage earners: Interior	460 ⎭	3,500	1.6 ⎭
4. Domestic servants[2]:			
a. Federal District	40 ⎫ 165	3,000 ⎫	0.3
b. Interior	125 ⎭	1,250 ⎭	
5. Government service	145[4]	10,000	1.5[2]
6. Agriculture:			
a. Remuneration of labor	750 ⎫	1,100	0.8 ⎫
b. Remuneration of capital and enterprise	150 ⎬ 900[5]	5,000	0.7 ⎬ 1.5[2]
7. Profits in industry, commerce, mining, services & construction	—[6]		2.15[2]
8. Rent & interest not elsewhere included	—	—	1.0[2]
Total	2,110	6,000	12.8[7]

[1] Doctors, dentists, veterinarians and lawyers only. Excludes those employed in Government service, by business concerns, etc.

[2] Source: Banco Central de Venezuela.

[3] Includes employers and workers on their own account, the average remuneration of whose labor (as distinct from their capital and enterprise) is assumed to be equal to that of wage and salary earners. See note 6 to this table.

[4] According to the estimates of the Banco Central, the total remuneration of labor in Government service rose by 43% between 1950 and 1957. During the same period the average rate of wages and salaries in industry, etc., rose by abour 60%; but salaries rose less than wages, and the proportion of salary earners is substantially higher in Government service than it is in industry. It thus seems reasonable to assume that employment in Government service is of the same order as it was in 1950 when, according to the Census, it appears to have been about 145,000.

[5] It is difficult to estimate the numbers engaged in agriculture. We give below two methods that may give high and low limits.

One method is to estimate the total active population and then subtract those accounted for in the non-agricultural sectors. In 1950, according to the Census, the total active population was rather more than 34% of the total population of the country. If the proportion was the same in 1957 and the population at mid-1957 as high as 6.6 million (see footnote 4 to this study), the total active population would be about 2.25 million. Subtracting 1.2 million already accounted for in lines 1–5 of the table (and ignoring unemployment) we are left with about 1,050,000 engaged in agriculture. This may seem high, as it is 50% above the number enumerated in agriculture in the 1950 Census, while agricultural production rose by only about 50% between 1950 and 1957 (Banco Central *Memoria* 1957, p. 102), so that no increase in productivity per worker is allowed for. (The 1950 Census may, however, have understated the numbers in agriculture.)

Another method of calculation is as follows. It is estimated in *Encuesta Agropecuaria Nacional 1956* that there were in 1956 nearly 400,000 units of exploitation in agriculture, of which about 320,000 were of less than ten hectares and nearly 80,000 of more than ten hectares. Assuming six persons to a family this gives a total population of 1,920,000 associated with the smaller units. Assuming that rather more than one-third of these were active (the proportion for the nation as a whole in 1950), we have 650,000 workers whom we may, as a first approximation, assume to be engaged on the family holdings and as workers on the larger farms. Adding 80,000 larger farmers and, say, 70,000 members of their families, and others not from the smaller holdings, working on their farms, we get a total of 800,000 engaged in agriculture. (Alternatively, we might assume rather fewer members of the average family on a small unit at work but rather more laborers on the larger farms and get the same total number.)

We have taken a figure between these two estimates, namely 900,000. In the light of the figures in the previous paragraph, and bearing in mind that they refer to 1956, we assume that the Bs.800 million estimated by the Banco Central as 'remuneration of labor' in agriculture (which is intended to include production of small holdings as well as wages of hired labor) is shared between 750,000 workers, and the Bs.700 million estimated as 'remuneration of capital and enterprise' between the remaining 150,000.

[6] In 1950, according to the Census, there were roughly 30,000 employers and 160,000 workers on their own account in industry, services, etc. Such people have, however, already been included in the first column under item 3. (See Note 3 to this table.)

[7] This is equal to the sum of the remuneration of labor and of capital and enterprise (as given in the Banco Central *Memoria* for 1957, tables 14.6 and 14.7 but brought up to 1957), excluding Government income from petroleum and other Government property, which should not be included in an estimate of private income. The small item 'employers' contributions to Social Security' has been ignored.

in the 1957 *Memoria* of the Banco Central (Tables 14.6 and 14.7), except that they have been further subdivided and brought up to 1957 through the courtesy of the Banco Central, who have provided us with provisional estimates. In the first column there are estimates of the number of incomes in the various classes. Most of these figures too are derived from information provided by the Banco Central with the exception of those for Government service and agriculture, where the method of estimation is explained in the notes below the table.

We have assumed that the active population was about 2,100,000 in 1957 or about one-third of a total population of perhaps 6-1/3 million (approximately the proportion in the Census of 1950). The remaining 4 million or so were dependents: wives, children, old people, etc. There is some uncertainty about the size of the total population of Venezuela but this does not affect the general picture.[4]

[4] The official estimate of total population at mid-1957 is 6,130,000, based on the assumption that the annual percentage rate of growth of the population since 1950 has been the same as that between 1941 and 1950 as shown by the Censuses of those years. On the other hand we have been given figures by the Dirección General de Estadistica of the Ministerio de Fomento which imply a population in the middle of 1957 of about 6.6 million. This is estimated by starting with the 1950 Census figure and allowing for subsequently recorded births, deaths and net immigration. Estimates made by 'Datos' for the end of 1957 imply a figure for mid-1957 between these two extremes of about 6.35 million.

The middle column shows the average annual income of the various classes, the average for the active population as a whole being Bs.6,000. Some groups are well above this figure but some are well below.

INCOMES WELL ABOVE THE AVERAGE

Let us start with those that are well above. First, there are 4,000—5,000 *independent professionals* — doctors, dentists, lawyers and veterinarians only — working on their own account (line 1 of the table) with an estimate average income of about Bs.80,000. The 46,000 *petroleum workers* (line 2) have an average income of Bs.20,000 a year. Some are well above this figure and, with a minimum wage of Bs.20 a day, every worker in regular employment must have an income far in excess of the national average when account is taken of various supplements and benefits.

In line 3a we find 60,000 *salary earners in industry, commerce, etc., in the Federal District* with an average income of Bs.16,000 a year. Since many of these are junior office staff, shop assistants and the like earning much less than this figure, there must be a substantial number earning far more. In the payrolls shown to us by the Ministry of Labor we did find a fair number of senior executives earning Bs.50,000 or more and a good many more earning less than this but still considerably more than Bs.16,000. There must also be a number of salary earners getting high figures in the Interior, but here the general level of salaries tends to be much lower.

While the average income of *wage earners in industry, etc.* (lines 3c and 3d) is relatively low, especially outside Caracas, there is a minority earning substantially more. In the Ministry of Labor's payroll figures we found some workers classified as wage earners who appeared to be earning between Bs.15,000 and Bs.20,000 a year, including supplements, mainly in large, well-managed firms. But Bs.20,000 seemed to be a virtual ceiling; we found only one wage earner with a higher figure. There are also some very high wage earnings in iron mining comparable with those in petroleum.

In *Government service* (line 5) we find 145,000 with an average income of Bs.10,000. A good many of these have an income little if at all above the national average, and some get less; but a fair number have salaries far in excess of Bs.10,000. According to the Budget for 1958/9 a Minister gets Bs.96,000 plus Bs.60,000 for expenses of representation; a senior official gets a basic salary of over Bs.57,000; and so on down the scale.

In line 6b, there are included some prosperous *farmers* earning good incomes and, as we shall see shortly, a small number of people owning huge estates from which they must derive very large incomes.

Finally, there is a very considerable number of people earning large incomes, some very large, from *profits, interest and rent* (lines 7 & 8).

INCOMES WELL BELOW THE AVERAGE

Let us now go to the opposite extreme and consider those who are earning well below the national average.

The first group that springs to attention is that of the 460,000 *wage earners in industry, etc. outside the Federal District* (line 3d) with an estimated *average* income of only Bs.3,500 a year. This means that a good half of the group is probably getting less. The fish-processing workers in Sucre, already mentioned, provide examples. There must also be a good many *salary earners in the Interior* (line 3b) earning very low incomes. For example, the Ministry of Labor showed us payroll figures for a store in Barquisimeto where the commonest rate for a female assistant was only Bs.100 per month, or Bs.1,200 a year apart from supplements. In Caracas, on the other hand, there seem to be rather few wage or salary earners with less than Bs.3,500 a year. This is the impression formed from a perusal of the Ministry of Labor figures, and it is confirmed by the results of the 'Datos' sample survey; of those interviewed only 5% reported incomes of under Bs.300 a month. It is true that only men were interrogated, but the Ministry of Labor figures suggest that, although there was a fair number of women in this group, the bulk of the women earned more; and it is estimated that even a domestic servant in Caracas (line 4a) gets, on average, about Bs.3,000 a year, including the value of board and lodging where provided; a chamber-maid in a first-class hotel may make substantially more. The bulk of the really low incomes, outside agriculture which we shall consider in a moment, are thus to be found among the wage and lower salary earners in the Interior, and with these we may include the 125,000 *domestic servants in the Interior* with an estimated average income of Bs.1,250 a year (line 4b). In Table I-5 below we estimate, from quite independent sources, that there were about 400,000 people living in towns of over 500 inhabitants who had incomes of under Bs.3,600 a year, a result that is broadly consistent with the analysis in this paragraph.

We now come to *agriculture*. It is here that the great bulk of the really low incomes are to be found. We estimate (line 6a) that there are around three-quarters of a million *campesinos* and agricultural workers (supporting a population, including themselves, of over 2,000,000) with an average income of little more than Bs.1,000 a year. This is earned partly by working for wages on the larger farms and partly by cultivating their own small plots. Let us consider these two sources of income in turn.

Agricultural wages

We are told that, in many parts of the country, not too near the cities or the oil camps where the competition for labor is greater, the usual wage for unskilled farm labor is around Bs.5 a day. But in many instances work is available during only part of the year, say 120—150 days during the period of the sugar crop. Annual earnings would then be only Bs.600—750 a year.

In the more modern, better-managed estates, however, especially if they are near cities or oil camps, the wage may be Bs.7—8 or even up to Bs.10 a day or more. (We have visited, or been told of, farms where a wage of Bs.10 or more was being paid, or at least demanded. These were all fairly close to cities or, for example, near Calabozo, where the irrigation works and influx of medium-sized farmers needing labor have helped to drive wages up.) A skilled worker, such as a tractor driver, may get Bs.12, Bs.15, or even up to Bs.20 a day, but often for only part of the year, and it is safe to say that exceedingly few agricultural workers will get as much as the national average of Bs.6,000 a year.

Production of small family plots

The bulk of the poor agricultural workers are, however, employed most of the time on the small family plots. (The Census of 1950, which is, however, not easy to interpret on this matter, showed only 245,000 employed workers [*obreros*] in agriculture.)

The National Agricultural Inquiry for 1956 estimated that there were about 320,000 units of exploitation of under 10 hectares. The sample survey of Dr. George Hill, to which we referred above, was concerned mainly with the *campesino* living on these small holdings. The survey, which was made in five different regions of the country, showed that the *campesino* 'tills the soil with his hands, aided sometimes with the traditional pico, planting stick and machete; 66% of them have no other tools.' Nearly half had gross sales of under Bs.800 a year. Since nearly one-quarter of the holdings in the survey were of more than 10 hectares, we may perhaps take Bs.800 as an average gross income from sales on holdings of less than 10 hectares. Dr. Hill has suggested to us that, on average, Bs.300—400 might be deducted for cash expenses of production and Bs.300—400 added for production consumed by the family, leaving a net income (including income in kind) of about Bs.800 a year for the small family holding.

Wages and production together

If we think of a typical family as consisting of six, with two working, of whom one works full-time on the holding and the other works for half the year as a laborer at, say, Bs.7 a day, we get a total family income of rather more than Bs.2,000 a year, or just above Bs.1,000 per person working. This also happens to be the average figure obtained if we take the Banco Central's estimate of 'remuneration of labor' in agriculture (which is intended to include production on the small holdings as well as wage-earners) and divide it by the estimated number of workers involved (see line 6a and note 5, Table I-3).

E. REASONS FOR THE INEQUALITY OF INCOMES

We have already seen that the inequality of personal incomes in Venezuela results in part from geographical differences: some regions are highly prosperous, others depressed; and incomes are generally higher in the larger towns than they are in the smaller ones or in the countryside. Secondly, there are industrial differences: income per head is much higher in some sectors of the economy than it is in others; and this helps to a considerable extent to explain the geographical differences. Thirdly, there are marked differences in personal incomes within a given economic sector in a given part of the country. These result, first, from differences in the earnings of labor (in the widest sense) and, secondly, from the uneven distribution of ownership of capital and land.

DIFFERENCES IN THE EARNINGS OF LABOR

These can be explained in part by differences in age, sex, length of service in a given employment, and luck. But most important are the differences in ability and skill. And the premium on skill is high in a country like Venezuela where many do not go to school, or stay only for a few grades, and where high school education is confined to a tiny fraction of the population.

Our study of the Ministry of Labor's payroll figures suggested that, leaving out young people and women, skilled workers in the most responsible positions typically earn some three to four times as much as the lowest paid general laborer in the same business enterprise, and that the top executives typically get three to four times as much again. We have seen that, in Government service, a Minister gets Bs.96,000 a year and a top official Bs.57,000; in the same Ministry a junior official may get only Bs.7,000 and a laborer or servant only half as much. In agriculture we have seen that a tractor driver may get twice as much as a general laborer.

THE UNEQUAL OWNERSHIP OF CAPITAL AND LAND

This is perhaps even more important in explaining the unequal distribution of incomes than differences in the earnings of 'labor.' It also helps to explain the latter since better-off families can afford better education for their children.

The great bulk of the population has little or no *capital.* Among those who have significant amounts, there is a vast difference between the considerable number of small shopkeepers and owners of workshops on the one hand and, on the other, the few families who control large businesses with profits running into many millions of bolivars a year. Moreover, given the very low income and inheritance taxes in Venezuela, these inequalities in ownership can be perpetuated, and even perhaps intensified, in a way that is hardly possible in countries with much more severe taxation. (Low taxation also, of course, helps enterprising, gifted and lucky people to move fairly rapidly from a lower income group to a much higher one, and a substantial middle class has grown up over quite a short period.)

AGRICULTURAL LAND

This is also most unevenly distributed. Table I-4 and the accompanying Diagram I.1 (which is based on the National Agricultural Inquiry of 1956) show that a mere 2½% of the 'units of exploitation' (those of over 500 hectares) account for 82% of the total area. At the other extreme we have 81% of the units of exploitation (those of under 10 hectares) accounting for only 4% of the total land. This is the share of the poor *campesinos* of whom we wrote above. It is possible that their share of the total value of agriculture output may be greater, and that of the larger estates smaller, than these figures would suggest. For the small holdings of under 10 hectares have as much as 23% of the area sown to crops and hardly any of the pasture land, the great bulk of which is in the large farms; and the value of output per hectare, other things being equal, is substantially higher in crop production than it is in animal husbandry. But against this must be set the inefficient methods and primitive equipment employed by the peasant farmer. In any case, it is clear that the very uneven distribution of agricultural land is bound to lead to great inequalities in income from it.

Table I.4

Agriculture: Size of Units of Exploitation, 1956 (Hectares)

	All sizes	Under 1	1—5	5—10	10—20	20—50	50—100	100—200	200—500	500—1,000	1,000—2,500	2,500—10,000	Over 10,000
No. of units (000's)	397.8	54.2	212.1	54.5	29.3	18.8	8.3	5.5	5.3	3.1	2.8	3.4	0.5
Per cent of total	100.0	13.6	53.3	13.7	7.4	4.7	2.1	1.4	1.3	0.8	0.7	0.9	0.1
Area:													
Sown	2,925	31	444	188	176	165	260	301	291	244	279	542	5
Fallow	864	—	12	24	30	68	41	45	78	71	118	194	181
Natural pasture	15,165	1	5	22	38	75	185	243	549	1,339	2,720	4,992	4,996
Artificial pasture	2,604	1	7	14	39	36	69	106	270	275	425	954	408
Other uses[1]	7,972	14	147	210	218	325	113	212	226	330	978	4,114	1,085
Total	29,530	47	615	458	501	669	668	907	1,414	2,259	4,520	10,796	6,675
Per cent of area by size of units:													
Sown	100.0	1.06	15.2	6.4	6.0	5.7	8.9	10.3	9.9	8.4	9.5	18.5	0.2
Fallow	100.0	0.03	1.4	2.8	3.5	7.9	4.7	5.2	9.1	8.2	13.7	22.5	21.0
Natural pasture	100.0	0.01	0.0	0.1	0.3	0.5	1.2	1.6	3.6	8.8	17.9	32.9	33.0
Artificial pasture	100.0	0.05	0.3	0.5	1.5	1.4	2.7	4.1	10.4	10.6	16.3	36.6	15.6
Other uses[1]	100.0	0.18	0.8	2.6	2.7	4.1	1.4	2.7	2.8	4.1	12.3	51.6	13.6
Total	100.0	0.2	2.1	1.5	1.7	2.3	2.3	3.1	4.8	7.7	15.3	36.5	22.5
Per cent of area by type of land use:													
Sown	9.9	66	72	41	35	25	39	33	21	11	6	5	—
Fallow	2.9	—	2	5	6	10	6	5	5	3	3	2	3
Natural pasture	51.4	2	1	5	8	11	28	27	39	59	60	46	75
Artificial pasture	8.8	2	1	3	8	5	10	12	19	12	9	9	6
Other uses[1]	27.0	30	24	46	43	49	17	23	16	15	22	38	16
Total	100.0	100	100	100	100	100	100	100	100	100	100	100	100

[1] Land productive but not cultivated; non-agricultural uses (houses, stables, corrals, buildings, granaries, mills, roads, etc.); woods; unproductive land. Source: Encuesta Agropecuaria Nacional, 1956 (Caracas, Sept. 1957). Ministerio de Agricultura y Cría.

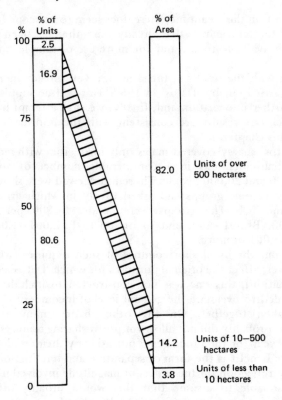

DIAGRAM I.1
Agriculture: Size of Units of Exploitation, 1956
(Source: Table I.4)

F. A QUANTITATIVE ESTIMATE OF THE PERSONAL DISTRIBUTION OF INCOME

We shall now attempt to make a quantitative estimate of the personal distribution of income. This is not easy, as the data are rather scanty. This is perhaps inevitable in a country like Venezuela where (1) the income tax covers only a small fraction of the population and, moreover, is levied on corporation profits but not on dividends, so that the personal distribution of the latter is not known, (2) the coverage of the Social Security System is as yet rather limited; in other countries this can yield valuable information about employment. The problem will be easier to handle as more basic data are collected but, in the meantime, there does seem to be scope for more analysis of the information that already exists than has been possible in the time available to us, and for more use of sample surveys of income.

We start with the results of the sample survey, already mentioned, that was carried out by 'Datos' in 1957. This will be supplemented later by further information and, finally, we shall attempt briefly to see whether our results are consistent with the information given earlier in this chapter.

The 'Datos' survey covered males only in all cities with more than 20,000 inhabitants and in a considerable number of towns of between 500 and 20,000 people. Those interviewed were shown a list of monthly income groups and asked to say in which group their own income fell. The groups were: under Bs.200 per month, Bs.201–300, Bs.301–400, and so on up to Bs.2,001–4,000 and, finally, Bs.4,001 or more.

Apart from the usual shortcomings of such inquiries (which did not, however, affect the original purposes for which 'Datos' collected the information), this one was not constructed to include females and so tended to overstate the general level of incomes of males and females taken together. On the other hand, many of those interviewed probably did not allow for profit-sharing bonuses[5] at the end of the year (or for funds being put aside by their employers for their future benefit is the form of separation and termination pay).[6] After some reflection on the orders of magnitude involved it seemed not unreasonable to assume that this would broadly offset the omission of women from the inquiry.[7] We therefore multiplied the monthly income ranges by twelve and assumed that the resulting figures would give a fair indication (apart from a further qualification to be mentioned later) of the distribution of annual incomes among males and females taken together.

We then estimated the economically active population in each of the towns of over 20,000 (taking one-third of the total estimated population at mid-1957[8]) and, applying the proportions in the

[5] *Utilidades.*
[6] *Antigüedades* and *Cesantía*
[7] Outside agriculture there are about three men at work for every woman. If women's earnings were on average, say, 60 per cent of men's, the average for men and women together would be 90 per cent of that for men alone. An overstatement of average basic earnings of this order would be broadly offset by the failure of a good many men to include supplements when saying what their earnings were.
[8] We used figures derived from 'Datos' estimates which implied a total population in the whole country of about 6.35 million. See footnote 4 above. The assumption that the ratio of active to total population does not vary with the size of towns may involve some error, but it is hoped that this is not quantitatively very important.

Table I.5
Estimated Distribution of Private Income in 1957 in Towns of Over 500 People[1]

Range of income (Bs. per annum)	Assumed average income in range[2] (Bs. per annum)	Numbers of incomes[3] (thousands)	Total income[3] (Million Bs.)
			((2) x (3))
(1)	(2)	(3)	(4)
Under 2,400	1,800	210	380
2,401–3,600	2,900	185	540
3,601–4,800	4,100	165	680
4,801–6,000	5,300	125	660
6,001–7,200	6,500	115	750
7,201–9,000	7,800	115	900
9,001–12,000	10,000	155	1,550
12,001–15,000	13,000	75	980
15,001–24,000	18,000	100	1,800
24,001–48,000	30,000	50	1,500
Over 48,000	80,000	15	1,200
Total		1,310	10,940

[1] This table does *not* cover those living outside towns of over 500 inhabitants. Moreover, the figures probably allow incompletely for income other than from wages and salaries. These omissions are discussed in the text and an attempt is made to repair them. The results are given in Tables I.6 and I.7.

[2] In estimating the average incomes in the various groups, account was taken of the fact that the original questions referred to groups such as Bs.201–300, Bs.301–400, etc., and that a good many monthly salaries are in terms of a round number of bolivars. The assumed average for the last group is partly a guess but seems reasonable in the light of various figures given earlier in this chapter and in a table in Chapter III of *The Fiscal System of Venezuela*, giving the distribution of salaries declared for income tax purposes.

[3] In round numbers.

appropriate samples falling within each income group,[9] estimated the actual number of incomes within each group in each town and then, by addition, in all towns of over 20,000. A similar procedure was followed with the smaller towns, which were divided into two groups of 5,000–20,000 and 500–5,000. But, here, since the sample did not cover all towns, we divided the country into a number of economic regions and then applied proportions based on the towns where the survey was made. When the results for towns of all sizes over 500 were added up we obtained the figures shown in columns 1 and 3 of Table I.5. Finally, we assumed average incomes for each income group (column 2) and thus obtained estimates of the total income in each group (column 4).

[9] The data were kindly supplied by 'Datos.'

Looking at the totals at the bottom of the table, it will be seen, first, that we have accounted for about 1,300,000 out of the total active population of about 2,100,000 shown in Table I.3. The remaining 800,000 comprise the active population in rural areas outside towns of 500 and over, areas which contain a total population of nearly 2½ million. Secondly, the total of incomes is Bs.10,940 million, compared with the total of private incomes of Bs.12,800 million derived from the Banco Central's estimates and shown in Table I.3, a difference of Bs.1,860 million. This does not look unreasonable since we still have two sums to add to the total shown in Table I.5. First, there is the income of dwellers in the rural areas. Secondly, some part of the income from profits, interest and rent was probably not included in the replies to the questions of the survey and not fully allowed for when we estimated the average income of those reporting incomes in the highest group. Almost certainly the *undistributed* profits of corporations have not yet been included in our figures although they must be included in an estimate of total private, as distinct from personal, income, and attributed to the shareholders on whose behalf they are being accumulated.

It is impossible to allocate our 800,000 people and Bs.1,860 million between the rather fine income groups in Table I.5, but we have made an attempt to do so between three broad groups — under Bs.2,400 a year, Bs.2,400—12,000 and over Bs.12,000. (The figure of Bs.12,000 has been chosen as a dividing line partly because it is the present income tax exemption limit for certain purposes.) The calculation is shown in Table I.6 and explained in detail in the notes to that table. Broadly speaking, we have assumed that most of the 800,000 in rural areas are poor *campesinos* and agricultural laborers in the lowest income group and that the bulk of the profits, etc. not reported in the survey (which are derived as a residual) is received by those in the highest group.

For clarity of exposition we have brought together the main results in Table I.7 where we also calculate percentages and round the figures off to avoid an impression of spurious accuracy.

This table shows that, according to our estimates, about one-eighth of the income receivers get one-half of total income. At the other extreme, 45% get about one-tenth of the income.

Looking at Table I.7 in conjunction with Table I.5, the broad picture portrayed does not seem inconsistent with the evidence given in the earlier part of the chapter and in other parts of the report. First, we have seen that there are good reasons for expecting a high degree of inequality of income in Venezuela. Secondly, to turn to more quantitative aspects, we have seen above that our estimates of

Table I.6
Allocation of Certain Incomes among Broad Income Groups

| Bs. per annum | Number of incomes (thousands) | | | Total income (Bs.million) | | | |
	In towns (from Table I.5)	In rural areas	Total	In towns (from Table I.5)	In rural areas	Profits, etc., not reported in survey	Total
(1)	(2)	(3)	(4)	(5)	(6)	(7)	(8)
Under 2,400	210	750	960	380	800	—	1,180
2,400–12,000	860	40	900	5,080	200	60	5,340
Over 12,000	240	10	250	5,480	200	600	6,280
Total	1,310	800	2,110	10,940	1,200	660	12,800

Note:

The task is to allocate to three income groups 800,000 members of the active population living in rural areas and Bs.1,860 million of income not included in the figures from Table I.5 shown in columns 2 and 5.

As a first step it seems that one would not go very far wrong in allocating to the lowest group the whole of the 750,000 people and Bs.800 million of income shown in line 6a of Table I.3 for the 'remuneration of labor' in agriculture. This leaves 50,000 living in rural areas to be allocated, in column 3, between the two higher income groups. Since a fairly high proportion of the larger farmers and landlords presumably live in towns, and in the light of the distribution of landholdings shown in Table I.4, it is likely that most of these 50,000 would be in the middle income group. Keeping to round figures we put 40,000 in the middle group and 10,000 in the upper one. The corresponding figures for total income in column 6 assume an average income of Bs.5,000 in the middle group and Bs.20,000 in the upper one.

We have now allocated Bs.1,200 million of the income, leaving Bs.660 million for profits, etc. not reported in the survey. It seems reasonable to put the great bulk of this, say Bs.600 million, in the upper group and the remaining Bs.60 million in the middle one.

Columns 4 and 8 show the final results when these additions are combined with the figures from Table I.5. They represent our estimates of the distribution of all private income among the whole active population.

Table I.7
Estimated Distribution of Private Income in Venezuela 1957
(In round figures)

| Income (Bs. per annum) | Number of incomes (thousands) | Total income (Bs.thousand million) | Per cent of total | |
			Number of incomes	Total income
Under 2,400	950	1.2	45	9
2,400–12,000	900	5.3	43	42
Over 12,000	250	6.3	12	49
Total	2,100	12.8	100	100

the number of low incomes (under Bs.3,600) in urban areas is not inconsistent with the analysis by social classes given in Table I.3. Thirdly, our figures for the higher income groups (over Bs.12,000 a year) do not seem inconsistent with the analysis in Table I.3. The reader who wishes will make his own comparison but we have shown in the footnote below, purely for purposes of illustration, one of various possible ways in which our estimated 250,000 incomes of over Bs.12,000 a year, yielding a total of Bs.6,300 million, might be distributed among the groups in Table I-3, in the light of the analysis earlier in the chapter.[10]

Finally, while our estimated number of incomes of over Bs.12,000 may seem high in relation to the numbers declared for tax purposes, the differences may be readily explicable. First, there is the possibility of tax evasion. Secondly, a good many salary earners getting between, say, Bs.12,000 and Bs.24,000 (who have already had schedular tax withheld by their employers) may fail to file a return for complementary tax since they know that they would not have to pay any on account of allowances for dependents. Thirdly, a corporation's profit counts as one income for tax purposes while it may distribute dividends to a number of shareholders.

G. THE EFFECTS OF TAXATION AND PUBLIC EXPENDITURE

Finally, it should be noted that all the incomes in this chapter are reckoned before tax and also exclude the non-monetary benefits of government expenditure. We have attempted to estimate the total burden of taxation, direct and indirect, on various classes of the community by considering the position of typical families. The main results are given in Table I.8.

This table, which should of course be used only as an indication of broad trends, shows that the tax structure in Venezuela tends to be

---

[10] We give only the results since it would be tedious to justify them in detail and because there are several plausible ways in which the totals might be made up. The 250,000 incomes of over Bs.12,000 a year might be distributed as follows:

(1) *4,500* independent professionals at Bs.80,000, total *Bs.350 million*.

(2) Two-thirds of the petroleum workers, one-third of the salary earners in the Federal District and one-tenth of those in the Interior in industry, etc., and one-fifth of those in Government service give a total of *95,000*. Assuming an average of Bs.25,000 a year yields a total income of about *Bs.2,400 million*.

(3) Six per cent of the wage earners in industry, etc. in the Federal District and two per cent of those in the Interior give *20,000*. Assuming an average of Bs.15,000 a year yields a total income of *Bs.300 million*.

(4) *30,000* farmers and landlords with an average of Bs.15,000 yields *Bs.450 million*.

(5) *100,000* business men [not already included in (2)], shareholders and receivers of interest and rent, with an average of Bs.28,000 yields *Bs.2,800 million*.

The total is 250,000 incomes yielding Bs.6,300 million as in Table I.7.

Table I.8

Taxes Paid Directly and Indirectly by Typical Families in Venezuela

	Assumed income of head of family[1] (Bs.)	Taxes as percentage of total family income[4]		Total taxes (round numbers)
		Direct taxes	Indirect taxes	
Conuquero and peon	1,500[2]	—	7.1	7
Domestic servant[3]	2,500	—	7.8	8
Unskilled laborer (*Caracas*)	3,820	—	10.1	10
Machine tender, textile mill	8,220	—	9.25	9
Petroleum field worker	15,000	0.2	13.0	13
Bookkeeper, food factory	15,750	0.2	12.0	12
Iron-mine worker	19,000	0.35	11.0	11
Wholesale grocery executive	28,000	1.3	16.4	18
Independent farmer	35,000	0.6	10.8	11
Attorney	80,000	2.9	15.5	18
Large landowner	100,000	2.8	10.6	13
Real estate speculator and owner	350,000	6.6	13.2	20

[1] Including fringe and extraordinary benefits.
[2] Assumed to have son earning Bs.500 a year as laborer, making family income of Bs.2,000 or Bs.1,000 per person working.
[3] This domestic servant, though assumed to be in the Interior, is earning much more than the average for that category shown in Table I.3, line 4b.
[4] Includes, in a few cases, income of other members of the family.

progressive, but only moderately so; and if the range of incomes in the table were extended further it would be seen that it is still possible to get an annual income, after all taxes, of several million bolivars. If taxes are subtracted from the figures of income given in Tables I.5, I.6, and I.7, it makes little difference to the general picture. We have attempted to estimate roughly the total tax burden falling on each of the three income groups distinguished in Table I.7, taking account of the data in Table I.8, and of the total collection of taxes from Venezuelan citizens. The results are given in Table I.9, which also shows, in the last column, the percentages of total private income, after all taxes, going to each group. It will be seen that these percentages are very little different from those relating to income before tax. The percentage going to the top group drops a couple of points and that going to each of the two lower groups rises a point; but that is all.

Moreover, as mentioned earlier, government expenditure probably tends to benefit disproportionately the larger — more prosperous

Table I.9
Income Before and After Taxes, 1957

(Bs.thousand million)

Income (Bs. per year)	Total income before taxes[1]	Total taxes	Total income after taxes (2) minus (3)	Percentage of total income after taxes
(1)	(2)	(3)	(4)	(5)
Under 2,400	1.2	0.1	1.1	10
2,400–12,000	5.3	0.4	4.9	43
Over 12,000	6.3	0.9	5.4	47
Totals	12.8	1.4	11.4	100

[1] From Table I.7.

— towns rather than the smaller ones and the countryside; and expenditure on trunk roads, hotels and the like probably tends to benefit particularly the richer classes. It is thus quite possible that taxation and government expenditure taken together have no redistributive effects.

11 National economic planning[1]

Governments in this country have for many years been engaged in national economic planning in the sense of looking ahead in quantitative terms and, in the light of their forecasts, making policy changes to achieve their objectives. Until about a generation ago the main objective was to balance the budget in the narrow sense of equalising Government expenditure and revenue, and the Government looked one year ahead. Since the war, under the influence of Keynesian ideas, governments have looked at the national accounts in a much wider sense; the main objectives have been to achieve a high level of employment, a satisfactory balance of payments and a minimum of inflation; and the Government has looked ahead one to one-and-a-half years. More recently still, during the 1960s, the Government has accepted the additional responsibility for economic growth and has been looking three to five years ahead; and some attempt has been made to fit together the forecasts of Government and of industry.

This latest phase reflects three developments. First, there has been a growing awareness that our rate of economic growth — though good by pre-war standards — has been relatively poor by post-war international standards. Secondly, in the early 1960s, we observed that rapid growth in France was associated with indicative planning, and thought there might be some causal connection. Thirdly, the Plowden Report of 1961 showed the need for the Government to look some five years ahead in formulating their public expenditure programmes.

We have had two experiments in national economic planning in the 1960s — the Neddy Plan of 1963 and the National Plan of 1965. In neither case was the growth objective achieved. The main reasons were:

> *First*, that both Plans deliberately set a somewhat ambitious target for the growth of productivity, in excess of past trends (though not greatly in excess).

[1] Abbreviated version of talk to Society of Long-range Planning, London, February 1969.

245

Secondly, both Plans recognised that balance of payments problems might prevent the postulated growth rate from being achieved, and both proposed ways of dealing with this constraint; but in the end the balance of payments problems proved too great to be solved without a marked slowing down of economic growth.

In the light of this experience, why — it may be asked — is another planning exercise now being attempted?

The simple answer is that there is a widespread recognition of the need for some such exercise — although opinions differ on the precise form it should take — and the failure of two previous attempts is no conclusive argument against a third, provided we learn from our past experience.

I shall now add something about the purposes and methods of national economic planning as I see them, and also give some indication of the lessons that may be learned from the two earlier experiments. Both the Neddy Plan and the National Plan contained a large number of proposals for action — by Government and by industry — both separately and in collaboration. Neddy published its so-called 'Orange Book' entitled *Conditions Favourable to Faster Growth.* The National Plan had its *Check List of Action Required.* Everyone accepts that agreed action of a general nature to improve our industrial efficiency, competitiveness and the balance of payments is an important part of national economic planning. But for the most part such general action does not depend on numerical projections of the economy over the years ahead. What then is the use of such numerical projections?

They are certainly essential to the *Government* in formulating its own *public expenditure programmes.* In order to determine how much public expenditure can reasonably be planned for *in total* it is clearly necessary to assess the rate of national growth and how much must be allowed for private investment and consumption and for the balance of payments. All these magnitudes are, of course, uncertain, and public expenditure programmes must therefore be flexible. One technique for preserving such flexibility, and to allow for unforeseen demands, is to set aside a 'contingency reserve'; and this is increasingly being done.

Another problem in public expenditure planning is to devise ways in which the Government can take rational decisions as between different forms of expenditure. This involves knowing more clearly, first, what result — or 'output' — can be expected from given sums of expenditure in various fields; and secondly, the economic impact of various forms of expenditure. A pound spent on one thing can have very different effects from a pound spent on another. It may, for example, involve much more, or much less, demand on manpower, on imports or on resources generally — and may thus require much more, or much less, taxation to offset it.

On all these matters, much work is needed to improve our accounting techniques and methods of economic analysis.

The Government also needs economic projections, looking several years ahead, to form a rational basis of decisions on the *investment programmes of the nationalised industries*, on such matters as energy and transport policy, on regional policy, and on its medium and long term strategy generally.

The case, then, for economic projections and assessments for the *Government's own use* is quite clear. Such projections can, of course, never be exactly right, and may sometimes go quite badly wrong. But that is not a reason for not making them. Rather it is a reason for attempting to assess the ranges of uncertainty and for taking this uncertainty into account in policy decisions.

Now it is tempting for a government to keep its projections and assessments to itself (just as companies do most of *their* planning in private). But there is also a case for making them public, so that there can be informed public discussion of the economic prospects of the country, of public expenditure programmes, and of Government economic policy generally.

So much, then, for the Government's *direct* interest in national economic planning. It is clearly essential for the proper management of the now very large public sector and as a guide to general economic policy.

But what about the *private sector?* Have they any interest in national economic planning, and can the economic performance of the country be improved by bringing the private sector into the planning process?

There is one way in which this cannot help, at least in present circumstances. It once used to be argued that, if you picked a national growth rate higher than had been achieved in the past — and divided it up into the performance required by individual industries and firms — then everyone would act accordingly and the higher growth rate would be achieved. While this argument might possibly be valid in some circumstances it is not applicable to Britain today.

A more hopeful approach is to regard the involvement of the private sector in national economic planning as helping firms and industries to make better projections on which to base their own decisions on investment, export policy and so on. If in this way they can be helped to make better decisions, this will also benefit national economic performance — because our limited national resources will be better distributed.

Now this aspect of national economic planning is sometimes greeted with a certain amount of scepticism from those in private business — for two reasons.

First, it is said, if the Government bases its projections on an unrealisticly high rate of growth, firms will pay little attention. I shall deal with this point later.

Secondly, even if firms accept the postulated rate, or rates, of national growth, some say that this has little relevance for their own business decisions, because of the double margin of error involved, first, in translating such national rates into the growth of demand for their industries, and then in estimating the share of the firm in the market for their products.

Be that as it may, many major companies in fact appear to go through the process of estimating the growth of national product, from that the total demand for their own products, and hence the demand for their firms. They may also be interested in projections of aggregates such as personal consumption or private investment; and they are interested in the planned purchases of the Government and of nationalised industries, and in the prospects of their customer and supplier industries.

With the rapidly growing interest in corporate planning, it seems inevitable that there will be a development of what might be called 'co-ordinated market research' in the years ahead; and it seems sensible for national and corporate planners to pool their information so far as possible in an attempt to improve their projections.

If this development is to take place, the co-operation of private industry — and private firms — with the Government is essential; because national planners, working in a backroom as it were, can go only a part of the way in making projections for individual industries, much less firms.

In this context, another form of mutual co-operation is in the collection and analysis of industrial statistics. A number of major changes are being planned by the C.S.O. and other departments to make industrial statistics much more up to date, complete and consistent. Broadly, we are aiming at what will be virtually an annual Census of Production system, plus quarterly figures of product sales which are of the most importance to business users. To ensure greater consistency, we are working towards a *central register of businesses.*

These new developments will require a great deal of effort from both industry and Government, working in partnership, if they are to be achieved. For its part the Government has created a *Business Statistics Office*, out of the old Census Office, charged with the functions of meeting industry's increasingly voracious requirements. We feel sure, from the great interest already shown, that industry is also anxious to help in this co-operative venture.

I have so far discussed national economic planning as a way of helping Government, on the one hand, and industry on the other, to make better decisions. This is sometimes called '*indicative*' planning. But I think this word does not quite do justice to the form of *co-operation* that seems to me to be needed *between* Government and industry, over and above the pooling of their information to which I have already referred.

It would seem to me sensible, and useful, for the Government to have continuing consultations with individual industries — and, where appropriate, with individual firms — not only on the national economic *prospects* over the next few years, but also on what *changes* need to be made if the national goals are to be achieved. For such consultations to be meaningful, the national prospects and goals would have to be translated — through discussions between Government and industry — into the implications for individual industries. It would then be easier, against this quantitative background, to see what obstacles lay in the way of the necessary changes — industry by industry — and what action was required, and was feasible, to bring these changes about.

The main theme of such consultations would vary from time to time. In present circumstances, the overriding need is to improve the balance of payments by switching resources from home consumption — both private and public — into exports and import replacement, and to keep the resources switched until we have repaid our debts.

While action by Government on the financial and fiscal fronts (devaluation, cuts in public expenditure, taxation and monetary policy) can set the scene for the necessary switch of resources, and is essential, it is not enough in itself. Action on the industrial front is clearly necessary as well. This means essentially action in the individual boardroom and on the individual shopfloor. But there are ways in which the necessary action can be helped by cooperation between firms within an industry, between related industries, and between industry and the Government; for the Government is now inevitably involved in the fortunes of private industry in a good many ways.

There are three lessons which I believe can be learned from past experience about planning discussions between Government and industry.

First, they should not be too rushed. The time allowed for consultations when the National Plan was being prepared was felt by many in industry to be too short.

Secondly, the consultations should be a continuing process, rather than a once-for-all build-up to a sort of grand national blueprint to be valid for the next five years. As with corporate planning, national economic planning needs to be rolled forward periodically to take account of changing circumstances and of new evidence becoming available.

Thirdly, it would seem unwise to concentrate on one single national growth rate or on single growth rates for particular industries — all based on rather optimistic assumptions. It would seem better to consider various possible outcomes — some more, some less, optimistic. This would be more acceptable to industry as a basis for discussion. It would also be more realistic in the light of the inevitable uncertainties ahead: both uncertainty about the course of events largely outside our control (such as the course of world trade and international monetary developments) and uncertainty about the extent to which we shall ourselves succeed in improving our industrial efficiency and competitiveness and capturing markets from our industrial rivals both at home and abroad.

I have come increasingly to the conclusion that any form of planning — or decision making — needs to take account of uncertainty. Only in this way can one properly weigh the balance of risks. I am sure this is as true of corporate planning as it is of national planning. To work only on single-line projections can be highly misleading and lead to wrong decisions. To take account of uncertainty does not mean that one is becoming more ignorant. On the contrary, it is a sign of greater sophistication and rationality.

12 The short-term regulation of the national economy[1]

HISTORICAL PERSPECTIVE

I should like to begin with a brief historical perspective. Before the First World War there was little or no conscious attempt at short-term regulation of the national economy. The main objects of *fiscal policy* had nothing to do with demand management; they were to keep public expenditure as low as possible and to balance the Government's budget. Nor was *monetary policy* concerned with regulation of the national economy but rather with ensuring the convertibility of paper money into gold at a fixed rate and with avoiding banking crises.

Whether because of this system or not there was, during the half century or so before 1914, a reasonably good record of long-run price stability; there was no balance of payments problem as we know it today; and there was a substantial growth of prosperity (though not as fast as most industrial countries have got accustomed to in the last 25 years). But, on the other side of the coin, there were wide fluctuations in activity and employment, with unemployment frequently rising to levels that would not be tolerated today; and also great inequality and much poverty. (Public expenditure and progressive taxation designed to mitigate these were only on a very small scale.)

In the years *between* the world wars, we continued to avoid inflation in Britain (apart from a spurt in prices immediately after the First World War); but we suffered from chronically high unemployment in the 1920s and this was intensified in the 1930s when nearly all the main industrial countries had a prolonged period of very heavy unemployment. The long-held economic doctrine that, apart from cyclical fluctuations, the demand for and supply of labour would, by and large, automatically reach a balance at a high level of employment was rudely shattered. We also had balance of

---

[1] Paper given to a conference of the Foundation for Business Responsibilities, at the Festival Hall, London, June 1970 (published July 1972).

payments crises that could not be resolved as they had been before
1914. There was in addition a growing demand for higher public
expenditure, especially on social services. Then, in the late 1930s, a
body of economic doctrine — associated particularly with the name
of Keynes — was evolved which argued that unemployment was *not*
inevitable and that governments *could* control the level of employment and prevent disastrous slumps.

And in 1943 the War-time Coalition did indeed accept, for the
first time, the Government's responsibility, not just for mitigating
the hardships of unemployment through social policy, but actually
for maintaining a high level of *em*ployment through economic
policy. This was a fundamental change of attitude towards the
Government's responsibilities; and a high level of employment has
been a central objective of demand management during the last
quarter of a century.

One of the main instruments has been fiscal policy; and its
potency has been greatly increased by the fact that public expenditure — and thus taxation — have been a far higher fraction of the
national income than previously. For this reason alone it would
hardly have been possible to ignore the effects of fiscal policy on the
economy as a whole, as in Gladstone's day.

Before long it became apparent that the pursuit of what was called
'full employment' raised problems of its own — and in particular that
of inflation, which had not been a significant peace-time problem
— in Britain at least — during the previous century; and also the
problem of the balance of payments, which had been unknown — at
least in its present form — before 1914 although it had emerged in
the inter-war years. (The White Paper on 'Employment Policy' issued
by the War-time Coalition Government had foreseen these problems
but only to a limited extent.)

OBJECTIVES
Thus, since the Second World War the main objectives of demand
management have been a high level of employment, a minimum of
inflation, and a satisfactory balance of payments. The last has been
in part an objective in its own right — because national solvency is a
necessary condition of national self-respect and of an influential
foreign policy — and in part an intermediate goal because balance of
payments disequilibrium threatens the level of employment and the
stability of prices.

More recently, since about the early 1960s, governments in this
country have accepted the further responsibility for economic
growth. This reflected a growing awareness that our rate of economic

growth — though good by pre-war standards — had been relatively poor by post-war international standards. Much of Government economic policy to promote growth must naturally be concerned with the *supply side* of the economy — with increasing the growth of economic efficiency and thus of our productive capacity: by better training of labour and management; by stimulating competition or, where appropriate, the rationalisation of industry; by encouraging technological development; by providing incentives to investment; perhaps by some form of indicative or consultative planning; and so on. But *demand management* also has an important role to play in growth policy. First, it must ensure that a faster growth of productivity leads to greater output and not just to higher unemployment. Secondly, the avoidance of undue fluctuations in demand can lead to a better utilisation of capital equipment and thus reduce costs and encourage investment. Thirdly, when demand management requires changes in fiscal or monetary policy, the *pattern* of these changes can be designed so as to encourage industrial investment and efficiency, or at least to avoid discouraging them.

It is also possible that demand management can contribute to faster growth by keeping the average pressure of demand at the optimum level for this purpose, but there is considerable disagreement about what that level should be; plausible arguments can be adduced for aiming at either, say, 1½% or 2½% unemployment as a long-run average, but the debate on this matter (which has been going on for some time) has not yet reached an agreed conclusion.

INSTRUMENTS OF SHORT-TERM REGULATION

As I have mentioned already, a major instrument of demand management has been fiscal policy — ie, changes in taxation and public expenditure. Another important instrument has been monetary policy, including changes in hire purchase regulations. There have, thirdly, been several attempts to influence or control prices and incomes, other than through fiscal or monetary policy. Fourthly, there have been measures to influence directly the balance of payments: through exchange rate adjustments (as in 1949 and 1967); through exchange control affecting foreign investment and other transactions: through restrictions on imports (by quotas, surcharges or import deposits); through export rebates; and in other ways. In the early post-war years there were other forms of direct control, such as rationing of consumer goods and allocation of materials; but these had been largely eliminated by the mid-1950s.

The Government thus has a large armoury of weapons at its disposal in its attempt to regulate the national economy. And the

British executive branch is considerably less restricted in the exercise of many of these instruments than is the case in a good many other countries where legislatures and central banks have greater independence and more control over fiscal and monetary policy in particular.

Now some might argue that this greater power of British Governments has been a disadvantage rather than an advantage, on the grounds that we have had too much rather than too little short-term regulation of the economy since the war. It has indeed almost become a part of conventional wisdom that short-term management has been destabilising in some sense rather than stabilising. But I personally do not believe that studies of this question have been at all conclusive, for the simple reason that it is virtually impossible to estimate what would have happened if policy had been in some sense much more neutral. (Nor incidentally is it at all easy to define what such 'neutrality' would have meant.) There certainly have been fluctuations in the rate of growth and in the balance of payments since the war. But it is difficult to tell whether these would have been greater or smaller in the absence of policy changes. The actual fluctuations in output have certainly been much smaller than they were in the inter-war years (although fluctuations in the balance of payments have admittedly been at least as great); the rate of growth has been substantially faster than it was before the war; and the level of unemployment has on average been incomparably lower. Now this does not prove that we might not have done still better if policy had been more neutral. But it should at least make us pause before concluding that we should henceforth renounce all deliberate short-term regulation of the economy.

It is interesting to recall that the War-time White Paper on 'Employment Policy' did in fact suggest a scheme whereby social insurance contributions should be *automatically* varied inversely with the level of unemployment; but it did *not* suggest that this would be sufficient in itself to maintain a high and stable level of employment; variations in taxation and public expenditure would be necessary as well. More recently, however, various sets of simple rules have been proposed that would, according to their proponents, themselves achieve – in the longer run at least – satisfactory levels of employment, relatively stable prices, a sound balance of payments, and relatively steady growth. My own suspicion is that this over-estimates the present state of economic knowledge, and under-estimates the complexity of the real world in which we live. But I do not wish to labour this point. Whatever the truth of the matter, and whatever changes there may be in the nature of economic policy, it seems only realistic – I think you'll agree – to assume that short-term regulation of the economy of a discretionary nature will continue, in some form or another, for the foreseeable future.

Our knowledge of the effects of the various instruments of policy that I mentioned a little while ago varies considerably. We think we can estimate with some degree of confidence the effects of changes in most, but not all, forms of taxation and public expenditure, and of changes in hire purchase regulations. These estimates are based on observed relationships between relevant economic variables in the past, and on knowledge of the administrative time-lags involved. We know a good deal less about the effects of changes in monetary policy. This may be because they are inherently more uncertain; but it may be merely because empirical work on this question has, in general, been going on for a considerably shorter time. We think we can estimate at least the order of magnitude of the effects of a good many of the measures directly affecting the balance of payments, although the margin of error is usually rather large and there is always uncertainty about the timing of the effects. When it comes to the effects of various forms of prices and incomes policy the estimates are necessarily still more hazardous.

FORECASTING

I shall now say something about economic forecasting.

Short-term regulation of the economy must be based on an assessment of how the economy is currently performing, and of how it is likely to develop during the next 18 months or so. Major short-term forecasting exercises are normally carried out within Government several times a year; and in between there is a more or less continuous assessment of how the economy is behaving, and of how the most recent developments might affect the latest major forecast. There is thus, in effect, a sort of running assessment and forecast.

Short-term forecasts are made for the domestic economy — including the development of the various types of national expenditure — and for the balance of payments. Forecasts are also made of monetary conditions and of financial flows between the various sectors of the economy; the results of these are fed back into the other forecasts I have just mentioned, and they are useful in the formulation of monetary policy. Forecasts are also made of likely changes in demand on various industrial sectors. These are useful in deciding on the nature of policy changes. To take a simple example, at the time of last April's Budget, the prospects of rather slack demand in the construction industries but a fairly buoyant demand in the engineering industries led the Chancellor of the Exchequer to give a temporary investment incentive in a form that was directed to industrial buildings rather than to plant and machinery.

Finally, longer-term projections are made from time to time, looking about 3—5 years ahead, and sometimes longer. These are relevant to short-term demand management, which must take account of longer term developments; and they are of course especially relevant to the formulation of public expenditure programmes where it is essential to look a number of years ahead.

In making a forecast the first step is to assess the current state of affairs; and strangely enough one of the most difficult parts of the exercise is the 'forecasting' (if that is the right word) of the recent past.

This is partly because a good deal of the relevant information becomes available only after a considerable time lag, since it has to be collected from a large number of businesses and other organisations, and then collated. A good deal of effort is now being devoted to getting quicker returns, to speeding up their compilation, and to ways of making preliminary estimates on the basis of incomplete information. For example, until recently the first estimate of consumers' expenditure in each quarter did not become available until about three months after the end of the quarter. Now the CSO publish a first preliminary estimate about four weeks after the end of the quarter, and a second preliminary estimate eight weeks after. This sort of development is very valuable for those in Government assessing the course of the economy; and I hope it is also useful to some in private business.

A second problem in 'forecasting' the recent past is that the evidence is not infrequently conflicting. A well-known example is that the three methods of estimating the gross domestic product — from data on expenditure, output and incomes — can give different results and can indeed move in different directions from one quarter to another.

Thirdly, the relevant statistics are usually subject to revisions and can sometimes be revised to such an extent that the picture of the past is very substantially altered. For example, some years ago the Index of Industrial Production suggested that output had been stagnant over a period of a good many months, but when the figures were finally revised it appeared that production had in fact been rising quite markedly all the time.

These difficulties involved in forecasting the recent past mean that a good deal of judgement has to be exercised, and it is valuable to take account of qualitative as well as quantitative information — and here, of course, contacts with those engaged in industry are important.

So much for the forecasting of the recent past.

Turning to the forecast of the future, the first step is to make preliminary estimates of the various elements of demand — exports, public expenditure, private investment and so on. The methods used vary from case to case. I shall give you a few examples.

The forecast of *exports* is based in the first place place on quite an elaborate assessment of economic prospects in the various parts of the world — and in this we are now considerably helped by the exchange of information between Governments through international organisations, especially the OECD in Paris, and by the work of the OECD Secretariat in collating and analysing this information. (There have incidentally been remarkable strides forward in this form of international co-operation since the war.) Then, having assessed world economic prospects, it is necessary to estimate the share of our exports in the various markets of the world, taking account of our competitive position and also of any supply constraints at home.

The forecasts of *public expenditure on goods and services* — by the Central Government, by local authorities, and investment by the public corporations — are based of course on the programmes of the relevant authorities. This should in principle be the easiest and most reliable part of the forecasts, but in practice it is quite difficult because of the need to take account of such things as short-falls and contingency allowances, and a good deal of effort is now being devoted to improving forecasting techniques in this field.

The forecasts of *private investment*, other than housing, are based largely on the official intentions surveys carried out by the Board of Trade and the Ministry of Technology.[2] But we also take account of other information such as CBI surveys, home engineering orders and approvals of industrial development certificates. It is also necessary to take account of the expected financial and monetary conditions, and to check that the forecasts look plausible in the light of past relationships between investment on the one hand, and output, profits, cash flow, and so on, on the other.

The forecast of *consumers' expenditure* is perhaps the most complex, and it is concerned with the largest single element of national expenditure. The first step is to forecast personal incomes. The most important part is wages and salaries but we also have to estimate income from Government grants, dividends, interest, rent and self-employment. From the total of these personal incomes is subtracted an estimate of direct taxes and national insurance contributions, to give what is called personal *disposable* income. This in turn must then be adjusted for the forecast change in consumer

[2] Now the Department of Industry.

prices — which itself involves a complicated exercise — to get *real* personal disposable income. Finally, it is necessary to subtract a forecast of personal savings to get a forecast of consumers' expenditure at constant prices.

These forecasts of exports, public expenditure, private investment, consumers' expenditure — which I have just discussed briefly — together with forecasts of investment in private housing and stockbuilding (which I have no time to discuss) give, when added together, a first estimate of what is called total final expenditure. A forecast of imports is then subtracted to get a preliminary forecast of the gross domestic product. Certain iterative processes are then required to get a consistent, final, forecast of GDP. From this it is also possible to deduce a forecast of unemployment, based on past relationships between output, employment and unemployment.

At the same time as these domestic forecasts, a forecast is made of the balance of payments which takes account of expected domestic developments. In addition to forecasting exports and imports of goods and services, it is necessary to estimate net investment income from abroad and various types of international capital movements.

UNCERTAINTY

From this very brief description of how the main short-term forecasts of the national economy are made it will be evident that the processes are complicated and the margins of error necessarily considerable. Let me give you some illustrative figures.

The turnover on the balance of payments — adding debits and credits together — is now around £25,000 million a year. An error of only 1% in both credits and debits, in opposite directions, would thus make a difference of some £250 million. The gross domestic product is running at over £40,000 million a year so that an error of 1% here is over £400 million.[3]

This means that, even if one attaches quite a small margin of error to the forecast of the balance of payments, the range of probable outcomes may quite often cover both a very satisfactory outcome and a pretty unsatisfactory one. Similarly even a small error in the forecast of GDP may be of the same order as the effects on demand of a typical Budget.

Now you might say that all this forecasting is therefore useless. But in my view this is emphatically *not* the conclusion to be drawn. What it does mean is, first, that great care must be taken to make the best possible *central* forecast, and, secondly — equally important —

[3] The current figures are much higher.

that one must try to *quantify* the uncertainties, and then to take policy decisions in the light of these uncertainties. It is certainly much better to base policy on a forecast than on no forecast at all. But to base it *only* on a *central* forecast can lead to the wrong decisions. In my view the rational way to make decisions is to base them on the likely *range* of probable outcomes, with a different range for each policy option. The original range, assuming no change of policy, is based on central forecasts of the national economy, together with the estimated margins of error. The ranges assuming various possible policy changes can then be derived from estimates of the effects of these changes.

The estimation of the various margins of error inevitably, in the last resort, contains a considerable subjective element. But some useful indications can be obtained by studying the degree of success of past forecasts. It is also valuable to have a number of forecasts made independently outside the government with which the internal ones can be compared, and we very much welcome the development of these independent outside forecasts.

Many of those here today will know that, in appraising investment projects – for example – within a company, it is important to have not only central forecasts of the rate of return on capital, but also some assessment of the probability of different rates of return, either higher or lower. The same is true, *mutatis mutandis*, when the Government is appraising the consequences of various lines of action in the field I am discussing today. In framing a budget, for example, it is important to know not only the central forecast of the growth of demand over the next 12–18 months corresponding to each possible policy package under consideration, but also the likely range of error in each case. It is then possible to take a more rational decision which balances the various risks and uncertainties.

If only central forecasts are made the reasoning has to be on the following lines, Policy I will lead to a growth of demand of X, and Policy II to a growth of demand of Y. I prefer Y to X. Therefore I choose Policy II in preference to Policy I. But if we also estimate the degree of uncertainty there is fuller information on which to base the decision. For example, we shall have some idea of the danger, under each policy, of the growth of demand being either unacceptably low (leading to unacceptably high unemployment) or unacceptably high (leading to over-heating of the economy). And this additional assessment of the uncertainty may lead quite possibly to a different decision from that which would be taken on the basis of central forecasts only – in other words an opting for Policy I rather than Policy II.

In fact, the problem is still more complex than this, for two reasons.

First, there are possibilites, whatever course of action is chosen, of taking action later to correct an undesirable state of affairs. These possibilities, which are of course limited, must be fed into the information on which the decision is based.

Secondly, there is more than one objective, and there tends to be a conflict, and a trade-off, between the various objectives. This may also be true, I suppose, of some decision making in private business. In the case of the short-term regulation of the economy one important conflict is that between the growth of home demand on the one hand, and the balance of payments on the other. In general the higher the growth of home demand — over a short period at least — the less satisfactory will be the balance of payments. But in addition, of course, the forecast of the balance of payments, for a given level of home demand, is itself subject to a margin of error.

Thus, if the decision maker is to make rational choices, he must have before him, for each policy under consideration, first, *central* forecasts of, among other things, the growth of demand, unemployment and the balance of payments. Secondly, because of the uncertainties involved he must have some idea of the chances of other possible outcomes — of various other possible combinations of the three variables I have just mentioned, and others such as the pace of inflation. Thirdly, he must know the possibilities of remedial action later.

It all sounds rather complicated, and in fact it is. This means that it is important to devise simple ways of presenting the risks and uncertainties — and the trade-offs — involved in various policy choices; and we have in fact been experimenting a good deal recently with techniques of this sort, some of which are graphical. There is no time now to go into further detail, but I hope I have said enough to show the importance of this approach.

It is the answer to those who might be tempted to say that, because of the inevitable uncertainty in forecasting, one might just as well spin a coin or stick a wetted finger in the wind. I am sure this would be a counsel of despair. Nor would it be right just to make central forecasts and forget about the uncertainties. The correct approach, I am convinced, is to make the best possible central forecasts; to recognise, and attempt to quantify, the uncertainties; and then to set out the prospects in such a way that a decision can be taken between various policy options in the light of the risks and uncertainties, and of the trade-offs between the various objectives.

A COMPARISON OF THE PROBLEMS OF GOVERNMENT AND INDUSTRY

I dare say that many of you here who are concerned with decisions in private business will have noticed a good many similarities between your problems and those facing government in the short-term regulation of the national economy. Both industry and government have to assess the current situation, to make forecasts, to weigh up the risks and uncertainties, and then to take decisions. But there are also important differences and I shall now suggest what some of these are. If I am at times a little provocative, this is with a view to stimulating discussion.

First of all, the *magnitudes* with which government has to deal are of course very much greater. For example, public expenditure of some £20,000 million a year, a balance of payments turnover of £25,000 million a year, and a national product of over £40,000 million a year obviously dwarf the turnover of any corporation in this country.

Secondly, while the margin of error is greater in absolute terms when forecasting national aggregates than it is when forecasting magnitudes with which companies are concerned, I suspect that it has to be much smaller in percentage terms in the national case if it is to be of use.

A third difference is, I think, that well-run businesses have more up-to-date reliable information about what has been happening in the recent past. The Government, it is true, has very up-to-date information on certain matters directly under its control. For example, it knows daily, or even hourly if necessary, about the authorities' transactions in the markets for foreign exchange and government securities. It has monthly information on, for example, unemployment and overseas trade with only a relatively small delay. These statistics are based on the operations of two of its own agencies — the Employment Exchanges and the Customs Offices. But when it comes to collecting returns from private businesses on, for example, production, orders, sales, investment or stocks — often on a voluntary basis — the delays are almost bound to be greater than in the case of a well-organised company collecting such information from constituent parts directly under its control.

A fourth difference, I suggest, is that private corporations have a fairly closely defined *objective* — the maximisation of the share-holders' profits (though I agree that this is not nearly so clear-cut as it sounds and that there are other objectives as well). But a Government on the other hand has many more objectives, and as I have already said they quite often conflict — full employment, price stability, international solvency, equity, incentive, regional balance, economic growth and so on.

Fifthly, while the policy of a company must take account of considerable uncertainty about the future development of market forces, its actual operations are, broadly, under its *direct control*. But national economic policy must not only take account of economic uncertainties such as the future course of world trade. In addition, many of the economic acts of Government can only influence, in a way that can never be predicted with accuracy, the decisions of corporations and individuals in the private sector — and even in the public sector the actions of local authorities and the nationalised industries are by no means wholly under the central Government's control.

Sixthly, many of the individual decisions of companies can be made to a considerable extent *in private*, with the shareholders kept very largely in the dark. But in national affairs this is, quite rightly, much more difficult — and Parliament, the electorate and the press normally scrutinise the detailed proposals and decisions of a Government much more closely than do shareholders those of a company.

TASKS AHEAD

These then are some of the main differences as I see them. But I believe that the short-term regulation of the national economy and short-term regulation of the affairs of a company have a good deal in common and also that we can learn from each other's experience. Those of use who are concerned with national problems certainly have a great deal still to learn. As I said at the beginning, short-term regulation of the national economy, in anything like its present forms, has been practised for less than a generation. Quarterly statistics of national income and expenditure, which form the basis of a good deal of the econometric work required to establish the relevant relationships, are available only from 1955. The whole subject is still really in its infancy.

There is much to be done on the practical problems of obtaining quicker and more reliable economic information.

We have only begun to appreciate the potentialities of modern computers in, for example, the exploration of economic relationships; in the quick production of variant forecasts based on different assumptions or different policy options; in the field of computable economic models, where it is now possible to combine a more complex system of economic relationships with the inevitable (and essential) exercise of judgment in the production of forecasts.

There is much more to be done in exploring the effects of *monetary* conditions on the national economy.

Better techniques for dealing with *uncertainty* need to be developed — and uncertainty will undoubtedly remain, however much our information and forecasting techniques are improved; for the social sciences will always be much less exact than the natural ones.

Quite different approaches to the problem of forecasting may be discovered — and quite different approaches to the problems of regulating the economy. It is almost certain that new problems will arise in the next 25 years that as yet we have hardly thought of, just as quite new problems have emerged during the last 25 years that had hardly been thought of before 1945.

The prospect, I suggest, is an exciting one, and the subject is important — both for the nation and for individual companies, many of which are represented here today. Demand management is certainly not the be-all and end-all of economic policy. It can make only a limited *positive* contribution to faster economic growth, the avoidance of inflation and the achievement of a healthy balance of payments. But sound demand management is a *necessary* — if not a sufficient — condition of all these things. For this reason the prosperity of companies, of individuals, and of the nation as a whole will depend in no small measure on the successful short-term regulation of the national economy.

Epilogue: In praise of economics

(Presidential Address to the Royal Economic Society, 27 June 1974)*

INTRODUCTION

It has been common in recent presidential addresses to bodies of this kind, as well as in numerous lectures and articles, for economists to criticise rather severely the present state of our subject, or at least to call in question some recent tendencies. This is by no means an unhealthy development. It is, I think, an indication that ours is a flourishing subject that can take such self-criticism in its stride (though I sometimes wonder whether such repeated pronouncements may not perhaps be a little discouraging to young men and women thinking of embarking on a career as an economist). I happen to agree with many of the criticisms that have been made; and if I had been giving this address a few years ago I might well have emphasised the failings and failures of our profession. But I think the time has come to redress the balance, and that it may be proper if on this occasion I do something to defend the profession, and for a change sing the praises of economists — and of our subject — even if I do so in rather muted tones, as befits a practitioner in a subject that has no need of self-advertisement.

Economics, and economists, have been subject to a good deal of criticism not only from inside but also from outside the profession. But I doubt whether this has been any more pronounced recently than it has been for the past few hundred years. Thus Clarendon, commenting on the economic advisers to Archbishop Laud, who was a sort of Finance Minister to King Charles I, tells us that Laud made it

> his principal care to advance and improve the King's revenue by all the ways which were offered, and so hearkened to all informations and propositions of that kind; and having not had experience of that tribe of people who deal in that traffick, (a confident, senseless, and for the most part a naughty, people,) he was sometimes misled by them to think better of some projects than they deserved.[1]

*Economic Journal, December 1974.

[1] Clarendon's *History of the Rebellion*, re-edited from the manuscript in the Bodleian Library by W. Dunn Macray, 1888, vol. I, p. 130. I am grateful to Mr Bensusan-Butt for drawing my attention to this passage.

Nor have economists' criticisms of each other changed very much during the past century and a half. Thus in 1820 J. L. Mallet wrote in his diary about no less a man than Ricardo (for whom in general he had the greatest admiration and respect):

> He meets you upon every subject that he has studied with a mind made up and opinions in the nature of mathematical truths . . . It is this very quality of the man's mind, his entire disregard of experience and practice, which makes me doubtful of his opinions on political economy.[2]

And G. K. Chesterton in 'The Napoleon of Notting Hill', when describing the human race's favourite game of 'Cheat the Prophet', wrote the following about economic forecasters:

> The players listen very carefully and respectfully to all that the clever men have to say about what is to happen in the next generation. The players then wait until all the clever men are dead, and bury them nicely. They then go and do something else.

Only now they do it while we are still alive and kicking.

Jokes about economists are almost as numerous as those about Scotsmen; but, like the latter, perhaps they are really sneaking tributes to a class of person that most people admire.

I find it hard otherwise to reconcile the apparently bad reputation of economists with the very strong 'revealed preference' for our services. Thus in Britain, for example, in the past dozen years or so the number of economists employed by universities has probably trebled; the number teaching the subject in schools has risen still faster; those employed by business have multiplied six-fold or more; the number of economists employed as such by the government has increased – admittedly from a low base – some ten- to twenty-fold according to the definitions used (and this takes no account of several hundred with economics degrees in what used to be called the Administrative Class). There has also been a welcome expansion in the number of economic journalists (and in the column inches given to their writings in the newspapers). In total I would hazard a guess that the number of professional economists in these various occupations has at least quadrupled.

Since the average price of our services has not, I believe, fallen – or at least not significantly – in relation to the general price level, the demand curve for economists, in real terms, has shifted very sharply to the right – though how far this reflects a high

[2] Political Economy Club Centenary Volume, 1921, p. ix.

income-elasticity of demand, and how far a sociological time-trend, I would not care to guess. In any case, we can only be as useless as some of our critics would have it if what used to be called the 'sovereign' consumer — and should now perhaps be called the 'satisficing' employer — has been even more ignorant of what he really wants and needs than his severest critics have claimed.

I turn now to some of the criticisms that have been made of our subject in recent years. These have been so numerous that I cannot deal with them all in the time available. I have also had some difficulty in classifying the criticisms but I shall try to deal with them under four very broad heads:

(i)   Our basic assumptions are faulty.
(ii) The balance of our research is wrong.
(iii) Our predictive power is weak and overrated by us.
(iv) The economic state of the world and the number of unsolved problems is a poor advertisement for the state of our art.

FAULTY BASIC ASSUMPTIONS
On the first point, it has been not uncommon for recent speeches by distinguished economists to argue that much of our subject is based on false or irrelevant assumptions and that it does not begin to take account of some of the really important facts of the modern world in which we live.

I recalled a moment ago that Mallet made much the same criticism of Ricardo and I need not spend long on this kind of questioning and criticism because it is not the sign of a sick subject but rather the lifeblood of a healthy, developing one; and there is probably no subject in which such questioning is more necessary that it is in economics, since the social behaviour and organisation of human beings changes so rapidly. Clearly we must take full account of such facts of modern life as the power of trade unions and large corporations, including multinational companies, of the Eurodollar market, of the increasing erosion of the money illusion, and whatever.

The questioning of our basic assumptions is a way in which important advances can be, and have been, made. But clearly those who do the questioning must guard against the temptation to inject policy conclusions in which they happen to believe, but which do not logically follow from the removal of some basic assumption, and are in fact based on explicit or implicit assumptions that may be just as vulnerable as those they have claimed to be unrealistic.

I have sometimes, too, detected a tendency — for example in the arguments about free trade versus protection in their various current mutations — for some economists to claim that, just because the real world does not precisely conform to the assumptions in an economic theory — which in the nature of the case it never could — therefore any public intervention they are in favour of must be justified.

I also feel that some of the criticisms of our basic assumptions and methodology are to some extent knocking down an Aunt Sally. For much economic analysis of particular real problems nowadays takes only as an implicit starting point, if that, what have been described as the irrelevant assumptions of equilibrium economics. Such analysis then relaxes as many of the assumptions as seems appropriate, including, among many others, that of constant returns. It may also attempt to quantify the effects of these relaxations where practicable, using what might loosely be called cost-benefit techniques (which, whatever their shortcomings, can at least give some idea of how far purely political considerations are affecting a particular policy decision).

The analysis can thus discard the concept of 'equilibrium' and, incidentally, be made as 'dynamic' as you like; and if you ask what I mean by this, I am afraid the best definition I know of the terms 'static' and 'dynamic' as used by economists is simply that 'your false theories are static while my correct ones are dynamic'. But, having said that, let me admit in all seriousness that the numerous theorems of static equilibrium economics can prove an obstacle to an understanding of what is really going on, unless we also try to take account of what has been called the process of circular and cumulative causation.

WRONG BALANCE IN RESEARCH

The second main criticism of the present state of economics is that the balance of our research is wrong and in particular that there is far too much emphasis on the refinement — including mathematical refinement — of theories that are sometimes based on flimsy empirical foundations and not infrequently of dubious relevance to anything; and too little emphasis on empirical work, the testing of hypotheses made by economic theorists and econometricians, and the analysis of actual economic problems; also that research of the former type is the more likely to lead to professional advancement in the academic field. I have for long had considerable sympathy with these views, partly perhaps because most of my own work has been in the latter category. But there are two arguments on the other side.

First, all economists must agree that, in the process of clarifying thought, it is necessary to carry out a great deal of theoretical analysis based on models that are recognised to be grossly over-simplified and unrealistic. There is a story — perhaps apocryphal — of Professor Hayek opening a seminar in the 1930s with the words 'let us assume full employment'. When a student protested that in the real world there was heavy unemployment, Hayek is reputed to have replied 'so much the worse for the real world'. This, however, by no means proved that his analysis was worthless but only that it would have been quite wrong to apply conclusions based on this assumption, unless it was suitably relaxed, to the real world of the 1930s.

Secondly, while there is very probably an excessive *relative* emphasis on theoretical refinement in university research — and perhaps teaching — one must not overlook the large *absolute* increase in empirical work, and in the study of real economic problems, during the lifetime of a good many here today. Those of us who first started to study economics in the early 1930s will remember how relatively little empirical evidence there was to go on and how much of our time had perforce to be spent on pure theory. I remember the delight with which I first discovered that someone had actually tried to *measure* the marginal productivity of, I think, fertiliser applied to an acre of land.

The great change for the better that has taken place since then reflects, I suppose, the very large absolute increase in the number of economists available to do research; greatly improved official statistics; advances in statistical methods; and the growing number of economists who are reluctant to accept a proposition unless it has passed an empirical check. This I regard as a healthy development, although it is a valid criticism that there is as yet too much reliance on purely econometric tests that are sometimes of dubious validity and too little on more direct, down-to-earth methods.

Another important factor has been that, while before the war most of the limited number of professional economists were in universities, there is now a large number outside: in government, international organisations, research institutes, trade unions, indus-try, commerce and finance. These are mostly engaged in work of practical relevance; and, moreover, a good many of them have a strong incentive to discover techniques and devise models that are not just intellectually or aesthetically pleasing, but which actually produce useful results. They have to make tools for particular jobs, not tools for their own sake that might or might not find a useful job one day to work on.

I regard this as a valuable discipline but, if I may digress for a moment, I shall always remember the horror of an academic economist, for whom I have the highest regard, when I suggested — half seriously — that in the allocation of public funds among those wishing to develop their forecasting models, limited sums should in the first place be given to all suitably qualified applicants, but that after a few years' experience of the forecasting performance of their models the funds available should be wholly allocated to the team that had proved most accurate.

As a result of the large growth in the number of economists outside universities, it is no longer true that all the significant advances in the subject are made in the academic world. A single government department in Britain, for example, may now have fifty or more professional economists of a high standard, and provide an intellectual atmosphere at least as stimulating as that in many university departments; and there are now many government departments with a substantial number of economists, whereas a dozen years ago there were hardly any outside the Treasury and the Agricultural Departments. Economists in government are now working on a wide variety of topics, both macro and micro; and I might mention here the rapid strides that have taken place in micro-economics reflected in, for example, all manner of project appraisal work — in government as well as in business. There is room in government for research as well as operational work and many economists are in fact engaged in both. They are also, in many cases, well integrated into the Civil Service machine. In addition there has been, and I hope there will continue to be, a considerable mobility of economists, in both directions, between universities on the one hand and government and other institutions on the other. This, I believe, should improve the quality and relevance of economic research in all these places, and of economic teaching in the universities.

POWERS OF PREDICTION WEAK AND OVER-RATED

A third main criticism of economists is that our powers of prediction are weak and that we exaggerate them. Now it is blindingly obvious that we shall never achieve anything like the certainty of the natural sciences for two well known reasons. First, we cannot conduct the same kind of controlled laboratory experiments (although experiments are beginning, for example in the field of poverty in the United States). Secondly, human behaviour is complex and changeable, fickle and sometimes perverse. But I do suggest that, given these severe constraints, it is no mean achievement to have made a subject so closely concerned with human behaviour, if not into a 'near science', at least into something less far from a science than most other branches of social study. We are thus, I believe, not doing too badly provided we do not claim too much.

Now non-economists tend to have an infuriating habit of complaining — sometimes almost in the same breath — first that we claim near-certainty, secondly that we hum and haw and say 'on the one hand and on the other'. There then follows the time-worn jibe about how nice it would be to have a one-armed economist.

This is a cross we have to bear. The truth is that, while I have known young, highly qualified, but inexperienced economists claiming near certainty for their results, it does not take much experience to instil in us a due sense of humility; and the process is hastened among those engaged, not just in constructing theoretical models, but in predicting the real world for practical purposes, where their forecasts can rather quickly be proved wrong or right.

A due sense of humility about our powers of prediction should not, however, lead to despair. It is true that in, for example, short-term macro-economic forecasting, the probable error in predictions of the gross domestic product may well be as large as the intended effect on demand of a typical Budget; and in forecasting the current account of the balance of payments — which is the relatively small difference between two much larger magnitudes — the margin of error is such that the band of probable outcomes can range, say, from a relatively satisfactory one to near disaster. But in my view this does emphatically *not* mean that forecasting is pointless and that one might just as well spin a coin or stick a wetted finger in the wind. Our forecasts may be bad but not, as careful post-mortems have shown, as bad as that.

What it does mean is, first, that we must continue our efforts to devise tools and techniques that will enable us to make better *central* forecasts. Secondly we must frankly recognise the inevitable uncertainties that will always remain, and — something I regard as important and on which not enough work has been done, though I recognise that some respected colleagues disagree — attempt to quantify them (for example, by reference to post-mortems on previous forecasts or to the range of forecasts currently being made by various expert groups). Policy decisions can then be taken in a considered way in the light of these uncertainties. It is better to base policy on a forecast than on no forecast at all. But, given the inevitable uncertainties, to base it *only* on a central forecast can sometimes lead to wrong decisions, however much economists may stress the wide margins of error. In my view the rational way to make decisions is to base them on the likely range of probable outcomes, with a different range being given for each policy option.

This is a complicated procedure and it is made still more complicated by the fact that there is always more than one objective of economic policy and there tends to be a conflict, and a trade off (which is often difficult to quantify) between the various objectives. There is the further complication that, for any set of policy decisions taken now, there are possibilities of further action later.

All this provides an important challenge to economists to devise simple ways of setting out the prospects for the policy maker in such a way that a decision can be taken between various policy options in the light of the risks and uncertainties, the trade offs between the various objectives, and the possibility of further action, in either direction, at a later date. This is difficult, but I believe it can be done. I have myself, for example, made a modest start in devising a graphical approach.

We cannot hope to achieve the precision of those sciences which have enabled men to guide spaceships to the moon. But we can, despite our much more limited powers of prediction, and provided we recognise these limitations and take full account of them, do quite a lot to help those who have to take what are in many ways more difficult – and more important – decisions about the ways of achieving a considerably more complex set of goals.

In recent years, observers both in Britain and in other countries have not infrequently claimed that all the so-called 'laws' of economics seem to have broken down because, for example, large-scale reflationary measures appeared to be failing to reduce unemployment, or because the depreciation or appreciation of a currency was failing to bring about the expected change in the balance of payments. But most of the good old 'laws' have usually come into their own in the end. Their only failing has been to take longer than expected to operate; and the delays naturally seemed much longer to the anxious and impatient observer at the time than they will do to the historian looking at the charts in later years. And, as an American economist temporarily turned politician recently remarked, 'an economist's "lag" may be a politician's catastrophe'.[3]

ECONOMETRICS

While on the subject of prediction, a word about what is now called econometrics but which until not so very long ago was called simply the application of statistical methods to economic problems.

[3] George P. Schulz, 'Reflections on Political Economy', *Challenge*, March/April 1974.

Practitioners of this branch of our subject have been criticised on various grounds:[4] for spending too much time devising more and more sophisticated methods of statistical inference without ever engaging in empirical research; or, when they do so engage, for using data – sometimes in a thoughtless or even careless way – that are quite inadequate to support their sophisticated superstructures; for undue reliance on indirect statistical inference as the *principal* method of empirical research, and for claiming too much for their powers of prediction.

I have already mentioned most of these criticisms in a more general context and there is much force in them. But they are not a criticism of the econometric approach as such. This is essentially, I suppose, one way of bringing together and formalising past events of a measurable kind in the attempt to establish causal ralationships which it is hoped will apply in the future. When those who do not call themselves econometricians attempt to predict they are consciously or unconsciously attempting to do the same sort of thing but in a less formal, and sometimes less quantitative, manner.

My predecessor, in his Presidential address,[5] argued that 'running regressions between time series is only likely to deceive'. It certainly can deceive, as witness the fate of the Phillips curve. But I think his statement is too strong if it is intended to suggest that we might as well give up running such regressions. Econometrics will and must continue to be a necessary part of the process by which we attempt to establish causal relationships and thereby try to predict the future and the effects of policy changes. But it will be only a part of the process and the importance of the part it plays will depend on the extent to which its techniques can be improved.

May I deal with this latter point first? There is a clear need to improve econometric techniques and to avoid the pitfalls of false inference. Such improvements will, I believe, take place, partly because predictions based on econometric work will be proved wrong – and being caught out in this way concentrates the mind wonderfully – partly as a result of the work of theorists in this field for whom there is certainly an important role, even though there may well be at present an excessive concentration on this type of work – and on irrelevant aspects of it – of the limited, high-quality

[4] See, for example, Professor Leontief's Presidential Address to the American Economic Association on 'Theoretical Assumptions and Non-observed Facts', in *The American Economic Review*, March 1971.
[5] E. H. Phelps-Brown, 'The Under-Development of Economics', *Economic Journal*, March 1972.

brain power available. Experience convinces me that marked advances have already been made during recent decades.

But the subject is still in its infancy as subjects go; and it is well known that infants have teething troubles. This is one reason for its much commented on misuse and failures — and I have done my fair share of railing against econometrics and econometricians. But it is also a reason for hope that there will be advances in the decades ahead, although the speed and extent of these advances is impossible to predict and it could be that they will be offset by an increasing irregularity in the behaviour of economic man so that the predictive power of econometric techniques fails to improve.

I emphasised a moment ago that econometric work is only part of the process of searching for causal relationships and of economic prediction. As an essential complement, and as a check, we need more direct enquiry into how economic man behaves, *qua* consumer, *qua* saver, *qua* worker, *qua* trade unionist, *qua* manager, *qua* trader. This may involve novel approaches and will require much painstaking work and descriptive studies of a type that does not always get the credit it deserves in our profession. We need better, and more up-to-date statistics. We need a historical sense and a detailed knowledge of recent history.

In this context my predecessor rightly remarked that 'different years have their personalities'. This reminded me that a considerable time ago two highly intelligent and well-trained economists who were working with me produced some econometric results that were repugnant to my common sense (which is incidentally another necessary complement to econometrics — and to economics anywhere, any time). When I asked whether they had taken account of the fact that in one of the years in their time series the Korean war had broken out, they regarded this question as jejune and irrelevant. It was only when I had spotted several elementary arithmetical mistakes in their calculations that they were shaken; and after forty-eight hours of more or less continuous work revised results were produced that were much less repugnant to common sense.

I am told that applicants for some courses in economic history are obliged to show prior qualifications in econometrics. I would also like to see the reverse, with economic history a compulsory subject for any student of econometrics, to make him more aware of the complexities of the real world and show him that his data consist of more than statistical time series. I recall that in the 1930s any candidate for the Honours School of Philosophy, Politics and Economics in Oxford who wished to take two further subjects in economics was obliged to take a paper in modern economic history as well. That, I believe, was sound common sense. I would not, however, push the case for a sense of history quite so far as the History Fellow of an Oxford College who criticised the reasoning behind the Bursar's investment policy on the ground that the last 200 years had been exceptional.

ECONOMISTS BLAMED FOR ECONOMIC STATE OF THE WORLD

A fourth, popular, criticism of economists is that they cannot be any good because the economic state of the country, and of the world, is so bad. This raises two questions:

   (i)   How far are economists responsible for our economic ills?
   (ii) Has economic performance really been so bad?

On the first question the presumption that economists are to blame for any or all of our economic ills is really rather flattering and suggests that our influence is great. (I sometimes feel that we are almost blamed for bad weather — though never praised for goods.) Now it is true that, as Mr Worswick has quite recently reminded us,[6] Keynes believed that 'the ideas of economists and political philosophers, both when they are right and when they are wrong, are more powerful than is commonly understood. Indeed, the world is ruled by little else.' But it is also possible, at the other extreme, to take a Tolstoyan view of economic events and believe that the degree of economic prosperity depends to an overwhelming extent on the actions of millions of individuals; that politicians affect it to only a minor degree and that the economists who advise them, or affect them by swaying public opinion, have an infinitesimal effect because neither the politicians nor the general public are very much influenced by what they say.

It is hard to form a judgment, but the truth probably lies between these two extreme points of view. Certainly economic, and political, developments have been very markedly influenced by such economists as Adam Smith, Maynard Keynes and, dare I add, our new President.[7] (I make no comment on other economic advisers to government.) On the other hand, the economic performance of a country and the quality of its economists are often held to be inversely correlated.

For the sake of argument let us assume that economists have a significant but not an overwhelming influence on current events and

---

[6] Presidential Address to Section F of the British Association, 'Is progress in economic science possible?', *Economic Journal*, March 1972.
[7] Professor Lord Kaldor.

move on to the second question: whether economic performance has really been so bad.

Now reading the press in our various countries one might get the impression that we are in a continuous state of economic crisis. This must be heavily discounted because it is well known that, to the popular journalist at least, good news is no news. But even the tiresome citizenry never seems to be satisfied. For example, a year or so ago British public opinion polls suggested that the majority of the population regarded themselves as financially worse off than they had been a year earlier. But the Central Statistical Office was saying at the same time that they were in fact 8% better off in terms of real personal disposable income per head. (My pet explanation of this paradox — and there are many other possible ones — is the rapid pace of inflation coupled with the fact that pay increases are normally granted once a year whereas the general price level rises more or less continuously. The average man thus feels considerably worse off than six months earlier when he had his last pay rise; and six months and a year are indistinguishable when a pollster interrogates you in the street or on the doorstep.)

Leaving aside the press and the people I think most of us would agree that the last thirty years, when economists have probably been listened to at least as much as ever before, have been a period of unprecedented prosperity in the world, with high levels of employment, at least in the developed countries, unprecendented rates of economic growth and of improvement in living standards in the world generally, and an unprecedented rate of expansion of international trade.

We have, it is true, had a succession of international monetary crises; but it can be argued that these have had much less effect on the mass of the people than on finance ministers, governors of central banks and their officials who, while they are reputed to have put in a plea for 'fixed week-ends with wider margins', may really, in secret, have rather enjoyed it all. And the fact that the man in the street has been so little affected — and he might have been much more affected had less intelligent and co-operative policies been followed — must be credited, to some extent at least, to the work of economists, including those in international organisations.

On the assumption that economists have some influence we have not, therefore, done too badly. It is true that economic growth in the United Kingdom has been less rapid than that in many other industrial countries; but it has been good by pre-war U.K. standards and our record in sustaining employment has been very good — so far at least — compared with pre-war performance. In any case, even if it were argued that the relatively poor growth performance of the U.K. compared with that of other countries reflected a poor quality of economists in Britain, this would not prove that economists in the world generally had performed badly.

All this, of course does not prove that economists have done well, but neither does it substantiate the popular view that we are a hopeless breed because economic performance has been so bad. Indeed I think that, whatever the future may hold in store, economists can take some credit for what has been a relatively good performance since the war. I am thinking of such things as the maintenance of high levels of employment; the progressive liberalisation of international trade, and, on the whole, the avoidance so far of beggar-my-neighbour policies; the advances that have been made during the period in adapting economic principles – in co-operation with other disciplines – to the practical problems of the less developed countries, so, hopefully, helping to some extent at least to speed their development.

UNSOLVED PROBLEMS

Having said all this I am, of course, the first to admit that there are many important questions to which we do not know the answer. But of what subject is this not the case? And might one not perhaps expect to find more unanswered questions at any one time in economics than in many other subjects because new and unforeseen problems are arising all the time?

It is true that when economists meet in conferences we often have to agree that we do not know the answers. But we should not be too depressed about this because we usually meet to discuss not things we know – and there are quite a lot – but things about which we are currently baffled.

How to raise the sustainable rate of growth of the British economy is one of the questions that is baffling most of us at the present time – one possible, and notable, exception being our new President. It is over eleven years since the National Economic Development Council published 'Conditions Favourable to Faster Growth', on the preparation of which I spent a good deal of time and which was, in effect, agreed by both sides of industry and the Government of the day, and I think broadly accepted by the then Opposition. I must confess to some disappointment that it is not yet easy to discern much improvement.

But I must not spend time on a little local difficulty because I wish to turn to a universal and urgent problem that is baffling us all everywhere and could have most serious social consequences if not solved or alleviated — the problem of inflation; and I cannot deny that economists must share part of the blame for the inflationary situation that has developed. There are some who claim to know the solution in terms of a proper control of the money supply, although I think most of them would admit that the process of reducing the present rapid pace of inflation to tolerable proportions through this route could well involve heavy unemployment, and this could have equally serious social consequences.

Economists have done an increasing amount of work on this problem during the past twenty years or so, and the dangers of inflation when a government is trying to maintain a high level of employment were recognised some thirty years ago, for example in the British war-time coalition government's White Paper on Employment Policy, and in the writings of Lord Beveridge and others at about the same time. We have learned quite a lot about some of the relationships involved and where relationships are weak, shifting or non-existent. We know a good deal about the operation of various forms of prices and incomes and other counter-inflationary policies in a large number of countries. A good many 'gimmicks' of an economic nature have been suggested to deal with the problem. But still there is no real solution.

This is not an unprecedented situation. In some ways it resembles that of the 1930s when there was no agreed solution to the problem of unemployment. It may be that further work by economists will reveal a mainly economic solution, as was the solution of the unemployment problem associated with the name of Keynes. But I suspect that most economists are coming to believe that this is less and less likely and that the solution will have to include important political and sociological elements involving major changes in attitudes and possibly in institutions.

The Keynesian solution to unemployment also involved changes in attitudes, but mainly the attitude of an élite to propositions that were not unattractive and, in retrospect (but only in retrospect), blindingly obvious, such as that when there is heavy unemployment it is right for the government to spend more and tax less rather than the other way round. The solution to the problem of achieving greater price stability without heavy unemployment could be much more difficult because it may involve changing the attitudes of a large part of the population and, moreover, persuading them to accept propositions that are far less obvious and much less palatable; and it may well raise questions concerning the distribution of the national cake that are more controversial than the objective of increasing its size.

None of this, however, means that economists can wash their hands of the problem. We have, on the contrary, important contributions to make, but we shall have to co-operate much more with other relevant disciplines, as indeed is very necessary in dealing with many other problems, such as the paradox I referred to a moment ago of the coexistence of popular dissatisfaction with the level of personal prosperity and the publication of official statistics purporting to show that the population had 'never had it so good'.

CONCLUSION

In conclusion, I hope I have persuaded you (if you needed persuading) that all is not rotten in the state of economics, that economists are not such a useless lot after all, and that the answer to the question, 'are economists really necessary?', is definitely 'yes'. We certainly talk a lot less rubbish about many economic problems than do other intelligent people without our basic training. The growth of demand for our services has been enormous. Our habit of self-criticism and of questioning our basic assumptions is a sign of a healthy, developing subject. It is wrong to suppose that our conclusions are all based on unrealistic premises. We do not all live in ivory towers and there has been a very large increase during the last few decades in empirical work on topics of practical importance. Our predictive powers are not so bad considering that we are dealing with human rather that physical behaviour; and our predictions can be useful for policy makers provided we take explicit account of the uncertainties inevitably inherent in them. We cannot be written off on the ground that the world economy is in a ghastly mess, if only because it has in fact been doing relatively well, although there are still many crucial outstanding problems such as inflation which, like others, will very probably have to be solved in co-operation with other disciplines.

So, to come back to a point I made at the beginning, young people with ambition, intellectual curiosity and a desire to advance human welfare will, I hope, not lightly cast aside the possibility of a career in a profession which has, I believe, proved its worth and which deals with a vital and challenging subject in which constant re-thinking is necessary in the light of new situations, new information, new techniques and new problems. In brief, I hope they may feel that a career in economics would not be at all a bad bet.

To end on a still more hopeful note — albeit a somewhat parochial, insular one — there is a little glee which I shall read — not sing — written by one Samuel Webbe at, I am told, about the time of the publication of 'The Wealth of Nations'.[8] It runs:

> My pocket's low, and taxes high;
> I could sit me down and cry.
> But why despair? The times may mend;
> Our loyalty shall us befriend.
> Propitious fortune yet may smile
> On fair Britannia's sea-girt isle;
> Then poverty shall take her flight
> And we will sing by day and night:
> God save the King.

What a brilliant forecast by a non-economist of the advent of North Sea oil. I wonder what assumptions he made about the arrangements for taxing the American oil companies engaged in this great venture.

---

[8] I am grateful to Messrs John Wright and Peter Davies, of the Government Economic Service, for drawing my attention to this glee which was recently sung by a small group of the Chapel Choir at King's College, Cambridge (England). Samuel Webbe (1740–1816) wrote over 300 glees, canons, catches and part songs.

Index